THE INCREDIBLE TRUE STORY OF

★ ★

BLONDY BARUTI

MY UNLIKELY JOURNEY FROM THE CONGO TO HOLLYWOOD

BLONDY BARUTI

WITH JOE LAYDEN

SIMON & SCHUSTER
New York London Toronto Sydney New Delhi

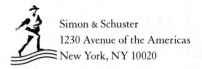

Simon & Schuster
1230 Avenue of the Americas
New York, NY 10020

First Simon & Schuster hardcover edition May 2018

SIMON & SCHUSTER and colophon are registered trademarks of Simon & Schuster, Inc.

For information about special discounts for bulk purchases, please contact Simon & Schuster Special Sales at 1-866-506-1949 or business@simonandschuster.com.

The Simon & Schuster Speakers Bureau can bring authors to your live event. For more information or to book an event contact the Simon & Schuster Speakers Bureau at 1-866-248-3049 or visit our website at www.simonspeakers.com.

Interior design by Silverglass Design

Manufactured in the United States of America

10 9 8 7 6 5 4 3 2 1

Library of Congress Cataloging-in-Publication Data:

Names: Baruti, Blondy.
Title: The incredible true story of Blondy Baruti : my unlikely journey from
   the Congo to Hollywood / Blondy Baruti ; with Joe Layden.
Description: First Simon & Schuster hardcover edition. | New York :
   Simon & Schuster, 2018.
Identifiers: LCCN 2017057729| ISBN 9781501164996 (hardback) | ISBN 9781501165009
   (trade paper) | ISBN 9781501165016 (e-book)
Subjects: LCSH: Baruti, Blondy. | Motion picture actors and actresses—United States
   —Biography. | BISAC: BIOGRAPHY & AUTOBIOGRAPHY / Personal Memoirs.
Classification: LCC PN2287.B3755 A3 2018 | DDC 791.4302/8092 [B]—dc23
LC record available at https://lccn.loc.gov/2017057729

ISBN 978-1-5011-6499-6
ISBN 978-1-5011-6501-6 (ebook)

*This book is dedicated to
my Lord and Savior Jesus Christ
and to my hero: my mother, Annie Baruti,
who protected me and never left my side
while going through some of the
worst moments of my life.*

PROLOGUE

"And you may ask yourself . . . How did I get here?"—Talking Heads

APRIL 19, 2017—

HOLLYWOOD—

id you know that the red carpet is not always red? Sometimes, like tonight, at the Dolby Theatre, it is purple. I had no idea! Then again, I had never attended a world premiere of a Hollywood movie. Not even as a spectator. So please forgive both my ignorance and enchantment; this is all a bit overwhelming.

Lights are flashing, stars are dazzling as the crowd outside the theater gasps and applauds at the seemingly endless parade of limousines that stretches before the theater, disgorging one celebrity after another. Chris Pratt, Sylvester Stallone, Vin Diesel, Kurt Russell and his partner, Goldie Hawn, just to name a few. They are all here to celebrate the premiere of *Guardians of the Galaxy Vol. 2*, the latest blockbuster in the Marvel Comics cinema franchise. And I am here with them, as part of the team, which in itself is something of a miracle.

As with all Marvel movies, the production was shrouded in secrecy and heavily laden with special effects, and I have yet to see a final print. So I do not even know how much screen time will be devoted to my character, a villain named Huhtar. Frankly, it does not matter in the least. It is enough to have earned a role in one of the year's biggest movies; it is, in fact, more than enough. As the movie unspools for the audience and I get the first glimpse of Huhtar, I must stifle the urge to shout, but I hear it in my head.

"I made the cut!"

Yes, that is me up on the screen. Blondy Baruti.

★

A 6-FOOT-8 FORMER REFUGEE from the Democratic Republic of the Congo; a basketball-player-turned-actor whose life story is only marginally less fantastic than a Marvel film. Not only shouldn't I be here, in Hollywood, I shouldn't be anywhere at all. I could have died many times over—as a child living in poverty in the Congo, or especially as a young boy fleeing the violence of a nation ravaged by war on a harrowing five-hundred-mile odyssey for survival.

Imprinted on my brain are images impossible to erase, and memories I cannot shake, and do not want to shake, for they have shaped me into the man I am today, a man of unwavering faith and hope. I will carry scars for the rest of my days, residual damage from the sheer volume of violence I encountered; the odor of death that burns the nostrils and seeps into your lungs; the screeching of machetes and unmistakable cocking of AK-47 rifles; the whistling of bullets as they cut through the jungle. My God, the savageness of it all. I can still feel the driving rain—only in the tropics is it so ceaseless and loud, and hear the harsh rustling of wind through the tall mahogany trees, a sound I could never differentiate from the sound of soldiers walking through the high grass.

Is it a cliché to say that children are resilient? I don't believe so. I believe it is true in the most fundamental sense of the word. What the boy lacks in physical strength—in size and musculature—he compensates for with a purity of spirit, and the blessedness of naïveté. Surrounded by cruelty and violence, the child is still capable of happiness and love. He can smell the rotting flesh all around him; he can hear the anguished cries of his mother; he can suffer for days on end with dysentery and fever, and emerge from it with a smile and an eagerness to play with his friends as if he doesn't have a care in the world.

Even when surrounded by death and confronted daily by the inescapable reality of the depths to which mankind can sink, the boy remains filled with life and light, his heart capable of feeling goodness and optimism in even the bleakest of situations.

Sometimes, the memories of the ordeals of my childhood come back to me at the strangest of times: not just in the early morning fog of a terrifyingly vivid dream, but when I least expect it. The hot, sticky smell that follows a summer rain will fill my nostrils, and suddenly I am back in the jungle, crawling on all fours, listening to my mother's urgent whisper:

Keep down, Blondy. Stay low. Stay quiet. They are close.

A car that backfires or a firecracker tossed casually on the Fourth of July—a joyous holiday that reminds me of the great fortune I have to now call America my home—can easily trigger an episode of post-traumatic stress, and I have to fight the urge to drop to the ground and seek cover from the crackling gunfire. In that moment, I am catapulted back in time. I can feel the jungle all around me. I can hear the cries of friends and loved ones. I can sense the danger deep in my marrow; it feels almost more real now than it did then.

But then I am back. As quickly as it comes, the anxiety dissipates, and I remember where I am, and that all of this happened a very long time ago, in another part of the world. A place of both uncommon beauty and brutality. A place I once called home.

I don't know what it is that allows some of us to survive the worst of horrors with our souls intact—with an ability to still see the innate goodness in our fellow man when experience shouts at us to be wary and cynical. But I am one of those people, and I thank God that he has made me this way.

I was raised Christian, but I believe wholeheartedly in karma. I have experienced violence and bloodshed on an epic scale. I have seen the worst that humans can do to each other. But I have also been touched repeatedly by the warmth of human generosity, and I choose to embrace this side of my species. Unlike so many of my friends, I survived the horrors of war. I got out of the Congo and came to America, a country so miraculous that it once seemed to exist only in my dreams. And along the way I made countless new friends and was welcomed into homes by families that had no reason to open their doors. I have lived when I should have died; I have succeeded against profound odds.

So you see, I am the luckiest man on earth.

My name is Blondy Baruti . . . and this is my story.

CHAPTER 1

The Africa of my ancestors, I am told by the elders in whose footsteps I follow, was a glorious and magnificent place. And the Congo, in particular, was as beautiful and bountiful as any region shaped by God's hand, as lush as Eden itself. A description of my homeland makes it sound like nothing less than paradise. Rich, fertile soil capable of sustaining vast and varied farmlands; geological richness producing thick veins of precious minerals and metals—copper, cobalt, gold, and diamonds, to name just a few; verdant forests and sub-Saharan plains sustaining a vast array of wildlife; jungle canopies so dense and fruitful one could simply raise a hand and pluck a veritable buffet of sweet sustenance. A land of brotherhood and peace.

This was the Congo of my people . . . the Congo shared wistfully in stories handed down from generation to generation.

The Congo of my dreams.

Alas, it is not the Congo I call home. The Congo of my youth was (and sadly remains today) a place of pestilence and poverty; of vengeance and violence so indiscriminate as to be almost beyond comprehension. How do you reconcile the tales of beauty and innocence I heard with the things that actually happened? How did the supposed Utopia of my ancestors become a land riven by chaos and bloodshed? A land where preteen boys are conscripted into military gangs and become drug-fueled killers; a land where rape is so ubiquitous that it is barely noticed as a crime; a land in which more than five million people have died since the outbreak of civil war in the mid-1990s. There is a reason the Congo is sometimes referred to as the "Trigger of Africa," and it is not simply because of geographic appearance.

There are no easy answers or explanations. But I can tell you the story as I know it, and my place in it. This, too, is in my blood, the tradition of finding one's place and identity through oral history. There is, among my people, an unwritten burden of responsibility to disclose one's past by discharging the truth with unflinching honesty and candor. A journey anywhere—whether across the village or to a distant land—must necessarily commence with a single step forward. And rarely is that journey made alone. There is an African proverb that says, "An ox's hind hoof treads where the front hoof has stepped." I stand and walk today where I am because my kin once stood and walked before me. Ugly or pretty. For better or worse. I am a product of the Congo, and of the people it has reared.

The family structure of any African society is blatantly and indisputably patriarchal. The man—the father and husband—is the head of the household. No one debates this hierarchy, and no one attempts to enforce upon it modern Western philosophies of equality and partnership. The man is the king of his castle, no matter how humble it might be. It has been that way from time immemorial.

My maternal grandfather, as the custom of the day dictated, was named Baruti Batilangani Boto Leyande. He was born in the Yangambi region of the Congo on May 28, 1939, when much of the world was being drawn into the vortex of World War II. This was a period well documented as one of the most turbulent in the annals of Congolese history, as the country continued to wrestle with the devastating consequences of the twenty-three-year reign of Belgium's King Leopold II, and his iron-fisted colonial oppression of Africans. Following the Conference of Berlin in 1885, Leopold acquired the rights to the territory of the Congo, and in a gesture of stunning grandiosity, took it as his personal property. As a result, Leopold personally "owned" a region that today is the second largest country in Africa and the eleventh largest nation in the world, a region nearly ninety times larger than Belgium itself. (This, too, was a sign of things to come, for the Congo remains even today a nation bullied and exploited by smaller and crueler neighbors and occupiers.) Leopold renamed the territory the Congo Free State. This was a cruel and oxymoronic name, as there was nothing "free" about it.

For every horror story captured by the media outlets of the West, untold tribulations were being perpetrated with vicious and unchecked recklessness in the Congo: epic construction and infrastructure projects undertaken with ferocious commitment, ostensibly designed to enhance and modernize life in the Free State, but in reality undertaken for purely venal purposes—to expand the wealth of Leopold himself. Railroad lines and roads were carved out of the jungle with breathtaking speed; rubber was extracted to help meet a rapidly expanding global market spurred by the burgeoning popularity of the automobile. Had the Congolese people profited in some way from this industrial movement, perhaps history might view Leopold differently. But in the land of my people he is rightfully considered an exploitative tyrant who viewed them as merely tools to be used in the procuring of resources, and then cast aside like rubbish. Natives who resisted the colonists' orders were beaten or butchered, their limbs hacked off by bloodthirsty soldiers in a terrifying and unforgettable show of might.

Untold millions of my people died during this period, the victims of violence or sickness or starvation. And so it became a part of Congo lore to accept with stoicism the cruelty of invaders, to understand that freedom was not our birthright.

The Congress of Berlin marked the germination point of the turmoil that later enveloped the continent, where European powers carved up Africa like a jigsaw puzzle, and divided it among themselves for their own profit and glory. When 1939 rolled around, and the world became embroiled in a war that affected every part of Africa, the Congo was among those nations pillaged to its core. Its young men were enlisted to fight enemies they didn't know. Family structures were permanently disrupted. The sixty years before my grandfather's birth was the incubation period for the harrowing unrest and violence that would plague the Congo from then on.

This was the world into which my grandfather was born. He was originally from Yawenda, a city in the territory of Isangi, not far from the Congo River. He was the son of Baruti Boyoma and Banzanza Sophie. In stark contrast to the expectations of the period, my grandfather was fortunate to receive a Western-styled formal education. Erudite and accomplished, he eventually graduated with a degree in law from what was then known as the University of Lovanium (the school later merged with other institutions of higher learning under the moniker of the University of Zaire; it subsequently became known as the University of Kinshasa). Through a combination of diligence, ambition, intelligence, and guile, my grandfather developed a lucrative business enterprise in the Congo, the fruits of which provided him the leverage and latitude to travel extensively.

As his accomplishments ballooned (along with his ego), Baruti bestowed upon himself the two last names and middle name, Batilangandi Boto Leyande, which in the vernacular means *Bazali na maw ate moto na moto na oyo yaye.* There is no direct English translation for this phrase, but the closest approximation is as follows: "They do not have sympathy (No mercy); every man for himself." It is a survivor's credo, befitting not only the spirit of the war-ravaged Congo, but of a man who endured and ultimately thrived in spite of a series of betrayals at the hands of friends and family members and business associates. Baruti was unique among his siblings in etching out a sustainable and successful business enterprise. While the fierce individuality of his name might suggest a coldness of the heart, for a time Baruti's generosity appeared to know no bounds. It was commonly known that he would readily disburse his massive wealth to anyone in need. I have been told that he spread his good fortune among both friends and strangers in virtually equal allotment. To his core, Baruti was apparently a good-hearted man who preferred to share rather than shun; a man who was charitable, compassionate, and sympathetic. I would like to believe so, anyway.

Baruti had left his hometown as a young man to go to Kisangani, before ending up in the capital, Kinshasa. There, he procured a sizable plot of land and erected a house for his sister Albertine Basasa. The house, which was affectionately referred to as "The Huge House," was a central and unifying locale for not only family, but for folks from all walks of life. True to tradition, Baruti's parents, my great-grandparents, found him a worthy wife, Christine Lofo Boyale. She was sixteen years old when they married in 1962, seven years younger than Baruti. While this age difference might raise eyebrows in Western culture, it was at the time normal in Africa. Indeed, tradition dictated that the woman in a marriage should be at least five years younger than her partner; a gap of as much as fifteen years was not uncommon. The purpose was primarily to demonstrate power and control on the part of the man, and to prolong and maximize the child-bearing years of his wife. If a young man fell in love with a young woman his own age, the two would undoubtedly face resistance from their families if they wanted to marry. This was no small thing, as parental blessing and approval is crucial to African marriages.

Cultural norms vary wildly from place to place, and are sometimes lost in translation. What is perfectly acceptable in one culture is deemed outrageous or even perverse in another, like polygamy, which was and remains commonplace in my homeland. And so it was that Baruti, following a long and protracted period of monogamous marriage with my grandmother, took a second wife. Like most African men, my grandfather had dreamed of raising a large family. (And by large, I mean *very* large!) Unfortunately, my grandmother was unable to fulfill this desire. Stemming from endless battles with health issues and periodic fertility complications, Christine did her best, but only

(*only?*) managed to birth three children: my mother, Annie, as the first-born, and then my uncles, Desire and Joseph Baruti.

My grandmother was the personification of a selfless African wife, driven by love for her husband and an unwavering commitment to family and tradition. It was in this spirit of generosity and cultural acceptance that she allowed my grandfather to take other women. I should point out that none of this occurred in a vacuum. Baruti consulted with family elders, as well as with his wife. Difficult as it might be for Westerners to understand, all agreed that my grandfather should wed a second time. Does this make my grandmother a fool or a saint? Perhaps neither: she was merely a product of her time and culture, and she did what she felt was in the best interests of her family. Christine's magnanimous presence and generous spirit opened the doors for her husband to bring his second and third wives into her house, under her roof, and accommodate them with their own rooms. While my grandfather went on to multiple marriages thereafter, these other new women lived in different parts of the city largely because, as my grandmother would later say, "The 'Huge House' only had five bedrooms!"

If the family dynamics were amicable and cordial (and from what I have been told, this was mostly the case), it was primarily because of my grandmother's munificence, and the warm and loving environment she cultivated as the first wife. She was inclusive and loving, but sensible in establishing boundaries. Christine slept with her children, my mother and uncles, in one part of the house, while the other wives shared sleeping quarters with their children. My grandfather, meanwhile, grazed nomadically, as befitting his stature as head of the household. His job was to sire children and to provide for them and their mothers financially. The spiritual and emotional care was left to the women, and my grandmother, true to form, embraced this role with all her heart. She took care of all the children as if they were her own, and the wives as if they were her sisters. They lived lovingly among each other as though they were biologically linked. Not surprisingly, the other women developed genuine admiration and respect for my grandmother, their natural trepidation and jealousy giving way to something like love as the years wore on.

Discretion was vital to the success of such an arrangement. Vast, sprawling homes filled with people related to one another either through blood or marriage were not uncommon, and unless you were to ask the women involved about their relationships, you never would have known that they were all wives. Indeed, they might have been sisters or cousins, so peaceful was their coexistence. The bickering and contention that could easily have ensued (and did, in many African households similarly structured) was mitigated also by my grandfather's own tactfulness, as well as his wealth, which naturally alleviated some of the complexities of such a diverse family arrangement. He had the means to provide everyone with a comfortable existence. It is a simple truth: poverty exacerbates all manner of problems, while money helps heal otherwise festering wounds. Baruti made sure that his children and wives were cared for; additionally, when any of the other wives gave birth, my grandmother would liberally expend her own resources to celebrate the arrival of a new family member. This was the type of woman she was: unfiltered and exceedingly giving of herself. Thus, while my grandfather may have been viewed as the head of the family, my grandmother was in a very real sense the lifeblood that pulsated through the organism and made it not just functional, but healthy.

★

AND THEN, BEFORE MY mother even reached her teenage years, my grandfather disappeared. Slowly at first, and then altogether. As the story is told, he aligned himself with a team of business colleagues and left the Congo for greener pastures in Ghana. His Ghana adventure, undertaken as a way to expand his business empire and care for his family, became long and unwieldy, and veiled in secrecy. Communication with his family in the Congo all but ceased; the once surging river of financial resources slowed to a trickle, and then dried up entirely. To say this threw the family into chaos would be an understatement. With not enough money to go around, and with many mouths to feed, the household fell apart, bit by bit. The wives Baruti had brought into the big home soon left, along with their children, and remarried. My grandmother, however, steadfastly refused to leave or to find another husband. Instead, she focused her efforts on taking care of her children and ensuring that they would have a loving and stable home, even in the absence of their father.

Many years later, while researching my family's story, I asked my grandmother about this period in her life. A dignified and private woman, she at first demurred, unwilling for whatever reason to discuss the inner workings of her heart. Like many grandmothers, though, she had a soft spot for her grandchildren, and I was not easily dissuaded. Why did you not leave? I asked. Why did you not move on with your life, away from the huge home with five bedrooms, most of them now sad and empty? Why did you not find another man to take the place of Baruti . . . a man who could have eased your financial and emotional burden? No one would have judged you harshly. Not even your own children, who by this point barely knew their own father.

My grandmother merely smiled and shook her head. And then, in a tone that somehow managed to reflect both the sweetness of a grandmother and the sternness of an army general, she offered an explanation.

"I did not marry your grandfather because of the lure of fame or money, but because of the love I felt for him. And that love was extended to our family and our home. Why would I leave? Just because the rains came and washed everything downhill? It was still my home and he was still my husband. And we still had children who needed me there. No, no, no. There was no reason to leave. None at all."

And so, when it was all said and done, when the brightness had faded away, only the first and legitimate wife, my grandmother, remained vigilant to the very end. She lives to this day in the home her husband built for her, the home in which her children, including my mother, were raised.

In 1990, word reached our family that Baruti had died in Ghana, leaving behind twelve children—seven males and five females—that we knew of. Later my grandmother discovered that while he was working in Ghana, my grandfather had also had at least two other children.

There is a West African proverb that seems appropriate to this situation: "Matters within the house are only known to mice." I do not know how my grandfather died, whether through sickness or accident or retribution from a wronged business associate or lover. Any of these possibilities seem plausible. But I would like to believe that in his final moments on this planet, perhaps he may have reflected upon the life he had lived, and in those moments, as darkness fell for the last time, he saluted with the firmness of a strong and determined hand the wife and woman he left behind: my grandmother, Christine Lofo, who did not wilt in the face of adversity, and who never vacillated in her loyalty to family and faith. Her roots were deep and firm, providing stability for generations.

And I am a limb that has branched from that tree.

CHAPTER 2

While the Congo is a place of great and undeniable natural beauty, it is also a harsh and unforgiving place that demands courage of its citizenry; only the strong survive.

I was barely two years old when my tiny body was ravaged by a mysterious virus. My mother watched helplessly as the fever soared and I lapsed into a state of delirium. I was rushed to the closest hospital, where doctors conducted a battery of tests and determined that I had contracted some sort of disease that was siphoning off my blood supply, preventing healthy cells from replacing dead ones, as is the normal physiological way of things. I do not remember this, of course, and I do not know the official diagnosis. I know only that my mother and grandmother told me repeatedly that they did not expect me to survive the devastation. Nor did anyone on the hospital staff.

But I did survive! To this day, there are pictures of me at the hospital— before-and-after photos of an emaciated toddler, alongside another photo of a healthy and smiling little boy. The photos are marked with the words: "Miracle Baby." And so it has been through much of my life—sadness juxtaposed with joy, survival beating back death.

I was born in Kinshasa. Like much of the Democratic Republic of the Congo, it is, on one hand, a bountiful city surrounded by river basins and magnificent vegetation rooted in dark fertile soil. But it is also a land of staggering heartbreak and unfathomable cruelty.

Even today, the drumbeat of horrifying news continues—dismal headlines about a country ripped apart by a seemingly endless civil war and the repeated encroachment of brutal and venal outside forces. A country where roadsides are littered with rotting, mutilated corpses; where the horrors of rape and torture go beyond the merely criminal to the outright inhuman (do some research, if you dare, and behold the nearly incomprehensible savagery of teenage boys violating elderly women with knives and guns and other instruments of mayhem; of disemboweling pregnant mothers and forcing them to eat their own fetuses). This is the stuff of horror movies. And it is utterly, shockingly real.

Indeed, the Congo often seems like some post-apocalyptic nightmare of death and desolation plaguing a region that has never known peace or prosperity—at least not in my lifetime. This is the Africa that I grew up in—the epicenter of some of the most appalling episodes of human mutilation within the last half century.

But while there is great poverty and violence in the Congo, there is also wealth, and my father, like my grandfather, was in fact a wealthy man. However, Francois Nseka, a banker and government official, was not a very good man, or at least not much of a father.

By the time I was three years old (and my sister ten), my father had officially and completely disappeared from our lives, and our family had relocated to Goma, a city in the far eastern portion of the country, on the Rwandan border. Goma is a city that has been largely shaped by violence, in particular the Rwandan genocide of the 1990s that resulted in millions of refugees flooding across the border. And yet, my early childhood was relatively uneventful. We scraped by as best we could. It wasn't easy, but neither was it unsafe. At least not in the early years of my life. My earliest memories are probably no different than those of most children. I was outdoors from sunrise to sundown. Like many in my community, I had dreams of becoming a professional soccer player. The absence of a father notwithstanding, it seemed like a normal childhood; I did not realize the enormous effort my mother expended in making sure that I felt safe and secure, and above all else, loved.

Like my grandmother, she talked often of the importance of education and hard work, and of making an honorable living. As testament to my grandmother's sturdy guidance, one of my uncles had become a successful attorney, and another had become a judge. My mother worked long hours in a local market selling goods, while at the same time raising her children, a burden that began when she was quite young, and that effectively prevented her from obtaining a high school diploma. She never complained, but she did make it quite clear that she wanted something better for her own children.

"Dream big," my mother used to say. "Anything is possible."

While a photograph is merely a glimpse of a particular time and place, and thus only a small piece of the story, there is undeniable truth in the image. Peruse the tattered and dusty pages of an old photo album of my family, and you will see a gorgeous young woman in her adolescent years. This is Annie Baruti. In these pictures, she is slender and erect, with deep-brown, confident eyes perfectly imprinted on a smooth mahogany face. Perhaps she is looking to the future with the same enthusiasm and promise as her male siblings, unaware of the harshness that lay ahead.

Regardless, my mother was, quite simply, a strikingly beautiful young woman, and not surprisingly the target of an endless stream of suitors. No doubt the absence of a reliably watchful father in her own life created a void wherein she'd later crave attention from an older and presumably strong male figure. I was born out of an illegitimate promise that started a chain reaction of oaths left unfulfilled by Francois Nseka. As he left when I was a toddler, I never knew my father nor his family. My mother, to the best of her ability and with the unfailing support of my grandmother, raised us amid a myriad of difficulties. She was a single mother who never gave up on her children, persevering mightily within a cultural environment that shunned women who bore children out of wedlock, and treated as second-class citizens the innocent and unfortunate offspring of these ill-advised unions.

My mother's resilience notwithstanding, our lives were unrelentingly difficult. Without the financial support and stability of a father, money was scarce. Most, if not all, of my birthdays as a toddler and youngster were spent in the corrosive seclusion of need and want. I can recall on several occasions witnessing my mother trying to make something special out of nothing in the weeks and days leading up to my birthday; or, worse, selling her own meager possessions—her clothes or furniture—to pay for some type of present. Her face, bowed down by the sheer weight of the needs of her children, couldn't mask the burden she carried. Her naturally erect posture would devolve into a defeated slump, as though to hide her face. Having nothing for my birthday was commonplace to the point that I barely even noticed. If anything, I felt for my mother, and the obvious stress that the impending day would bring. I wanted only for her to be happy, and on some level, I knew that my birthday provoked feelings of sadness, and so I wanted it merely to pass quickly.

If poverty is harsh, though, it is nothing compared to the grim reality of life during wartime, and war has sadly shaped the Congo for much of its existence. The Rwandan genocide of 1994 began with a brutal and determined effort by the ruling Hutu tribe to exterminate the Tutsi, a minority tribe, but one that wielded considerable wealth and power. In a little more than three months the marauding Hutu forces, armed with machetes, hacked their way across the country, invading villages and slaughtering more than 800,000 Tutsis, along with more moderate Hutus who refused to cooperate with the genocidal madness. Eventually, Tutsi forces who had been exiled to neighboring Uganda regrouped and pushed the Hutus out of Rwanda, ending the slaughter but prompting the mass exodus of an estimated two million refugees, most of whom settled in the eastern Congo. Refugee camps became de facto military training grounds for the exiled Hutus, who terrorized the local population, in particular Congolese nationals who were of Tutsi descent. In essence, the people of my country were subjected to ethnic cleansing as a fallout of the Rwandan genocide.

But as is often the case, tribalism was little more than an excuse to obtain power and wealth. In 1996 military forces from Rwanda and neighboring Uganda allied in an effort to invade the Congo and expel or destroy the Hutu forces that had been responsible for the Rwandan genocide, and in the process overthrow the government of President Joseph Mobutu. Also at stake were the vast natural resources and untapped mineral reserves of the Congo. So you see this was a practical war, as well as one born of nationalism and vengeance. With the help of Congolese oppositional forces led by Laurent Desire Kabila, the Alliance of Democratic Forces for the Liberation of Congo marched into Kinshasa. Mobutu fled the country and Kabila anointed himself president.

Kabila was hardly a man of great intellect or patience, but rather an impulsive drunk who quickly turned on his allies; in 1998 he enlisted help from Zimbabwe, Angola, and other neighboring countries to expel Rwandan and Ugandan forces from the Congo, which led to the First Congo Civil War, which in turn gave way almost immediately to the Second Congo Civil War, a massive and multinational confrontation involving multiple countries—indeed, it is with good reason that the first and second Congo wars are often referred to as "Africa's World War." Together these conflicts involved nine nations and resulted in the deaths of some five million people. At the dawn of a new century, war, that most evil of man's creations, was raging like wildfire across the continent on a scale and brutality not seen since Hitler's extermination of six million Jews more than a half century earlier. In the Congo, neighbors became adversaries; friends and relatives took up arms against each other as chaos and bloodshed engulfed the region.

In January of 2001, Kabila was assassinated—by one of his own bodyguards, no less—and succeeded by his son, Joseph, who despite being only thirty years of age and having spent most of his formative years in

Tanzania and Zimbabwe, was better suited temperamentally to the job. By late 2002 he engineered a cease-fire and by 2003 the Second Congo Civil War had come to an end; four years after that, Kabila was elected president following the first democratic elections held in the Congo in more than four decades. The Congo has continued to be plagued by political and economic unrest and remains one of the most unstable regions in the world. But it was in the late 1990s and the early 2000s that the bloodshed and violence reached a peak.

★

I WASN'T QUITE TEN years old when the war finally reached my backyard; when rebel soldiers spilled over the border and made their way into Goma, and our lives instantly devolved into chaos and a nightmarish exodus into the jungle, where survival was the only goal. There was little warning or preparation. In the preceding months, my mother had become more cautious about making sure we did not stray far from the home, especially at night, but if she was expecting some sort of attack, she did not share her concern. Indeed, this day was much like any other. I had come from school and played soccer with some friends from the neighborhood; my sister and I were both doing homework when my mother came into the house and began screaming.

"We have to leave now!" She offered no further explanation, but it was clear from her tone that something was very wrong. I had never seen her in such a state.

I tried to pack up some clothes, but my mother said there wasn't time. Instead, I took my sister by the hand and ran out into the street, where panic reigned. People were running everywhere. I could hear the sound of bullets echoing in the distance. And then something louder, more ominous: the rumble of rocket-propelled grenades.

Though I was just a child the day we left Goma, I remember it vividly—the look of fear on my mother's face, the way my sister's hand felt in mine, so clammy and tight, the way the whole world seemed to be falling apart in front of me. Instinctively, almost as if she had anticipated such an act and therefore had an escape plan in mind, my mother hurriedly led us to the outskirts of town, away from where the fighting was heaviest. I remember her pushing me to the ground, driving my face into the brush, and holding a finger to her lips.

Quiet . . .

For several hours we stayed there, silent and practically motionless, like prairie rabbits frozen by fear and self-preservation, until darkness fell and the crackling of automatic gunfire began to ebb. I realize now we were more fortunate than clever, but of course there is no small measure of luck involved in surviving the indiscriminate whims of war.

When the moon rose high in the sky, my mother pulled me and my sister from the ground and with a simple nod of her head implored us to begin walking. In an instant, she had been compelled to choose between two ghastly outcomes: remain in Goma and face the likelihood—if not certainty—of being overrun by rebel forces; or disappear into the dark, immeasurable jungle. What I knew at the time was only fear—crippling and unexplainable; fear of pain and death in that rudimentary way of childhood. I knew what guns could do. I knew that bombs and grenades could destroy homes and families.

But my mother? She was driven by more than just the possibility of death, or even the maternal instinct that compels a mother to do anything to protect her children. My mother knew there were worse things than death, and it was this possibility—of witnessing her children subjected to torture or rape—that led us out of Goma and into the jungle. She heard the gunfire and grenades and recognized the inevitable outcome: Not merely a bullet to the head or a machete blade cleaving her children before her eyes. More likely, she knew that my sister would be raped and mutilated before being left to die. And me, her only son? The soldiers might have been quick and callous in their snuffing of my life; or, more likely, they would have conscripted me into their ranks, put a gun in my hand, and ordered me to fight, or even to kill my own friends and family. Facing this Hobson's choice, which was really no choice at all, my mother opted to flee, and to take her chances with the jungle.

And so, as though in a scene from a documentary about the great Serengeti migrations, a mass evacuation ensued: an exodus of black, downtrodden faces filing out of the city and into the vast and unforgiving African wilderness—a trek out of Goma.

The plan, such as it was, involved simply running away from the center of the violence, hugging the Congo River as we made our way to the northwest, our destination being Kisangani in the north-central portion of the Congo (Goma is actually about 325 miles from Kisangani if you can take the most direct route. But by following the river we lengthened our journey by a considerable distance, heading first to the south, and then north to Kisangani). Kisangani was our goal largely because, my mother explained, a handful of our extended family members lived in the city. They would take us in and provide us with food and shelter; they would help us rest and recover; and then from Kisangani, we would take a boat down the Congo River, all the way to Kinshasa, where there would be more family and we would hopefully be a safe distance from Rwanda and the fighting in the east.

I had no idea how long the journey would take or what we would encounter along the way. There were thousands of people trying to escape the city, with approximately one hundred in our initial group. I knew some of these people, but most were strangers thrown together by desperate circumstances. We were civilians, trained in neither wilderness survival nor combat. We were, for the most part, unarmed and unprepared for the rigors of life in the jungle. Forget about GPS devices or cell phones—we did not even have the most basic of outdoor equipment. We had no shelter, no food, no weapons, no medicine, no clothing beyond that which we wore on our backs. Under these conditions, it would be difficult to survive more than a few days in the jungle.

Sure enough, very quickly people began to die. Some had been wounded before the journey even began. I saw them in our group, staggering along, ashen and sickly; at first, I was uncertain of what had happened. Were they ill? Exhausted? I did not know. And then I would look down and see a gangrenous stump where a hand had been, or notice a shirt soaked with blood. These were people who had been hacked with machetes or knives on their way out of Goma, and while they may have escaped the city, they did not last long.

There were, it seemed, a thousand ways to die: starvation, dysentery, malaria, just to name a few. There was the ever-present threat of being shot or maimed by soldiers, which was only slightly more terrifying than the prospect of being killed by one of the jungle's apex predators. I would wade into the river sometimes, just to cool off, only to be scared off by the sight of a crocodile's snout breaking the surface of the water. Sometimes I would step over a corpse in the jungle and wonder for a moment how he had met his end. I would stand there and stare, my senses assaulted by the stench of rotting flesh and the buzzing of flies. The first few times this happened, naturally, I was so overcome by revulsion that I vomited onto my feet. After a while, though, these encounters became so commonplace that they barely provoked a rumble of nausea. In such a cold and brutal world, it's easy to understand how children become reluctant warriors; how they are compelled to take up arms against their neighbors and become hardened killers at an age when they should be playing soccer or basketball with their friends.

The loss of innocence is at once heartbreaking and terrifying.

We trekked from village to village, stopping to sleep or to ask for sustenance. Sometimes it was provided, oftentimes not. Most nights we slept outside, under the stars, our bellies empty and aching. Five hundred miles might not seem like a long journey, but on foot, through the jungle, while hiding from armed soldiers? It might as well have been five thousand miles. We crept along quietly, almost stealthily, our progress as slow and thick as the muddy banks of the Congo River itself.

Desperate for food, we would eat rotten fruit. Delirious with thirst, we would drink from fetid swamps and rivers, ingesting water polluted not merely with human and animal waste, but with the disintegrating corpses that floated forever downstream, like a horrible moving graveyard. "I don't know how you made it," my mother said to me repeatedly in the months that followed. "You were so sick, fevers every week. Vomiting . . . diarrhea. You were so weak."

But no, I was not weak. I was strong. Stronger than I ever imagined. Or maybe just blessed. I don't know. In the beginning, I cried every day; I cried for my home and for food and shelter. I cried out of fear and discomfort. But soon I hardly cried at all, no matter how terrible the sights placed before me.

A bomb went off in a village where we were staying. It happened with no warning whatsoever. One moment everything was peaceful, and the next moment there was carnage everywhere. Body parts dangling from trees; a pink mist hanging in the air. Mothers crying for lost children; children crying for missing parents. I was sick and exhausted, and sadly accustomed to the sight and smell of death, and so I barely reacted. My mother found me, pulled me to my feet, and off we ran.

Days turned to weeks and weeks to months, as we walked and walked and walked some more, for hundreds of relentless miles toward our destination. We did this despite the fact that we did not know, and could not have known, whether Kisangani was any safer or less turbulent than Goma. We had no way of communicating with anyone outside of our small and ever diminishing circle of travelers. But still we trekked on, buoyed only by hope and faith that things would somehow be better.

A full year passed before we arrived at our destination. I remember my mother being excited as we approached the city, the way she allowed herself to smile for the first time in months. There was a bounce in her step, and a quickening of pace as she dragged me along, not for safety, it seemed, but because a goal was in reach.

"Here will be different," she whispered. "We will be safe."

But as the jungle receded and Kisangani came into view, I could tell that something was amiss. At first it was just a feeling, a sense that we were no longer skipping along, but rather trudging wearily as we had so often in the past. My mother's shoulders began to sag. She loosened her grip on my hand. Finally, she bowed her head.

Ahead of us was Kisangani, a sprawling city of more than one and a half million citizens. And yet it seemed so quiet. Time in the jungle had taught me to be wary of silence; and indeed, Kisangani seemed foreboding, rather than tranquil.

"What is it, Mama?" I asked. "What's wrong?

left her numb. Or, perhaps, this was her way of demonstrating strength and resolve in the face of adversity and immeasurable sadness.

I remember begging for a chance to rest, and for food. I remember throwing myself on the ground and refusing to move, like a toddler in the midst of a tantrum.

My mother simply shook her head.

"Keep walking."

And so I did. As she disappeared from view, I scrambled to my feet and ran after her and my sister, crying and complaining every step of the way. If we were to live and not become statistics of the war, casualties of the slaughter, the only option, my mother explained, was to keep on trekking. I did not ask a lot of questions, although I knew that the plan had not changed.

"We will find a boat soon," my mother promised. "And it will take us home."

Where this miraculous vessel was located, or if it even existed, I did not know. I envisioned a giant sailing ship, with full masts, like those I had seen in books and movies. The kind that ventured out into open seas, where adventure waited. Maybe there would be pirates! A battle to be fought and won!

From the very beginning of our journey, even as we trekked along the Congo River, I had envisioned a seaside rescue of epic proportions (though we were nowhere near the ocean). My mother's goal of securing a spot on a simple, flat-bottomed riverboat packed with uncomfortable refugees was much humbler, but equally noble. And it must have seemed in the dreary moments after arriving in Kisangani nearly as unattainable. For me, the entire ordeal, while it stretched out over the course of more than a year, unfolded like a dream—at once endless and brief. Events both tragic and mundane bled into one another, the suffering and boredom so relentless that one day became almost indistinguishable from the next. It all comes back to me now, all these years later, as a sort of collage, scenes splattered against a canvas.

CHAPTER 3

H ow quickly hope gave way to despair.

Instead of a city teeming with life, we discovered in Kisangani that the raw reality of war had reared its ugly head once more, and to an even greater extent than we had witnessed in Goma. The city had been ravaged by conflict, with neighborhoods dilapidated and virtually empty. The evacuation of Kisangani had apparently been just as swift and devastating as it had been in Goma.

As we wandered about the city, searching for our relatives, vainly calling out their names, there was barely a soul to be found. Instead of walking into the waiting arms of aunts and uncles and cousins, we were enveloped by the familiar stench of decaying flesh. As bad as this smell had been in parts of the jungle, it was much worse in Kisangani, filling the air with rot, as if the skies had opened and poured death upon the land.

We did not linger long in the center of Kisangani; driven out by sadness and nausea, we marched to the edge of the city, where we spent some time before plunging back into the jungle. In my memory, I can see the look on my mother's face, an expression of despair and grief so heavy that it registered almost as a kind of impassivity. So deep was her anguish, and so committed was she to the task of keeping her children alive, that she betrayed not a trace of outward emotion. Maybe there was no feeling left to be wrung from her heart; the war and the jungle had

Throughout our journey, through one of the darkest periods of the war, through one of the world's most impenetrable jungles, I remember mainly a feeling of hunger. Raw, primal hunger. Thanks in part to having grown up in the country, my mother did her best to keep us from starving to death. She was able to concoct bush remedies to ward off infection and ease the symptoms of dysentery and other illnesses. She picked berries and scavenged for leaves and foliage to make a thin and acrid soup for our daily meal. Despite my mother's efforts to infuse this brew with love, it was the foulest thing you could imagine. The bitterness notwithstanding, my sister and I devoured the soup as though our very lives depended on it. I do not recall either of us complaining about the taste. Hunger is a powerful motivator and an unrelenting enemy. We somehow devised internal mechanisms to trick our brains and our taste buds into believing that the food wasn't that bad. On the nights when my mother could not make soup—and these were plentiful—we foraged with varying degrees of success from the jungle's natural resources. There were many nights when we went to sleep with only rainwater and mango in our bellies.

It is a common misconception that the jungles of the Congo are nourished by a nearly ceaseless stream of rainfall. While the region is generally lush and humid and torrential downpours are common, it is not unusual for many days to pass with no rainfall at all. Under normal circumstances this is not a problem, but when one is homeless and on the move, trying to live off the land, rainfall is the only source of safe drinking water. This left us at times in the unenviable position of waiting for the skies to open as our bodies ached from malnutrition and dehydration. Invariably, when the pain became too much to bear, we would walk to the river's edge, stare into the turbid water, and use our hands as ladles. This was a willful act of self-harm, as the Congo River teemed with all kinds of parasites and bacteria. Dead bodies frequently washed ashore or floated lazily along the same waters that we consumed. But what choice did we have? A choice between likely sickness or certain death is no choice at all, really. And so we drank from the river and hoped for the best.

The river was at once our friend and foe. It guided us as surely as a road map. We bathed in it and drank from it. And it sickened us and threatened us with disease and death. It was a constant reminder of how small and helpless we were, and of how far we had strayed from our home.

Still, each night we gave thanks to God. Before the civil war sent us running from our homes, church had been a vital and stabilizing force in our lives. We were a Christian family, and we not only attended service each week, we kept God in our hearts and our house. My mother and grandmother had both been left to raise families on their own, and they had never known anything but poverty, and yet they still spoke often of God's warmth and generosity. We were a family of faith, and that faith went with us into the jungle. My mother made sure that we all gave thanks every night, praying beneath the stars, for despite our dreadful circumstances, we were alive. And we had each other. As my mother pointed out, we were lucky.

And yet, it didn't always feel that way. Like wild animals at a shrinking waterhole, fights between desperate refugees were not uncommon. Sometimes the skirmishes would escalate for no reason other than boredom (while there were times when our trek through the jungle was fantastically violent and harrowing, there were long stretches when it was simply dull and exhausting) and our mother would quickly guide us away from the scene, hiding our faces in an effort to shield us from the horrors of what people can and would often do in their darkest moments of desperation.

In the best of circumstances, the Congo had for years been a place in which order was a fragile and tenuous thing. Governments were toppled, rulers ousted and replaced, and the citizenry treated no better than the feral inhabitants of the jungle. But this was different. Even in a country with as much dark history as the Congo, the second civil war represented an unprecedented descent into madness and mayhem. Africans grow up believing in the importance of community—*it really does take a village to raise a child*—but when the community is ripped apart and every man is left to fend for himself, what becomes of the individual? What happens to his humanity?

I still see in my mind's eye the unforgettable image of my country-men raining violence upon one another at the slightest provocation; men beating each other with rocks and sticks, or stomping each other to death over the smallest morsel of food. People would literally fight and kill each other for scraps that in another time might have been tossed to a family pet. What once would have been deemed unthink-able behavior became ordinary, if not acceptable.

In many ways, people (and not just the machete-wielding rebels), especially strangers, were as unpredictable and dangerous as the wild beasts we encountered in the jungle. It still can give me a wave of anxiety to recall how my mother would spot a house, how she would cautiously knock on the door in the desperate hope of eliciting compassion. Often, she would have us wait in the background, some twenty feet behind her, so that we could not hear the conversation, but only try to follow its course through body movement. My mother would put her hands to-gether, as if praying, and bow her head in subservience and desperation. Then one of two things would happen: she would either turn and ges-ture for us to join her, with a broad smile on her face, or she would walk wearily toward us, defeat and sadness etched into her every step.

Always, though, she would recover. My mother's courage and resil-ience were extraordinary. The Congo at this time was as deadly as any place in the world, particularly for a woman. War, after all, victimizes women first because of their vulnerability in the face of testosterone-fueled aggression. Men are killed or beaten; women are raped and muti-lated; they are robbed of their dignity; and then they are killed. I feared for my mother every time she walked to a stranger's door. Who would answer? How would they respond? And what would become of me and my sister if my mother were taken away? I had witnessed countless acts of brutality levied against women on this journey, and instinctively I wondered if my mother would meet a similar fate. There are nights even now when I will wake from a dream drenched in sweat, the cries of a faceless woman echoing in my head: a woman fighting vainly and valiantly to stop an attack in broad daylight, while others stand by watching.

Every door represented both hope and horror, and yet my mother never wavered. If we were turned away, she would explain calmly that the strangers were not being cruel, but merely trying to safeguard their own interests. There would be other doors; maybe the next one would present a different outcome.

We walked until the soles of our bleeding feet went numb, until we couldn't feel the sting of the sunbaked soil. Exhaustion was a persistent state, fatigue so deep that it settled in my bones and made me drop to the ground and fall fast asleep in the middle of the day. Sometimes my mother would pick me up and carry me or drag me along. Other times I would wake and discover that I had been slung over the shoulder of a stranger. Sometimes we were virtually alone; other times our group would swell to hundreds or even thousands, a veritable army of refugees trekking single file, like thirst-stricken wildebeests migrating across the open plains. We stepped over dead bodies without giving them a second thought, as if they were human barriers in a slow-motion steeplechase race. The lines of humanity were sometimes so long you could not make out where they began or where they ended. The middle of the pack seemed to be the safest area because one was never too exposed (although this may have been merely a false sense of security).

I have no pictures of myself on this entire journey, but I do have memories of other boys roughly my age, and I don't doubt that looking into their faces was like looking into a mirror. Tiny, emaciated children with sunken, yellow eyes and protruding teeth, clinging to life by the thinnest of threads, the skin stretched across their bones like a carcass rotting in the sun.

The toll of the journey was overwhelming as I fell sick frequently and repeatedly. I remember many nights falling asleep in my mother's arms, listening to her whisper to me softly as I melted into a fever dream.

"Always keep the faith and spirit of our ancestors with you. Keep the flame of the love of The Creator near you no matter what befalls you in your life. No matter where you go or what you become, always call upon the one who gives us life and thank the great spirit for the blessings bestowed and never waver in the knowledge that you were spared the carnage of this horrendous journey for a reason. We won't die here . . . we will survive."

And then again . . . over and over, until the words faded away and I fell asleep.

"We won't die here!"

Her words were my strength, bringing hope when hope felt lost. And after she would tell me something like this, I would look her straight in the eye and tell her, "Mama, one day everything will be all right. One day I will buy you a big house and a nice car like the cars we see on TV from America."

She would simply smile and stroke my forehead.

In Africa it is often said that a mother holds a knife by the blade side. Loosely translated, this proverb implies that there isn't anything a mother would not do to protect her children, and my mother's unwavering spirit is proof of this adage. Despite having no medication with which to nurse her gravely ailing children, and neither the physical strength nor the tools to fight off potential aggressors, my mother kept her children safe. Simply by staying alive, she ensured that we, too, would have the best chance for survival. So she gave every ounce of her being, going for long periods without food or sustenance so that we would have enough to live. Always she promised that there was light around the corner, that the worst was behind us. Even if this was not true (and really, how could she know one way or the other), it was enough to simply hear it. If my mother said we would be okay, then we would be okay. How could it possibly be otherwise?

It seemed like my mother rarely slept, for in sleep there was isolation and danger. I worried every night that if I fell asleep, I would not ever wake. My mother assured me that this was not the case, for she would watch over me and make sure that no harm would befall me or my sister. To that end, she would often stay up all night, watchful and vigilant, repeatedly checking on us to be sure of our safety and good health. She trained herself to get by on the briefest of naps, often during daylight hours when others were around. She would sleep, quite literally, with one eye open. I saw her do this! It was both disconcerting and awe-inspiring. She would lean back against a tree and seem to drift away, almost as if under a spell. One eyelid would droop to half-mast, while the other would remain open, gazing off into the distance.

"Mama," I would say, fearful that she had fallen into a trance, or that some sort of odd sickness had overtaken her. "Are you all right?"

With that she would open both eyes and smile.

We had to be aware of the faintest of noises. A ruffle in the brush might be nothing more than a wandering animal; or, it might signal the approach of rebel soldiers. The slightest commotion could, and often did, erupt at any moment into mass hysteria.

Even within our own ranks, safety and security were fragile concepts. There were bad people embedded in our group—not rebels, perhaps, but men of questionable morality. They were thieves and opportunists, and they were to be viewed with suspicion. I remember quite vividly striking up a friendship with another boy, slightly older than me, whose family was part of our pack. Together we found distractions from the endless trek, sometimes through conversation or games, and occasionally through mischief. There were two men in our group who both were mean-spirited and opportunistic. They would bully other members of the group or steal food and supplies. They were, I realized even at that young age, dangerous and despicable men concerned only with themselves.

My friend suggested we teach the men a lesson.

"We'll start a fight between them," he said. "Let them tear each other apart."

I will admit that while there was a certain cruelty to his scheme, it was oddly appealing. A great many good people from our group had died. Why were these two selfish and hateful men drawing breath? It seemed unfair.

"What do we do?" I asked.

My friend smiled. "You'll see."

That night, while the two men were sleeping, my friend and I exchanged some of their belongings, so that each would wake to discover that something was missing, and was in the possession of the other man. This was an extremely dangerous stunt, as either of the men would surely have beaten us had they caught us in the act. But I don't remember being scared; I remember mainly the thrill of executing the act perfectly, and of anticipating its outcome.

The next day, just as we hoped, the two men confronted each other. They accused each other of stealing and wound up getting into a nasty argument that escalated into physical violence. Neither of them was seriously injured, but by engaging in a ridiculous fight that produced no winner but rather two losers, they both were made to look foolish and pathetic in front of everyone else, which was exactly what they deserved. It was a small victory, but it tasted so sweet!

On the days that we felt up to it, my friend and I had a lot of fun together. We would play soccer, or climb in the trees, or just sit around and talk. Unfortunately, he did not complete the journey. I don't even know what happened to him. One day he was just . . . gone. As were his parents.

"What became of them?" I asked my mother.

She shook her head.

"It is better not to think about it."

A month or so passed after we left Kisangani. Eventually we came to a village where my mother was able to secure for us a ride on a boat that would take us the rest of the way downriver to Kinshasa. Refugee boats were common along the river by this point, but as often as not, there was no room. Somehow my mother was able to get us on one of the boats. It was not a safe way to travel, as the boats were rickety and overcrowded and open to the elements. Children would run about the deck and their parents were always trying to grab them and make sure they did not tumble overboard. Nevertheless, it happened with some frequency. If the child knew how to swim and the current was not too strong, and an adult was close enough to jump in and rescue him, a tragedy could be averted. But sometimes the child did not know how to swim and would be pulled beneath the water in the blink of an eye. Regardless, the boat would not slow down or change direction. What was lost was lost. Forever.

We spent an additional three months on the boat, traveling hundreds of miles to Kinshasa. It was a long and slow journey. We stopped most nights to rest. If we were lucky, we might also get a small piece of fruit to quiet our grumbling bellies.

Sometimes we would leave the next morning. Sometimes we would stay in one place for several days, presumably because the river had become dangerous. Most of the time we slept on the boat, for fear of giving up a spot that we could never reclaim. Eventually we reached Kinshasa. After not hearing from us for so long, my grandmother had assumed we were dead. So imagine her surprise and happiness when we showed up at her door, bedraggled but alive! That day there was a big celebration, lots of hugs, and food. Plenty of food. So much food I almost did not know how to react. It had been a year and a half since I'd eaten much more than a few bites of mango or rice in one sitting. It was a miracle! We were alive.

And we were home.

CHAPTER 4

I guess you'd call it post-traumatic stress disorder. I had celebrated (or endured) my eleventh birthday in the jungle, and so, for many weeks, even months, after we arrived in Kinshasa, I did not want to venture beyond the walls of my grandmother's home. Unlike most boys my age, I just wanted to sit in my room all day. I was happy to do nothing but eat, and to stay close to the side of my mother or grandmother. I was like a puppy fearful of being weaned. After so much time in the jungle, sleeping beneath the stars, with death never more than a few feet away, I found comfort in staying indoors. Here it was safe. Outside? Who knew?

A couple weeks after we settled in, a strange thing happened. Instead of growing stronger, I began to weaken. I would sleep for twelve hours at a time. My appetite diminished. It's not as though my grandmother was able to fatten us like lambs for slaughter, but certainly there was enough food to keep us happy and healthy, a revelation after so many months on the brink of starvation. Oddly, though, I lost interest in eating. I found it difficult to get out of bed in the morning. At first these were the only symptoms, but soon came the fevers, the torrential night sweats, and then the persistent bouts of nausea and diarrhea. Often, I could not even make it to the bathroom; I would simply lay in my own waste until my mother came to clean me up.

Days passed in a dreamlike state. I thought I was back in the jungle. In the safety of my own room I could hear the staccato chatter of approaching soldiers, and the thwacking of machetes as they sank into flesh. I saw things in my mind that had happened months before—the lifeless eyes of a friend cut down by gunfire; the bloated carcasses that chased our boat down the Congo River. I tried to scream, but not a sound came forth. I could not speak. I could not move.

One morning I woke in a hospital bed, with a nurse standing over me, offering a cup of water.

"Welcome back," she said with a smile.

My mother later told me that I had spent several days in the hospital and had come perilously close to dying. Whatever infection had taken root in my body had weakened me to the point of my being comatose. How ironic it would have been to survive a year and a half in the jungle and on the river, under the worst of circumstances, and then die after finally making it home; to pass away despite the love and sustenance of my family, and the care of trained medical professionals. But life is nothing if not strange and unpredictable.

"God must have a plan for you, Blondy," my mother said in the hospital. "There is a reason he has not yet taken you."

★

EVENTUALLY MY MOTHER MADE me go to school, but I was socially awkward and had trouble making friends. I had spent a year and a half mostly in the company of adults, running through the jungle, battered by death and destruction. As devastating as the civil wars had been, the fighting had been mostly confined to the eastern portion of the country, so many of the children with whom I now went to school had been spared the worst of it. They could not imagine the horror I had witnessed, and I certainly did not want to share this with them. I was a nervous, anxious boy, my head always on a swivel, trying to look in all directions at once, in anticipation of harm. To this day, if someone approaches me from behind, I respond with alarm. I'm not sure that will ever change, but I've learned to live with it.

Childhood can be a lonely time for even the most well-adjusted boy. I was damaged and maladjusted. In the safety of my grandmother's home, surrounded by relatives, I was okay, but once pushed out the door I struggled terribly to fit in. War had changed me; the jungle had changed me. While I was quick to adapt to some of the comforts of civilization, like having a bed on which to sleep and good food to eat, there were other aspects of life in Kinshasa that left me cold and isolated.

For one thing, I had grown accustomed to a spartan existence. Like my warrior ancestors, I had traipsed through the jungle barefoot and nearly naked, left only with the tattered remnants of the clothes I had worn when we escaped from Goma. Although there might have been a degree of discomfort to this exposure in the beginning, by the time we reached Kinshasa, it seemed normal to me. The soles of my feet were as hard as bamboo and callused to the point of numbness—I could walk across creek beds or shimmy up a tree using my toes like fingers. And there was no pain at all. In the first few months our bodies were so ravaged by insect bites and scratches from various plant life that my skin seemed to be covered with a type of pox; the itching was maddening. By the end I barely noticed the bites or the bugs that inflicted them.

I had become part of the jungle, and the jungle had become part of me.

And so, owing to a combination of familiarity and boyhood stubbornness, I resisted the efforts to acclimate that were foisted upon me. I walked around the house either naked or nearly naked. When I went outside I wore only ragged shorts. No shoes, no shirt. Even then it was all I could do to resist the urge to peel away the layers and sprint into the jungle, unprotected, exposed . . . free.

This behavior alone would have been sufficient to arouse suspicions and provoke contempt from other children in the neighborhood, but what really set me apart was an almost pathological aversion to hygiene.

On our exodus from Goma, we cared not in the least if we were clean or dirty—the stink allowed us to blend in with the surroundings and provided a measure of safety from human and animal predators alike, although, to be honest, I didn't even think about that. After a while, I just got used to being dirty; it seemed natural. The occasional Congo River bath was short and dangerous, as the river teemed with crocodiles and snakes, as well as parasites looking for a warm host. Better to be mud-caked and fetid than eaten.

Unfortunately, while it might have been perfectly acceptable to smell like a wild beast while living in the jungle, a more traditional approach to personal hygiene was required in order to blend in with other children. My reluctance to shower or bathe made this a bit of a challenge. In school, other kids would laugh at me, or run away while scrunching up their faces and pinching their nostrils closed in mock disgust (or actual disgust).

"Here comes Shaka!" they would shout. "Stay away from Shaka!"

"Shaka" was a reference to Shaka Zulu, an early-nineteenth-century warrior. There was at the time a South African Broadcasting Corporation television miniseries airing about his life that was enormously popular throughout the continent, and particularly in the Congo. The series was set more than a hundred years earlier, and told the story of the tribal leader, so of course he appeared frequently on-screen wearing very little clothing or warrior garb; moreover, his skin was quite dark, even by African standards. The other kids at school got a whiff of me, and a look at my own dark skin, and in that uniquely cruel way of childhood bestowed upon me a nickname.

"Shaka!"

I suppose there are worse things than being mocked for resembling a legendary African warrior, but certainly the nickname was not a term of endearment but rather of derision, intended to make me feel lonely and isolated and weird. And it worked.

"Do not listen to them," my mother would say. "They are foolish children. They know nothing of your past."

She also suggested I take a shower and put on some clothes; both messages were slow to sink in.

At school I barely spoke, which led to further ostracization from my fellow students, and frustration on the part of my teachers. School in the Congo, you see, was very traditional, consisting of lessons often taught in a Socratic manner. The teacher, or professor, as he was often known, would stand at the front of the room and ask questions of the students. Sometimes he would wait for volunteers, but just as often he would simply call on someone and demand an answer. It was a tense environment in which students were expected to be prepared for class by having read the assigned material and completed all other homework. To show up for class unprepared was to risk humiliation. Yet, I was often unprepared, and even when I had done the work, and knew the answers to whatever questions were asked, I was incapable of sharing this information with my classmates. It was almost as if a temporary paralysis came over me when I would try to speak in front of others.

While my teachers were generally sympathetic to my plight, there were limits to what they would tolerate. Periodically they would show up at my grandmother's home to speak with her or my uncle Joseph, and sometimes to my mother, about concerns over whether I was even educable.

My family insisted I was in fact a reasonably intelligent child, but that our experience on the long trek had left me traumatized.

"Give the boy time," they would explain. "He will come around."

The truth? I did not want to "come around." I did not care. I wanted no part of school or even a life that others considered normal. In some strange way, I think, I wanted only to return to the jungle, where at least I would be accepted. My family, thank God, would not let this happen and went to great lengths to make sure I had top-notch schooling.

In the Congo, when I was growing up, good education was not free. Tuition was paid to schools, and naturally the better the school, the higher the tuition. I was fortunate to be raised in a home where education was treasured; unfortunately, it was also a home of meager means.

The burden of tuition fell on my mother, and she did the best she could to come up with the necessary funds. But it was a never-ending struggle. It wasn't long after we settled into my grandmother's home that my mother began building a small business selling goods to the locals. This was a common way for people to make a living in the Congo. It required little formal education or equity (if you were willing to start small), but it did require a significant amount of energy and resourcefulness.

My mother was not lacking in either of those traits. She began by buying and selling products locally—clothing, food, and basic home goods. But there was tremendous competition for this type of business in Kinshasa, and my mother did not have the means to expand her business and compete effectively. We frequently missed tuition payments, which resulted in my being discharged from school on numerous occasions. Again, this did not bother me in the least; I was content to stay home and avoid the stress and pressure of school. But my mother was not so easily dissuaded.

She expanded her business in the only way possible: by taking it on the road. She would purchase goods in Kinshasa for a reasonable price—mostly shoes and clothing for children—and then travel to provinces closer to the central or eastern part of the country, places that had been hit much harder by war. These were poorer towns and villages to begin with, less civilized places that suffered from extreme poverty even in times of peace. My mother would pack as much as she could carry and bring it to the provinces. These were long and arduous journeys, if not as dangerous as our trek from Goma, still far from safe for a woman traveling on her own. But my mother was both fearless and smart. Once she had sold her stock in the provinces, she would take most of the money and purchase goods that would be valuable and less available in the city: corn, beans, other types of food. These she would haul back to Kinshasa and sell at a substantial profit.

Then she would repeat the entire process all over again.

These were not brief trips. My mother would be gone for many weeks, or even months at a time. Every time she left, I would cry hysterically, for

I knew there was the possibility that she would never return. Although civil war had ended, the Congo remained a deadly place, and the further one strayed from Kinshasa and the western part of the country, the more likely it was that violence would be encountered. You could easily argue that these excursions represented a callous or foolish disregard for safety on the part of my mother, but that would be missing the point. She was a survivor . . . a fighter. Nothing was going to prevent her from trying to provide for her family, not even the prospect of being killed or raped.

And so it was that my mother would trudge off into the wilderness, traveling on foot or by boat or bus, or some combination of the three. Often, she would arrive at her destination and discover that there were hundreds or even thousands of people in line ahead of her, waiting for a chance to buy and sell their goods. She would sleep outside on the ground for days and weeks on end before boarding a boat for her next destination. We never knew when she was coming home, as there was no way to communicate with her while she was away, and so each time a boat arrived in Kinshasa, we wondered if she might be aboard. More than once we stood at the dock, waiting and watching, only to hear horrifying tales of boats that had been attacked by guerrillas or flooded en route, killing everyone on board.

"Is Mama okay?" I would ask my grandmother.

"Yes, Blondy . . . God is watching over her."

Apparently so, for my mother survived every one of these adventures, which allowed me to continue in school, albeit with periodic interruptions for nonpayment of tuition. Such disruptions were not unusual; indeed, many of the children in my neighborhood also missed a lot of school, and in fact I was one of the few to complete my degree. I do not take credit for this; had it not been for my mother's industriousness, and her steadfast determination to take care of her children, in spite of enormous obstacles, I surely would have been just another casualty of the rampant poverty and violence of the Congo. Additionally, I was fortunate to have an extended family that not only cared for me, but demanded of me more than I expected of myself. My grandmother and my uncle Joseph insisted I go to school and do my homework so that I would not become like the rest of the neighborhood boys—uneducated, impoverished young men fathering multiple children when they lacked both the maturity and the resources to care for them. It was a brutal and seemingly endless cycle of poverty and heartbreak.

"Where are you going?" my grandmother or my uncle Joseph would say as I tried to sneak out the door in the evening. "It is time for homework." They would stand over me for hours on end, until I had finished every lesson precisely in the manner that it had been assigned. No shortcuts. No laziness. Uncle Joseph would beat me with his belt if I didn't remember what was taught at school that day, so you can imagine there was a lot of pressure to learn and remember everything to avoid that prospect. If one of my teachers sent home a negative assessment, or indicated that I wasn't paying attention in class, my uncle would also furnish a punishment, making me kneel under the sun, hands held high until my shoulders went numb, and I would cry like a baby. Sometimes my grandmother, concerned that my uncle was too harsh, would try to intervene. My uncle would yell at her: "Stay away. I know what I am doing! He has to learn." I should stress that while this might sound brutal, it was normal for African boys. In most cases it was the father who administered punishment and made sure that schoolwork was completed. In our house, Uncle Joseph assumed that role. At the time, I resented both their oversight and the tedium of schoolwork. In retrospect, however, I am grateful.

Nearly a year passed before I became comfortable with school and began to make friends. One of the things that eased my discomfort was an introduction to the arts, specifically theater. I'm not quite sure what it was that attracted me to the stage. Perhaps it was all the time I had spent in my own head, while out in the jungle, fantasizing about a different and better life. Theater was an escape, a chance to be part of a new and exciting world, a world far different from the one in which I seemed to be trapped. And I liked the other kids, as well. They were playful, smart, sensitive. I felt at home in their company.

I suppose it helped that my first real crush was also involved in the school drama program; her name was Peggy Nkunku, and she was pretty and talented. Part of my motivation for joining the program was a desperate attempt to spend more time with her. And it worked! I tried out for one of the lead roles in a production called "Commandment Jesus." I went after this part because it would allow me to play Peggy's husband onstage. I was not quite thirteen years and hopelessly infatuated with my costar. I guess this made my performance better. It sure made the experience more fun.

But at some point, my love for theater became more than just an excuse to be near Peggy, and I'd say that moment came the first time I was onstage in front of a real audience. To see the faces in the crowd, and to hear people applauding and laughing. It made my heart swell! I knew I was home.

Theater quickly became my passion. I was far more interested in the school play than I was in the mundanity of academic work. But there was an understanding from the beginning, made clear by my entire family: if my grades slipped, I would not be allowed to participate in the theater program. It was all well and good that I enjoyed "playing," as my grandmother called it, but school came first; school was what really mattered. I made sure that my work was done, and done properly, in order to ensure that I would always eligible for drama productions.

Our theater program was quite good. We even took second place in a national middle school theater competition, and I was named "most improved actor." The acting bug bit me hard and fast. Everyone thought it was the strangest thing. What had become of the boy who didn't want to leave the house? The boy who had been virtually mute when he first came to Kinshasa?

What had become of *Shaka*?

I don't know how to explain it, except to say that when I was standing on the stage, my fears and trepidation melted away. I could be anyone, and in the pretending, there was comfort and safety. There was a world far from the Congo—a world in which people were not mutilated or killed; a world in which children were safe—and I could be part of it. At least for a little while.

To make sure that I could continue to be part of it, I not only kept pace with my studies, but I also did what I could to contribute to the family budget. I no longer feared going to school; I feared the prospect of having school taken away. Losing school meant losing the theater program; it meant losing my friends; it might as well have meant losing my life. When my mother or my grandmother would tell me that money was scarce and that my tuition was late, I would begin to hyperventilate.

"What can I do?" I would ask.

"Work" was the customary answer.

There weren't many avenues for a middle school boy to earn money, but I did what I could. I would fill plastic bags with water and carry them in a basket on my head to the local market, where I stood outside for hours in 110-degree heat, selling the bags to thirsty shoppers for the equivalent of a few pennies. On a good day I might clear two dollars. Often, I would trade some of my school supplies for peanuts or other snacks from a local vendor, just to squelch the rumbling in my stomach. Everyone sacrificed so that I could go to a good school. I had an obligation to help in any way possible, and I took it seriously.

One of the hardest things about living in Kinshasa was knowing that my father lived only ten miles away, and yet had nothing to do with his children. He never stopped by on birthdays or holidays, never sent presents or cards. Christmas was particularly painful. Instead of having fun, I was sad, and not just because a lack of money meant we had few gifts. My mother would sell her own clothing so that she could buy food and make a big meal on Christmas, which is depressing, of course. But it was all the worse knowing that my father was so close and could have made things better for us, but apparently did not care enough to help.

I would sit there on Christmas Day, looking enviously at some of my friends hanging out with their fathers; even though they didn't have much in the way of material possessions or gifts, they had love to share with one another. Their fathers were there for them, and mine wasn't. He was with his other children, and with another wife. I was hurt more than you can imagine. I was also angry at my father. I repeatedly asked myself these questions: Why does he not care about me? Am I lacking in comparison to his other kids? What have I done so wrong for him not even to stop by and wish me and my sister a simple "Merry Christmas" during one of the most important days in the life of an African child?

There was one time, when I was in middle school, when we were having particularly challenging economic struggles that my mom contacted my father. I couldn't attend school because we didn't have money for tuition, and my mother must have been desperate to reach out to my father, because she was a proud woman and I imagined it pained her to have to do so.

My mother and I took a bus to my father's office; she hoped to convince him to help with tuition so that I could resume my education. I was excited merely at the prospect of seeing him, regardless of the outcome. I remember sitting outside his office for hours, waiting for him to meet with us. Finally, he appeared. He did not even look me in the eye. Instead, he stared down my mother and angrily said to her, "This kid has nothing to do with me. I didn't plan to have him. It was a mistake." Then he walked straight back into his office, closing the door behind him. I was stunned by both his actions and his words, which felt like someone putting a knife straight through my heart.

That was the last time I ever saw him. Last I heard, he was still alive and struggling in the Congo. I hope I will get to see him again, so that I can say to him, "Father, I love and forgive you, no matter what you have done to me."

And yet, there is a difference between forgiving and forgetting. I was born with my father's name—Blondy Nseka—but changed it to Blondy

Baruti out of respect for the person who raised me and cared for me, and who did everything in her power to keep me alive. My father played no role in any of this; I see no reason to honor him by bearing his name.

★

KINSHASA WAS A HARD place for a boy to grow up in, and many of my friends wound up in jail or dead. They used drugs and alcohol, and turned to stealing to support their habits. I could easily have gone this way, as well, if not for the love and intense oversight of my mother and grandmother. Despite frequent and extended absences, my mother's influence was always felt. I adored her and I wanted her to be proud of me. Likewise, I wanted the respect of my uncles, my mother's brothers, as well. My uncle Joseph, as I said, was a tough but supportive influence, while on the other hand my uncle Desire was often mean and spiteful. He would call me a "son of a bitch" in front of my mother, just to make us feel bad.

"You're nothing," he would say to my mother. "Your kids are nothing. Their father abandoned all of you, and these kids don't even deserve to be in our family."

While my older sister would often argue with him, I rarely said anything. Since I had no father, my uncles represented traditional male authority in my eyes. These men were my mother's brothers. Fighting with either of them would have been disrespectful to my mother, so I bit my tongue, no matter how hurtful the insult. Like when he would tell me, "You're never going to amount to anything in life."

For him it was a disgrace that I had changed my last name to Baruti. He felt that I didn't deserve to carry the proud family name because Baruti was a man of dignity and respect, a powerful man. I wasn't a child from love or marriage. I was a bastard in his eyes and worthy of nothing but contempt. This man would make me run errands for him, and I don't mean simply taking out the trash. He would give me a twenty-dollar bill and tell me to deliver it to one of his girlfriends, a trip that might stretch to ten miles in each direction. And I did it, because I didn't want to incur his wrath, or risk harm to my mother or grandmother or sister. This was the way it worked in Africa—the male held a position of power over all females in his family, and while it mystified me, I felt helpless to do anything about it.

I believe this is the reason why my sister went on to make some bad decisions in her life: she had four children with four different boys, and they all ran away from her. In the Congo, a girl is not supposed to have kids before marriage and my mother and my grandmother had to take care of the kids, which reflected poorly on our entire family. People would point fingers at me and say, "That's her little brother, Blondy." And I would respond by shaking my head and denying any association. This accomplished nothing, for I felt not only shame about my sister's behavior, but about my refusal to acknowledge my own family as well.

"No, she's not my sister. You have me mistaken."

But there was no mistake. One cannot hide from one's family, any more than one can hide from the past. We are shaped by both, for better or worse.

CHAPTER 5

I was introduced to basketball at the age of fourteen. Soccer is the game of choice for most children in the Congo, as it is in most of the world, but I had grown taller than my friends and thus found myself being nudged toward a game more befitting my changing physical stature. Soccer players are smaller and quicker; by age fourteen, I was approximately 6-foot-2 and thin as a reed, a bit clumsy but determined to get better. I was taller than many of my professors at school, prompting the other kids to give me a new nickname: "Giant."

"Forget about soccer," some of them said to me. "Forget about acting. You should be playing basketball."

At that point in time the Congo had produced just one world-famous basketball player, the great Dikembe Mutombo, who had been a star first at Georgetown University and then in the NBA. Mutombo was more than seven feet tall, with the wingspan of a 747 jet and an uncanny ability to rebound and block shots. He also had an ever-present smile and a huge personality that made him a fan favorite. Mutombo was a hero in the Congo, especially to children. He was an example of what you could accomplish with hard work and discipline, and with a little bit of luck. He was also a window into the glamorous life of America, the life we all dreamed about and saw on television, movies, and the Internet. A land where everyone lived in a mansion and had enough food and clothing to sustain a small village; where people drove pristine cars on perfectly maintained highways; where they smiled and laughed and were happy all the time.

A fantasy? Of course. But to a boy growing up in the Congo, playing basketball in sandals or even in his bare feet, with a persistent rumbling in his stomach and an unshakable memory of violence and hatred in his head, the America depicted in popular culture was a fantasy worth pursuing. As much as I loved acting and playing soccer, maybe my friends were right. If I had a chance of escaping the Congo and getting to America, basketball would be the ticket.

And I knew it right away, the very first time I picked up a ball. I had enjoyed playing soccer and other games, but there was something about basketball that instantly captured my heart. It felt natural to me. It was a game that valued athleticism and size. It was a game that could be played in solitude, just a boy and a ball and a hoop, and I took to it like a bird to air. I would spend endless hours dribbling and shooting and pretending that I was Mutombo or Michael Jordan, or some other great American superstar. I felt at home on the basketball court, and I also believed that the game could take me far from home—all the way to America—so I threw myself into it with a passion I had never known.

Initially, I had trouble getting into games because I didn't know any of the guys playing basketball on the local court—and by "court" I mean an uneven cracked surface (a mix of asphalt and concrete, often covered with loose sand)—known as Foyer Social, some four miles from my grandmother's house, in the neighborhood of Bandal. So I would sit there and wait until they were done playing, and then I would practice by myself, sometimes for two or three hours, until the sun dipped behind the skyline and I could no longer see the rim. I had no basketball shoes, so most of the time I would play in my school shoes or sandals, but these were uncomfortable, so sometimes I'd just go barefoot, until the ground burned through my skin and blisters erupted on my soles.

"I've got to get better," I'd say to myself. "I want to be part of these games."

I was allowed into pickup games only when there weren't enough players and a body was needed to fill out a team. Consumed by nervousness and clueless as to how the sport was actually played, I repeatedly embarrassed myself. I would dribble the ball off my foot or miss a shot so badly that it wouldn't even hit the backboard. Meanwhile, I noticed that many of the other players were capable of slam-dunking the ball. They would leap high into the air and throw down thunderous stuffs that would provoke howls of approval from their teammates and spectators. I was tall enough that I should have been able to dunk, as well. But I was clumsy and awkward; I would lose control of the ball on the way up or get it smashed back down onto my head by an older, more seasoned opponent. He would laugh and wag a finger at me—Dikembe Mutombo's signature move—as if to say, "Get that shit out of here!"

I was so bad that the first few times I played, my teammates kicked me off the court. They would mockingly refer to me as *"Mulayi ya busoba,"* the rough translation of which is "Stupid Tall Man." I could have just given up, or succumbed to pride and ego and said, "Okay, the hell with these games. I am out!" But for some reason I didn't look at it that way. I wanted to get better. I wanted to prove them all wrong. So I persevered. When I wasn't practicing by myself, I would aim to get into games with the more junior players who took over the court when the better players left. They were mostly younger and smaller than me, but were much more experienced and fundamentally sound. They were patient with me, and by playing with them I naturally began to improve.

On some nights, the older players would hold a dunk contest. It always drew a huge crowd. While only a few players from the Congo have made it to the NBA, the country's junior ranks are filled with tall, athletic basketball players, many of whom are spectacular dunkers. Among the best in these contests was a young man named DMX Kisenga. I liked Kisenga a lot: smart and funny, without ever being mean, he was one of the few older players who treated me with compassion and respect. I think he recognized my love for the game and my willingness to work hard.

"Keep practicing, Blondy," he would say. "Good things will happen."

Kisenga was already 6-foot-7 and probably 230 pounds. Although he was still in high school, he looked and played like a grown man. Although he never made it to the United States, he did eventually leave the Congo to play professional basketball in Europe, an accomplishment that not only made me happy for him, but gave me further hope about what I might accomplish. If Kisenga thought I had potential, then maybe I really did.

Sometimes during the dunk contests Kisenga would walk over to me on the sideline and ask me for a suggestion. One time he even invited me to join the contest. I looked out at the older players, soaring through the air and ramming the ball with such authority and confidence. I lowered me gaze and shook my head.

"No, I can't."

Kisenga gave me a pat on the shoulder. I looked up. He was smiling broadly.

"Do not worry about these people," he said. "They don't know anything about you. Do what you must in order to get better."

His words of motivation had a great effect on me. Not so much that I was brave enough to join the contest that night, but such that I nursed a kernel of hope that someday I could. And so I continued to watch and wait and work.

Inspiration is wherever you can find it; similarly, knowledge and wisdom can come from the most unlikely source. After the games were all through, I was working out on the court all by myself, practicing my dribbling and shooting, occasionally trying unsuccessfully to dunk like the older guys. Suddenly I was approached by a small boy. He was maybe ten years old and was, like me, shooting around by himself. He was so young that he rarely got a chance to play, so he would wait for the courts to clear, no matter how late it got.

"I can help you," he said after watching me lose control of the ball on another failed dunk attempt.

I looked at him dismissively. "Shouldn't you be home, little boy? It's dangerous out here after dark."

This was true—when darkness fell, soldiers would patrol the city and surrounding villages, enforcing curfews in ways that had less to do with ensuring public safety than with extorting and terrorizing the citizenry. A child or adolescent caught outside after dark would be stopped and questioned. Inevitably, he would be asked to turn out his pockets and hand over anything of value. If he had nothing—which was often the case—the mere fact of his impoverishment might provoke a violent outburst from the soldiers. I knew many boys who were beaten and robbed by soldiers. I knew some who disappeared altogether. Thus, my question to the little boy at courtside was legitimate, although my motive for saying it had less to do with concern for the boy's safety than with the fact that I was offended by the notion that I had anything to learn from one so small and young.

The boy smiled and shrugged.

"You look like you're having trouble."

I gave him a hard look.

"And you can do better?"

He nodded. "Yes. I mean . . . I can't dunk, but I know how it's done."

Was it possible? Could this little boy, a foot shorter and five years younger than me, have secrets worth hearing? I thought about it for a moment. I remembered the classmates who had called me Shaka, and the older basketball players who wouldn't let me on the court. I knew what it was like to be judged (or misjudged) by people based solely on appearance. How many times had I felt diminished by the treatment I had received. Why should I be like those people? Why not be more like DMX Kisenga, who saw good in other people, and value in those whose worth was routinely questioned.

"Okay, little one," I said, trying hard to smile. "Teach me."

And so he did. He showed me how to hold the ball so that it would not come loose when I turned my hand over to dunk. He showed me how to time my approach to the basket, and how to leap naturally off one foot, rather than stopping in front of the basket, planting both feet, and trying to explode upward. This is the hardest way to dunk, for it robs you of all forward progress and results in the equivalent of trying to get upward momentum from a standstill. It was amazing that the boy knew so much, simply from having watched a lot of basketball. Despite his diminutive stature, he was smooth and graceful, and I had no doubt that he would become a very good player in his own right. Already he was an amazing teacher!

On my first attempt, I lost control of the ball. On the second I slipped and barely got off the ground. On the third, I soared higher than I had ever soared before and became so overcome with excitement that I slammed the ball off the back of the rim. The fourth, fifth, and sixth attempts were all close. Soooooo . . . close.

Finally, on the seventh try, with my legs beginning to burn, I timed everything perfectly. The approach, the takeoff, the dunk itself. I knew as I brought my hand up, the ball tucked tightly into my palm, that this was the one. I could see the rim, twisted and netless, glistening in the fading evening sun, approaching fast. It seemed so close, closer than ever before, and suddenly my hand was in the sphere. I flicked my wrist downward and released the ball.

"YESSSS!" I shouted, as I fell to the ground, arriving at almost exactly the same time as the ball.

And from the edge of the court my voice echoed in the little boy.

"YESSSS!"

CHAPTER 6

Time would melt away on the court.

Even when it was just me and a ball and a hoop, with no one else playing and no one else watching, I would become lost in my own little world. In my head I could hear the roar of an imaginary crowd, and the announcer calling the game.

Baruti drives to the basket; he goes up over Mutombo . . . and throws it down! Oh, what a dunk by Baruti!

I loved the rhythm of the game, the sound of the ball, and the feeling of a perfectly executed shot. I wanted nothing more than to be out there playing and practicing, every waking hour.

But opportunities for basketball players were few and far between in the Congo. In some African countries—Nigeria and South Africa, for example—basketball is played with passion by many young men, and their promise is identified early and nurtured through sports academies and corporate sponsorship. Although there is talent in the Congo, the political unrest makes it far more difficult (and dangerous) to foster these types of programs. This was especially true more than a decade ago, when I was introduced to the sport. But if you are serious about playing sports, it is understood that you must join a private club team like ONATRA, a respected organization sponsored by the Congo's Office National des Transports ("ONATRA"). It was one of the best club teams in the whole country, although it was more than ten miles away and designed for older boys. Still, I made up my mind to practice as hard as I could and become a member of this team. It was that simple . . . and that preposterous.

And so I played ball . . . hour after hour. If I wasn't in school, I was playing basketball. I would get home at eight or nine o'clock, and have to wait until eleven o'clock to eat. This was the one family meal, and it was designed to sustain us for the next twenty-four hours. I'd go to school every morning with my belly rumbling. All I knew was one meal a day; lunch was available in school, but my grandmother could not afford to give me any money, so most days I went without.

It wasn't so bad, really. Living in the jungle, on the run, had changed me. While many of my classmates complained whenever they got hungry (or worse, complained about the quality of the food that was served), I said nothing. Hunger becomes a habit, a source of strength, even. There was no food in the jungle, and the memory of that ceaseless hunger gave me power to cope with almost anything. Even today I can go two or three days without eating if necessary. It doesn't bother me; it simply reminds me that anything is possible.

Throughout the summer months, I kept playing ball, either by myself or with the younger kids. I began pushing the envelope in terms of how late I would stay at the court. One night I did not return home until after nine o'clock. When I left the court, the sun was fading into the horizon. By the time I reached my grandmother's house, it was pitch dark. Uncle Joseph met me at the door, his eyes filled with fury and fear.

"What are you doing, you stupid boy! Do you not understand what could happen out there?"

I lowered my head, apologized, and went off to complete my homework. I understood precisely what could happen, and I realized on some level that my behavior was selfish. But I was willing to take the risk; I loved basketball so much that I was willing to put my life on the line for the sake of a silly game.

more subtle and laborious aspects of the game: defense and rebounding, for example. These are often overlooked by the casual fan and treated with indifference by the players themselves. Scoring is fun. Defense is . . . well . . . hard. If you get a rebound and pass the ball ahead to a teammate, and he drives to the basket and scores, who gets the credit? Who gets the accolades from the crowd? Not the player whose rebound started the entire sequence. But that's okay. Other players notice the hardworking defender and rebounder, and they want him on their team. Coaches want him on the roster, as well. There is a place for the unselfish, industrious player who is content to do the job others find unappealing.

I decided very early in my basketball career that I would be that player.

So even though I rarely scored, I gained the respect of my teammates simply by outworking everyone else. By making sure that I was in position to rebound, and that I attacked the rim on every play. I developed a knack for sliding away from my man at the last second when another player drove to the basket, so that I could challenge his shot. I remember the first time I blocked one of the older player's shots, and the rush of adrenaline I felt as the ball exploded off my palm and into the night air, eventually landing in the dirt, some twenty feet off the court. I remember the howls of approval from my teammates, and the look on the other player's face, a mix of anger and grudging respect. And the way he nodded subtly, as if to say, "Good job."

After a few weeks of playing in these games every night, I was invited to take part in one of the dunk contests. The time had come, I would have my chance! When my turn came, I was so nervous that I felt like I was going to throw up. My hands were so wet that I could barely control the ball. I thought briefly about withdrawing; then it occurred to me— what was the worst that could happen? I would miss the dunk and everyone would laugh. So what? No one ever died from being laughed at.

I started about fifteen to twenty feet from the basket, on the left wing. I took a deep breath and tried to calm my racing heart. Sweat poured from my brow and into my eyes. I wiped it away and looked

Except it wasn't silly. On the basketball court I felt free, at p both mind and body. And with that freedom came hope—hop new and better life.

By the end of the summer, I was allowed into some of th pickup games with older players on a more regular basis. By this had become savvy enough to know what I could or could not do court, and I used those limitations as a guideline. For example, I w awkward and unskilled; my body was growing and changing so q that my mind could not keep up with the changes. It sometimes though one arm was longer than the other, with fingers that looke tendrils; or that my feet were like those of a clown—five sizes too b the body they supported. Such is the nature of adolescence, but i case the development seemed particularly fitful and frustrating. I time I began to sense a natural equilibrium, something would cha And then I would find myself struggling against my own body, figh just to stay upright without tripping over myself.

Discretion being the better part of valor, I took few chances wh was allowed to play with the older guys. I knew that my offensive sl were poorly developed, so I rarely shot and only when wide open i in close proximity to the basket. The last thing I wanted was to thr up an air ball from twenty feet and get kicked off the court for be both arrogant and a poor teammate. Instead, I concentrated on playi good defense, moving my feet as quickly as possible to make sure I stay in front of my opponent. Athleticism is required to play defense—t stronger and quicker you are, the harder it is for an opponent to get I you. But defense is less about natural talent than it is desire.

I quickly discovered that ego plays a huge role in basketball. It a game of artistry and beauty; of lightning-quick moves to the baske and no-look passes that would make a magician envious. But it is also a game of strength and will. Everyone likes to put the ball in the basket Everyone likes to score. These are the things that people notice and for which praise comes easily. But just as important to the outcome are the past the edge of the court, past the crowd of onlookers and players, and toward the sun fading into the horizon. It was such a beautiful night! A surge of confidence and adrenaline rushed through my body. I lowered my head and dribbled hard two or three times before catapulting myself toward the basket. I knew as soon as I left the ground that I had it nailed. As I threw the ball down I could hear the other players (and some spectators) erupt with applause and cheers. I turned to face them, with a huge smile on my face. No longer was I "Stupid Tall Man." Now they were chanting my name.

"Blondy! Blondy! Blondy!"

It was a moment I will never forget.

★

SOME OF THE BEST games occurred on Sunday afternoon, when everybody got out of church. These contests included not just teenagers, but veteran players from around the region, some of whom were extremely talented and experienced, but for one reason or another had not escaped the Congo to further their basketball careers. Some of them had played with Dikembe Mutombo, or at least claimed they had. It sometimes seemed as though every basketball player in the Congo had a story to tell about having shared a court with the great Mr. Dikembe. This was not true, of course; it was all bluster. For this reason and others, I disliked many of these veteran players. They were pretending to be best friends with Dikembe to boost their own egos. Some of them did indeed have connections to help young African kids who wanted to reach the U.S. through basketball scholarships, but I never saw them put this influence to use in my neighborhood.

The first few times I showed up for the Sunday games, I was not allowed to play. These games were highly competitive—usually the veterans would insist on playing together as a team against the younger players, and I longed for a chance to show that I belonged. Eventually my patience was rewarded and I was welcomed into the game. Again, I did not push against the boundaries of what was permitted in this setting. I was one of the youngest and least experienced players on the court, so I deferred to my older teammates and worked as hard as I could while trying to defend opponents who in some cases were a decade or two older than I was. They may have lacked the fitness and energy of youth, but they were big and strong, and incredibly tough. They pushed me around and made fun of me, but I said nothing and betrayed not a hint of emotion.

I kept growing and improving, until one day, at the age of fifteen, I decided I was ready. It was time to try out for ONATRA. I had to take an hour-long bus ride with many stops to attend evaluation sessions in the neighborhood of Matonge. ONATRA had plenty of funding, which meant quality coaching and uniforms and practice facilities. Mutombo had been a product of the ONATRA program, and his legacy continued to help attract the majority of the Congo's best basketball players. I wanted desperately to be a part of ONATRA.

Every day, when school got out, I would run straight to the bus station in order to get to practice on time. Classes did not end until 1 p.m., and practice for the Division II players (the younger players) began at two. I had little time to spare. I would get off the bus and run straight to practice. Sometimes I was late, but the coaches believed in the importance of education and therefore didn't give me a hard time.

For three months I worked my butt off in practice. I didn't expect anything to be handed to me; I felt like I was playing well and had a good attitude. But there were lots of talented and ambitious young players who wanted to be part of ONATRA, and most of them not only were from Matonge, but came from families with far greater resources. They had access to better shoes, clothing, training, and food. In every way, they had advantages over me, so I knew it would be a challenge to make the team.

Finally the big day arrived: the final practice before cuts would be made. I played well and hard. I did my best. Afterward, the coach told us to hang around for a little while. Then he met with each player in person to deliver the good or bad news.

"I'm sorry, Blondy," the coach told me. "You played very hard, but right now there are too many players ahead of you."

I said nothing, just nodded and blinked back a tear.

"Keep practicing," the coach said. "Maybe next year."

I was disappointed, but not terribly surprised. I saw it coming.

Rather than sulking about something I could not control, I decided to try out for another club team in Matonge. This one was a rival of ONATRA called Molokai, which, although in lowercase letters, was an acronym comprised of the first letters of some of the busiest streets in Matonge. On the very first day of tryouts, I was less nervous because I had already practiced with ONATRA. I was thrown into a game with other boys who hoped to join the club. There were five of us at the tryout, playing games of two-on-two and two-on-three. When we finished I was invited to stay. A man told me that he thought I had promise (I was by now 6-foot-4, which was probably my strongest attribute). Molokai had three different levels of teams: A, B, and C. I was assigned to the C team, and could not have been happier. Finally, I was a real basketball player!

We practiced four or five days each week. My family did not have enough money for me to take the bus every day, so many times I would make the ten-mile trek on foot. As soon as school ended (around 12:30 or 1:00), I would start walking or jogging. I learned a few shortcuts that cut the trip to maybe six or seven miles, which I could cover in roughly an hour. After practice I would walk home. I realize that probably sounds incredible, but it really isn't all that uncommon in Africa. Most people do not have cars, and they become accustomed to walking great distances simply to go about the business of daily life. I did not consider it a big sacrifice to spend two hours a day walking just so that I could play basketball. I considered it a privilege. I would have walked twice that distance if necessary.

There were other, smaller, inconveniences. For example, I had at that time only one pair of underwear, and I wore them to school and to play basketball. At night I would remove my underwear, soaked and stiff with sweat, and wash them by hand and hang them to dry so that I could wear them again the next day. After a few months, my lovely underwear had faded from blue to gray, and was pockmarked with holes. I developed a rash in my groin area from wearing the same bedraggled shorts every day. But I didn't care. That's how much I wanted to play.

If there were ever moments where I felt beaten down by my circumstances, like putting on damp underwear or feeling my toes poking out of my fraying basketball shoes, I would hear my mother's words in my head: *"Don't let anything hold you back. Have faith. Believe. You're not alone out there. God will always have your back."* It was a familiar refrain from our exodus through the jungle and throughout my childhood and adolescence.

I loved basketball so much that on the days when we did not have practice, I would play pickup ball. Sometimes I would walk or jog directly from practice with Molokai back to my neighborhood and jump into pickup games. Yes, even after walking twelve to fifteen miles round-trip and practicing with my club team for two hours, I still wanted to play pickup ball with my friends! In some ways I enjoyed the pickup games even more than playing with Molokai. The games were informal but intense, with lots of trash-talking and acrobatic play. Every night most of the same guys would show up and we would always try to play together.

I became one of the better big men in the nightly pickup games. I became proficient at dunking the ball, both in games and during contests. My favorite dunk was one made famous by Michael Jordan, in which he would run from half-court and take off at the foul line. It took me a long time to master this dunk, but eventually it became my specialty. Nobody else could do it; my friends were so impressed that they gave me yet another nickname: "ShakaFly," because I could hang in the air for such a long time.

There was a dunk contest in which I had to face one of my best friends, a very gifted player named Serge Ibaka. He came from the Republic of the Congo (a smaller African country not to be confused with the Democratic Republic of the Congo), but had begun spending lots of time in the DRC, where he was considered a basketball prodigy. Serge was seventeen years old and already 6-foot-10, with a massive wingspan and the strong, muscular build of a young man headed for the NBA. He was a beast in pickup games, an immovable force in the lane who could do anything he wanted—block shots, rebound, score, pass. Many people were legitimately afraid of guarding Serge: they didn't want to be embarrassed by having him dunk on them, nor did they want to catch an elbow to the face, which sometimes happened if you got too close. Everyone figured Serge was headed for great things. But to me he was more than just a tremendous athlete; he was like my brother. While our dunk competition was serious, it was also filled with joy, as Serge and I tried to one-up each other.

So it was that night. I took off from the foul line for my signature dunk. Serge looked on and smiled and then he did the exact same thing. When he placed two people in the foul lane, on their hands and knees, and then jumped over them on his way to the rim and a thunderous dunk, the crowd went crazy. I stood there and applauded. Then I put three people in the lane and jumped over them on my next dunk. This time Serge applauded and smiled. He waved a finger of admonition and summoned a fourth person from the crowd, and then easily cleared this human hurdle for yet another spectacular dunk.

"Your turn, ShakaFly," Serge said with a laugh.

As the four spectators started to walk off the court, I summoned them back.

"Where are you going?" I asked. "We're going to do this again."

Gamely, they walked back into the foul line and got down on the ground. I walked back to half-court, took two quick dribbles, and then ran full speed toward the foul line. As I soared above the four brave spectators, I glanced briefly at Serge. Then I threw the ball down and pumped my arms furiously in celebration, as Serge came over and gave me a hug.

"Well done, my brother," he said. "Call it a tie?"

I shook my head. "Not while there is daylight."

It went on like that for another hour, until we were trading dunks in the fading light. Eventually we did decide to end the contest and call it a tie. It was one of the best nights I have ever experienced on a basketball court. Afterward Serge and I walked off together, his arm around my shoulder like I was his little brother.

What I admired most about Serge (in addition to his personality) was his ambition. Like me, he loved playing basketball and saw it as a ticket out of Africa: a way to change circumstances for himself and his family. And, like me, Serge had grown up in poverty, which helped to fuel his desire for a better life.

One night, we were walking off the court together when Serge betrayed just a hint of despair over his lack of resources, something he rarely did.

"Shaq," he said, using a shortened version of my nickname, one I liked because it reminded me of Shaquille O'Neal. "I'm not sure what to do. I do not have shoes to play ball anymore." He paused, ran a hand along the tattered soles of his shoes, which had become separated from the upper. "I only have one pair of shoes left, and they are for school. But I might have to start hooping with them or I won't be able to play."

I didn't know what to say. Sometimes there are no easy answers. I myself had frequently played barefoot or in sandals or school shoes. You do what you must.

"Keep your head up, brother," I said. "It will pay off. I know it will."

I thought of this conversation a year later, when Serge's sacrifice and hard work did pay off as we had both hoped and dreamed. He was selected to play in the U-18 division of the Africa Cup tournament, where he was seen by influential scouts and offered a contract to play professionally in Spain. I was sad to see Serge leave, but excited and happy for him at being offered such an amazing opportunity; it also gave me confidence that I might follow in his footsteps. He was my inspiration: my brother from a different mother, connected by history and hardship and hope.

CHAPTER 7

❝ It was like a war!"

My teammate said this with something like bloodlust, his eyes filled with excitement. We were sitting together in the locker room, right before a game, and I didn't know how to respond.

After less than a year I had been promoted to Molokai's B team, where most of my teammates were several years older and far stronger. I was nearly 6-foot-7 now, skinny but quicker, with the good sense to focus on what I could do well. I was still a somewhat weak and unpolished offensive player, not particularly smooth or skilled. But I could play defense and block shots. I could rebound. I could outwork almost anyone. Unlike most kids, I didn't care about the glory that came with scoring; I just wanted to be on the court. I wanted to play. There were games when I would barely score at all, but I would block ten shots and grab ten rebounds, which was more than enough to please my coach.

I became eager to join the A team, to get a chance to play with Molokai's best athletes. Some days I was invited to practice with the A team, and I did my best to show I belonged. One day after practice I was told that I was being promoted for the next game, against a club team called Heritage. The last time that Heritage and Molokai had played, the previous season, there had been a controversial ending and a fight that started on the court and spilled over into the stands. Many people were injured. Understandably, there was a lot of tension heading into the rematch, which made me feel both excited and apprehensive.

The next night, before the game, the players all got together to discuss strategy, but most of the conversation centered around what had happened the last time Molokai and Heritage had played. And it wasn't about basketball. It was about fighting and bloodshed.

"We wanted to kill each other," someone said.

"It was like a war . . ."

Everyone nodded in agreement. They seemed to relish this idea, of fighting for something so passionately. But I couldn't help but think to myself, *No, this is not a war, even if people get hurt. This is just basketball. It is just a game. I have lived through war. There is nothing that compares.*

Despite this affirmation, and my best efforts at meditative reasoning, I found myself nearly overcome with anxiety as game time drew near. In warmups, as the other players bumped fists or patted each other on the back, and exchanged words of encouragement, I could barely speak. My heart was racing—beating so hard that I felt it might jump out of my chest. Oddly, I was not even sweating. My skin was cold and dry.

As the game began, I took a seat near the end of the bench. I was the new kid on the team and did not expect to play very much. To my surprise, the coach called my name at the end of the first quarter.

"Blondy! Let's see what you can do."

Not much, as it turned out. I had never felt so lost on a basketball court. A place that had been a sanctuary to me suddenly felt foreign and overwhelming. Everyone was so big and strong and fast. The intensity of the competition was like nothing I had experienced. I felt like I was moving in slow motion. I could not stay in front of my man on defense. I tried to get in position for a rebound, only to have two players from the other team leap over me and grab the ball. Not necessarily because they were more talented than me (although this was probably the case), but because I was glued to the floor. I don't know how to explain it, except to acknowledge that I suffered from a catastrophic anxiety attack. It was almost as if I had forgotten everything I had learned about the game of basketball. My mind went dark and my body became immobile.

"Blondy!"

The voice came from the sideline. My coach wore a look of exasperation. He held out his hands, palms facing the ceiling, as if to say, "What are you doing?" I had no response. I didn't say a word, didn't even move. The coach shook his head, pointed to one of my teammates on the bench. Then he pointed at me. The buzzer sounded and the substitution was made. I walked sheepishly to the end of the bench, without making eye contact with any of my teammates or the coach. I did not return to the game. My entire shift had lasted less than one minute.

After the game, the president of the club came over to talk with me.

"You were scared."

I shook my head defiantly. "No sir. It was just . . . different than I expected."

The president smiled. "I could see it in your eyes, son. You were frightened."

I hung my head. "Yes, sir. Maybe a little."

He nodded. "It happens sometimes . . . when we ask too much of someone who isn't ready."

So that was my chance, an opportunity squandered in what felt like a heartbeat. The next day I went back to practicing with the B team. I was upset and embarrassed, but I knew it was the right and fair decision; I wasn't ready to be promoted, so I went back to my old team and worked hard to improve. I became one of the best rebounders and shot blockers in the entire division. In many games, I would block more than ten shots. It became my greatest source of pride. I felt like I was on the verge of being promoted to the A team again when I made a poor decision.

My friend DMX convinced me that we should leave Molokai temporarily and join another team located several hundred kilometers away, in Matadi. We would be gone just a few days while playing a couple of games with the team to help them qualify for the Congo Cup, a national championship tournament featuring the best teams in the country. If we were successful, DMX explained, we might be paid a nice bonus and maybe given a chance to join the team for an extended period. I never received a salary for playing club ball, but such bonus payments, while not strictly in accordance with amateur guidelines, were not uncommon. I had never known anything but poverty; the chance to make even a small amount of money for playing basketball was appealing. In order to make this happen, I had to convince Uncle Joseph. This was not easy since, it meant I would miss a few days of school, but Uncle Joseph was supportive of my basketball career and agreed to let me go. My mother was traveling for work at the time, so I did not have to seek her approval. I did have to come up with an excuse for missing some practice time with Molokai.

"I have a family emergency," I told my coach, which wasn't entirely a lie, but certainly wasn't the truth, either.

Unfortunately, we split our two games and the team did not make the Congo Cup. DMX and I received no money at all, not even bus fare for the trip back to Kinshasa. We ended up staying in Matadi for more than a week, trying to figure out how to get home. Eventually, when we got hungry enough, I decided to call Uncle Joseph and explain to him that things had not gone exactly as planned. To put it mildly, he was not happy, but in the end he agreed to send us money so that we could buy bus tickets and return home.

I finished the season with Molokai's B team, and wound up with respectable numbers: sixteen rebounds, eleven points, and eight blocked shots per game. When the season ended, I did not take a break, but instead played every day—usually twice a day!—with my friends at Foyer Social. Throughout the summer, I would get up at five in the morning and lift weights in an effort to put some muscle on my slender frame. On Sunday mornings I would join several of my friends for a long workout. We would run several miles to Tata Raphaël, a fifty-thousand-seat stadium in Kinshasa. Once there, we would run the massive and steep stadium stairs until we were ready to collapse from exhaustion. Then we would rest for a few minutes and run back home. The entire workout consumed nearly three hours and more calories than any of us could spare. I would get home and fall on the floor. (I didn't even know what "calories" were until I moved to the U.S. It was only then that I realized that the more you run, the more you burn calories; you have to eat and drink healthy food to replace the calories burned. But back then I had no clue.)

"Can I have something to eat?" I would ask my grandmother.

"We will have dinner later," she would say.

"But I am hungry now," I would plead.

"I am sorry, Blondy. There is nothing else."

On the occasions when I was desperately famished, I would visit a neighbor's house and ask for food. It was humiliating, to go begging this way, but in the battle between hunger and pride, hunger will usually win the day. You do what you must to ease the sting of an empty stomach. Often dinner was nothing more than a bowl of rice cooked over an open fire fueled by fallen tree limbs I had gathered for my grandmother. I saw less and less of my mother, as her business trips grew more frequent and longer in duration. Still, there was never enough money or food. This was just the way it was for me and for many people in my neighborhood.

Basketball, with its promise of a better life in America, sustained me. Whenever I would get depressed or hungry or begin to feel sorry for myself (and I am ashamed to say this happened frequently), I would go to Foyer Social and play ball with my friends. In those games, on that court, my problems and fears melted away. I was young and naive, without a clue as to how I would make my dreams come true. I had no connections, and no knowledge of the mysterious inner workings of the machinery that could potentially take one from the Congo to the basketball team of an American university, or, God willing, the NBA. I just knew that my destiny was to achieve these goals, and somehow it would all work out.

Many people felt I was indulging in a pathetic fantasy.

"Blondy, why are you wasting your time playing that stupid game?" some of my neighbors (and even my own relatives) would say when they saw me leave the house in my basketball shorts. "It will never bring you anything. Focus on school."

"There is room for both," I would respond with a smile. And this was true, although it is also true that I was far more devoted to basketball than I was to my studies. But I worked hard enough in the classroom to get decent grades and to ensure that if I had a chance to attend school in the U.S., I would not be deemed unworthy of the opportunity. But I didn't love schoolwork (what sixteen-year-old boy does?). I loved basketball.

That summer I played pickup ball with Serge Ibaka on many nights, and afterward we would walk home together and talk about what we needed to do in order to improve, and how we could make our dreams come true. Serge was definitely more talented than me, but he was endlessly encouraging and thoughtful. He would kick my butt all night, scoring as many points as he wanted and swatting my shot if I had the temerity to challenge him inside. Afterward, though, he would shake my hand and tell me "good job." Within a few months Serge would be in Spain, one step closer to fulfilling his dream. I remained in the Congo, following his exploits from a distance, and determined to follow the same path.

★

THE FOLLOWING YEAR ALL of my hard work paid off and I was promoted to the A team. Sometimes practices were early in the morning, before school, so I would rise before the sun to take the bus or walk to the practice facility. By the time classes started, I was exhausted. But I was willing to make any and all sacrifices in pursuit of my goal.

By the start of the season I worked my way into the starting lineup. A few older and more experienced players, who were naturally protective of their turf, responded angrily to my ascension. A couple even quit the team in protest. I did not care. I knew I had earned my playing time.

Unfortunately, there were some things I simply did not understand. For example, I ran afoul of the club administration, and some of my teammates, because of my unwillingness to participate in certain pregame rituals. You see, superstition plays a big role in the Congo, and that extends to sports. There are ties to the occult and to ancient ways of life that carry over to this day, and so it is not unusual for players to be asked to engage in certain rituals in the spirit of fostering good luck. On our team, the players were expected to rub totems before every game. To deny this ritual was to provoke the gods and risk a poor performance. As a Christian, I thought this was silly, if not downright blasphemous.

"I cannot do this," I explained to everyone as they gathered in a tight circle before my very first game with the team and implored me to join them. They were dancing and chanting, trying to pump themselves up before the game. I suppose, to them, it seemed innocent enough. But to me it was sacrilege. I had grown up as a Christian. My mother invoked the name of God and instructed me to turn to him for courage and guidance when we were trekking through the jungle, so close to death every day. And when my mother went away on long business trips, my uncles and grandmother made sure that I went to church service regularly— and by regularly, I mean several times a week.

"There will be times," my mother always said, "when there will be obstacles placed in front of you. Do not submit. Have faith in God. He will show you the way."

When I refused to join the pregame ceremony, some of my teammates were perplexed; others were angry.

"This is what we do before the game," one of them said. "If you don't do it, then you don't play."

"I'm sorry," I stammered. "My mother would not be happy."

"Who cares what your mother thinks?" the other player scoffed.

This made me angry. And it gave me strength. "I do."

For quite some time they continued to yell at me and taunt me and call me a "little baby." I did not care. I might have been the youngest player on the team, but I was not going to be bullied into taking part in what I perceived to be a pagan ritual. So I stood my ground, off to the side, as the players shouted at me and called me names. Eventually, one by one, they grew weary of the abuse and peeled off into a different part of the dressing room. They completed their pregame ritual without my involvement, and then we got on with the more important business of playing basketball.

It is a truism of sports that winning will cure most problems, and certainly this seemed to be the case on opening night. Any animosity my teammates might have felt toward me melted away once the game began. I started, played about twenty-five minutes, and finished with thirteen points and fourteen rebounds. I also blocked six shots. We won the game and everyone was happy. I was foolish enough to think that was the end of any controversy surrounding my abstaining from the pregame ritual.

A few days later I learned that my refusal to take part in the ritual was deemed insubordination by the club president, and resulted in my being suspended for a couple of games. My coach, however, fought on my behalf; in the end, I was allowed to play without taking part in any of the rituals. This was probably because the team fared poorly in my absence. Winning trumps everything, doesn't it?

Once I became accepted as part of the team, and continued to play well, I had a lot of fun playing for Molokai's A team. I was still not the most skilled or offensive-minded player, but I competed with great intensity, especially on the defensive end of the floor. The fans who came to our games liked my energy; they also liked my "look." You see, I was one of the few players in the league who wore his hair in an afro. As a result, the fans and some of my teammates began calling me "ShakaFro." (I must say, I enjoyed the fact that my nicknames kept getting better and better!)

Still, there were obstacles to my fitting in with the A team. Most of the players had fathers who were active in their lives, and came from families that had more money. They would wear nice clothes and nice shoes before the game, and I didn't. Some of them would even question what I was wearing (usually just sandals and my typical old school clothes), and sometimes make fun of me. Luckily, I wasn't alone. I had a dear friend named Shako, which means twin in some of the African languages (he had a twin sister), but his nickname was Ebende, which means medal, because he was a gifted jumper and a very strong, athletic young man. We supported each other in every way. Like me, Ebende was poor, and sometimes we would fight back against our teammates if they tried to make fun of us. We didn't have much, but we had our eyes on the prize: America. We would say to each other after a long walk home from practice, "Let's not get discouraged. This hard work will pay off someday."

Molokai did very well that year, qualifying for the playoffs and getting all the way to the semifinals of the season-ending Kinshasa Cup. It was a best-of-three series. Our opponent was a team called Kauka, whose best player was a young man named Momo Ntumba. In fact, Ntumba, a very muscular and physical player, was perhaps the best young player in all of the Congo. But you know what? I was not intimidated. In the first game, the stadium was filled with people who wanted to watch my matchup against Momo. The young, promising Blondy against the best player in the Congo: Momo Ntumba. I wanted to show him that a skinny kid with less experience could shut him down. Against Ntumba, I played the best defense of my life, and Molokai won the game. You cannot imagine my elation! It was quickly diminished over the course of the next two games, however, as Ntumba showed why he had such a great reputation. He kicked my butt on both ends of the floor. Not only did I have trouble getting off a shot, but I felt helpless to stop Ntumba around the basket. He was so strong and polished. I remember getting pulled from the game and sitting on the bench next to my coach, hurt and humiliated. That night I learned a valuable lesson: never let it go to your head when things are going well. Stay focused and keep working hard. But I had no experience in such matters at the time.

Kauka won the next two games and eliminated us from the playoffs. I took this personally because Ntumba was clearly the reason Kauka won, and I was the person responsible for defending him. But the truth is, he was simply better than me in that series. He was bigger, stronger, and more skilled. He was also a couple of years older, which obviously helped. There was no shame in being outplayed by Ntumba. He eventually left the Congo to play for a junior college in the U.S. Then he transferred to the University of Southern Indiana, a Division II program, before eventually embarking on a professional career in Australia. By any reasonable measure, Ntumba was a success. I wanted to be just like him, but that would require a great deal more work.

Actually, I wanted even more. My ambition was to receive a scholarship to play Division I college basketball in the United States. Not since Dikembe Mutombo, some two decades earlier, had anyone from my country achieved this goal. I dreamed of playing in the NBA, as well, but I also wanted an education. I wanted to play college ball in America.

"I am going to be the next Dikembe Mutombo," I would tell my friends.

"You are a crazy boy," they would say.

"Just watch. You'll see."

CHAPTER 8

I can honestly say that I never got into any trouble as an adolescent—not because I was a perfect young man, but simply because I didn't have the time. Every day was filled, from sunup to sundown, with the routine of basketball, school, and church. I was always busy, especially when Molokai's owner decided to move the team's practice headquarters to a different location even further from my house, in early 2008, in the hopes of attracting some new players. It worked; there were some roster changes and we got a few players who helped us improve. But we also lost some players who did not want to travel to the new practice court. The move also angered many of our fans in Matonge who considered Molokai to be a team that was intended for the young men of that region. Some were bitter when the team was uprooted, and they withdrew their support.

For me, personally, the move was challenging because it extended my travel time for practice, with even fewer opportunities to take public transportation (which I often could not afford anyway). By the time I got home in the evening I was so exhausted and hungry that I could barely stand up. Someday, I thought, the suffering will all be worth it.

One day after practice, I was approached by a man named Dr. Lissa, a trainer for a local soccer club who also spent time with Molokai.

"Your name is Blondy," he said. It wasn't a question.

"Yes, sir."

"How old are you, son?"

"I just turned seventeen, sir."

He nodded. "I've been watching you the last few months. You're young and you're not very strong, but you have good size and a lot of energy." He paused. "And I notice that you smile a lot when you come off the court." This was true. Off the court, I was happy. I smiled and laughed a lot. I told jokes. But on the basketball court? That was a different story. I played ferociously; all of the anger that I kept inside me—the anger over being poor, and what I went through in the jungle, and the uncertainty about my future—came out on the court. Every time I stepped between the lines, it was like I was fighting for my survival. That's how I saw the game of basketball.

I shrugged (I think I smiled, too). "I love to play."

"That is apparent. Don't change. Love of the game is important, especially as you get older and it becomes a job."

I nodded.

Again, there was a pause, as if the man was sizing me up.

"I want to help you, Blondy," he said. "I have an acquaintance in America who is looking for college players. I'm thinking of recommending you."

It seemed too good to be true, and indeed many of my friends told me that it probably was too good to be true. There was no shortage of people in the Congo who would pose as intermediaries capable of brokering deals for promising and often gullible young athletes who dreamed of traveling to Europe or the United States. More often than not, they failed to produce results, or perhaps did not even try. Sometimes they would collect a fee up front and disappear. I did not know whether Dr. Lissa was a friend or a fraud, but I soon found out that I was not the first person he had solicited—several other boys on the club had previously rejected his offer. I was merely next in line.

"Don't trust him," some of my teammates said. "He's using you."

This could have been true. I had no way of knowing; however, I was willing to take a chance. Again, part of this stemmed from my faith in

God, and a steadfast belief that he would not lead me down a dangerous path. But it also speaks to the fact that I was so hungry to leave the
Congo and get to America, so desperate that I was willing to overlook
the possibility of being exploited or swindled.

I asked Dr. Lissa what he needed. Usually, he explained, American
coaches wanted to see video of a player in action. I had nothing like that.

"Bring me your academic transcript," Lissa said. "And a picture
of yourself. Something that shows your size. And remember to smile.
Maybe that will be enough."

He gave me his address and told me to come by the following week.
(He did not ask for any money, which we all viewed as a positive sign.)
The next week, transcript in hand, I made the fifteen-mile walk to Dr.
Lissa's office. I didn't mind. We met for maybe thirty minutes, during
which time I presented him with the information he needed. We also
talked more about my dreams and aspirations; I could tell Dr. Lissa was
trying to figure out whether I was truly committed to this journey, and I
made sure that I did not disappoint. In the end, Dr. Lissa said he would
do everything in his power to facilitate my journey to the United States.

"I believe I can help you, Blondy," he said. "Please try to be patient.
This won't happen overnight."

"Yes, yes, of course," I said, nodding and smiling. "I understand.
Thank you, Dr. Lissa."

We shook hands and I left. Once outside, I began walking. Then I
broke into a slow jog, and finally into a full sprint. I ran with a smile on
my face, so happy that I could hardly even hear my own labored breathing.

It's happening, I thought to myself. *I am going to America.*

★

AS I WAITED TO hear from Dr. Lissa regarding my American prospects, I
tried to put the dream aside and focus on the things I could control: basketball, training, and school. Molokai had a very good season in the top

division. We won the championship, beating a team called Terreur in the finals. By this time, I had started to grow into my body and become one of the best post players in the Congo. I had eleven points and fourteen rebounds in the championship game, and was named All-Congo. During the game, I remember hearing fans in the crowd singing my name, and cheering for me on every play. It was thrilling to know that I was close to becoming the type of player I had always wanted to be.

If there was any sadness to the victory, it was only that my family was not there to share it. Not for lack of wanting, but simply because the tournament was too far away and they lacked the resources and time to make the trip. I was not angry or disappointed, as they had made many sacrifices on my behalf over the years. I only wished that I could have thanked them as the championship medal was draped around my neck.

On my first day back at Foyer Social after winning the championship with Molokai, everyone was proud of me. Even the older players who once refused to allow me to participate in pickup games applauded and congratulated me. I felt proud, but I didn't let it go to my head. I had one goal: to get to America. And that dream was still far off.

The spring brought more basketball and more opportunities. And the occasional brush with danger. I was invited to play with ONATRA in the Africa Cup, and despite an infection on the sole of my foot, I did pretty well. I was a starter in most of the games and did not back down against many of the best players on the continent. I knew I still had to improve considerably if I wanted to play college basketball in the U.S., but my confidence had grown along with my stature.

I rarely missed a day of training. I would run and lift weights in the morning, and play pickup ball at Foyer Social in the afternoon and evening. Sometimes the games stretched out until the sun had faded. As always, we knew this was dangerous, but as adolescents will sometimes do, we pushed the boundaries of safety and common sense. On the basketball court and at school, I felt protected; it was easy in these spaces to forget that the Congo remained a fierce and deadly place.

One night, I walked home from Foyer Social with three or four of my friends. In the gray of approaching night, we laughed and talked about the games we had just played, and how we had ruled the court again, and our plans for doing it all over again the next day.

It must have been close to 9:30 when the soldiers stepped out in front of us at a roadside checkpoint. There were at least ten of them, heavily armed, and unsettled merely by the sight of us. I was immediately gripped by a sensation of helplessness, a fear that ran deep in my bones and stretched back to my childhood, provoked by many encounters with soldiers and guerrillas and rebel forces, and of knowing what they were capable of doing; how the slightest misstep could be interpreted as disrespectful and inspire a firestorm of bullets or the unsheathing of machetes. In the worst of it, entire families were massacred and villages razed in the name of genocide. But even now, in less horrific times, bloodshed was common, and death a daily threat. Military rule was the norm, and the soldiers charged with maintaining order were often undisciplined, lightly trained, agitated by drug use, and emboldened by the notion that they were the law of the land. Essentially, they had been a given a license to kill, and it was not unusual for them to exercise this right.

One of the soldiers stepped ahead of the others and raised his rifle.

"Where are you going?" he asked in a tone more accusatory than curious.

I would like to say that I spoke first, that I took charge of the situation. But this would not be true. I was frozen with fear, my heart beating as furiously as it had when I was a little boy, hiding in the reeds by the Congo River, praying I would not be discovered.

"We were just playing basketball," one of my friends said. "We are going home now."

The lead soldier shook his head. "I don't think so."

The others moved forward and raised their rifles, as well. I looked at my friends. Their faces betrayed a fear as crippling as my own. Was this the end? Were the soldiers going to kill us simply for being out after darkness had fallen? Was life so inconsequential in the Congo that we would forfeit our existence for such a trivial offense? It seemed so. I reached for the hand of one of my friends. We stood there, motionless, waiting to be cut down. Remember, in the Congo we didn't have the same sort of laws that exist in the U.S. If the soldiers had killed us, there would have been no investigation. In the Congo, if you get shot or killed by the police or the military, that's it. Life continues, with no repercussions. The reason why police and soldiers behave this way is because the government pays them so little, and provides precious little oversight. So when they come across a civilian, robbery is often part of the interaction. And if you try to resist, you lose your life, as well as your money. We knew all of this as we cowered before the soldiers.

Finally, one of them spoke.

"Money. Give us whatever you have."

Again, we exchanged glances. Then we turned out our pockets, revealing that we were penniless, a revelation that only served to heighten the anger of the soldiers.

"What is this!" the lead soldier shouted. "You have nothing? I should kill you all right now."

My friend put up his hands and pleaded for mercy.

"We are young and poor," he explained. "If you need money, ask the government for help. We have nothing to give. I'm sorry. Please, don't hurt us."

From the left another soldier took a couple quick steps forward, reversed the grip on his rifle, and drove the butt end into my friend's face. He grunted and fell to the ground. Within seconds, the others did likewise, beating all of us with their rifles until we were bloody. As we cowered together, one of the soldiers pointed the barrel of his rifle at my head.

"Let's just shoot them. They have no money anyway. They are useless to us."

A few of the soldiers nodded in agreement. But a couple others shook their heads in protest.

"No, they're too young. Let them go."

Predictably, and almost comically, this exchange prompted a vigorous argument between the two factions, with some of the soldiers apparently eager to empty their weapons into living, breathing flesh, at the slightest provocation, with no concern whatsoever for the moral ramifications, and the others seemingly disinclined. My friends and I knelt in the dirt, our hands clasped behind our bloodied heads, listening to this insanity, wondering which faction would win out, and whether we would live or die.

Finally, the bickering ceased and one of the soldiers told us to get off the ground. We did as instructed, slowly, methodically, so as not to show even the slightest hint of aggression.

"Get out of here," he said. "Now! Before we shoot you."

Frozen with fear, we did not move, until one of the soldiers dropped the barrel of his rifle a few degrees and squeezed off a few shots in the dirt near our feet. We recoiled in horror but still did not retreat.

"Go home!" the soldier shouted again, as the others laughed. He fired again at the dirt, and this time we turned and ran, stumbling and falling over each other as gunfire strafed the ground all around us. We ran for perhaps a mile, as fast as we could, before finally stopping to rest, and to check ourselves for bullet wounds. We all were bleeding from the face and head, thanks to the beating we had endured, but none of us had been shot. It was something of a miracle. For whatever reason, through God's will or sheer luck, the soldiers had extended mercy to us and allowed us to see another day. With a full moon illuminating the sky, I looked into the eyes of my friends. Almost in unison, we began to cry.

When I got home, my mother was anxiously waiting (this was one of the rare times when she was not on a business trip). She saw the blood and dirt on my face, and began screaming at me.

"Why are you so foolish? Haven't I taught you well?"

I nodded sheepishly. "I'm sorry, Mama."

Then she pulled me in and held me close, like I was still her little boy, despite being a foot taller than she was.

"I cannot lose you, Blondy. You must be smarter."

I looked down at her; she was crying, too. "I thought living here would bring us peace." I said. "Isn't that what you told me in the forest? Will life ever be easier?"

My mother shook her head. "I don't know."

s spring gave way to summer, I wondered whether Dr. Lissa had forgotten about me. I had nearly given up when he suddenly showed up at our home.

"I have a scholarship for Blondy," he said. "He's going to America."

It wasn't a college scholarship. Because I was only seventeen years old and lagging behind in both academic and athletic development (in comparison to my American counterparts)—and because I did not speak English—it was determined that I would benefit from two years at Golding Academy, a prep school in the American Northeast. But I would be on an athletic scholarship so money for school was not an issue. If successful in prep school, then perhaps I would be offered a basketball scholarship in college. This, in fact, was a path followed by many Division I basketball players in the United States. I was thrilled, of course; so was my mother.

We kept this a secret. No one knew what was going on except my mother, my uncle Joseph, and my grandmother. We didn't want to tell my sister because she had trouble keeping things to herself. In the African culture, especially the Congo, if you are planning to travel outside the continent, you shouldn't tell anyone beyond your own family, because jealousy is a huge risk. Sadly, people do not always like to see others prosper. If people find out you are leaving, they might want to put your travel in jeopardy, or perhaps even try to end your life. This was a very real possibility, so we kept our plans very quiet. We had to swallow our excitement and enthusiasm, which were substantial.

Until we learned that in order to travel to the U.S., I had to obtain a visa, a process that was both mind-bogglingly complicated and expensive.

The first step was an interview at the American embassy. But even the interview was not without cost. We had to come up with $150 as part of the application and interview fee. Now, while this might not sound like much to you, or to most people in the United States, it was a princely sum to my family. Remember, we could barely afford food or clothing. But my mother was determined to support my dream, and so she sold some of our furniture and other meager belongings. Whatever she could not raise on her own, she borrowed. Somehow, she came up with the interview fee. I was so excited! But again, there were obstacles I had not anticipated.

★

I WENT TO THE interview with my friend Christian, who, thanks to Dr. Lissa, was also interviewing for a visa with the hope of playing basketball in the United States. I had planned and prepared for the interview, knew how to explain why I wanted to go to school in the United States. I dressed in the finest clothes I owned: a pair of jeans (my only pair) that I saved for special occasions, and a clean T-shirt. Very early in the interview, conducted by a woman only a few years older than me, I was asked whether I understood that my coursework would be taught in English.

"Yes, I know," I responded (in French, which was my native tongue).

"Do you speak English?" the woman asked.

"No, but I will learn."

She pursed her lips and sighed. "Okay."

But it wasn't okay. At the end of the interview, the woman stoically delivered the response I feared: my request for a visa was denied. I was very upset, but my mother was devastated. Can you imagine selling all your belongings, everything of value that you own, only to have your son's application rejected? I could see the pain in my mother's eyes, and it made me feel terrible. I felt like I let her down. But I still had faith. I told myself that being denied a visa was nothing compared to slogging through the jungles of the Congo for a year and a half. I would survive and hopefully get another chance.

But how?

Christian's application was also rejected. With nowhere else to turn, we both reached out to Dr. Lissa and explained what had happened.

"Don't worry," he said. "I'll take care of it."

And he did. One month later the prep school responded with a promise to provide additional services to support my language differences, and I was granted another interview at the embassy. When it came time for the interview, everyone on the Molokai team was at a camp getting ready for a big tournament to qualify for the Africa Cup. The team rented out space at a nearby Catholic school that had a nice basketball court on the premises. Our schedule was quite busy—with practice sessions every morning and evening. We ate meals at the school and showered there, as well. There were no days off. It was serious business.

I was faced with a difficult decision: to ask my coach for permission to leave for my second interview, not knowing how long I would be gone, or whether permission would be granted (which seemed unlikely), or come up with some other type of excuse. I did not consider skipping the interview. As much as I loved basketball and wanted to help Molokai win the Africa Cup, it was not as important as obtaining a visa. And this interview was my last chance. So, once again, I told the coach that I had a family emergency: my grandmother was sick and I was needed at home. The coach was upset with me, and I suppose some of my teammates were disappointed as well. I was Molokai's best big man, and they needed my help in the tournament. I still feel guilty sometimes when I think back on that decision, but I find comfort in the words of Michael Jordan, the greatest player in the history of the game: "To be successful, you have to be selfish, or else you never achieve. And once you get to your highest level, then you have to be unselfish."

In this moment, I had to do what was best for my future. I had to be selfish.

After I left the camp I contacted Christian and asked if he was willing to pay the fees necessary for a second interview. He said no, and said that he believed the whole thing was a scam; he wasn't going to waste any more money on a fantasy. It's hard to explain, but for some reason I did not share his cynicism. I am a man of faith, and I believed that God would provide for me this time. But there was still the challenge of having to pay another $150 application fee, and there was nothing left to sell, so my mother borrowed the money. She went to every family she knew and asked people to contribute in whatever they could. She did this surreptitiously, explaining not that the money was intended for my visa application, but rather for help with a family health crisis. I know this was dishonest, but we were desperate. I also asked for help from some people I knew; I told them I needed money but did not explain how I would use it, because I was not sure they would approve. As I said, it is a popular dream in the Congo to exchange the poverty and bloodshed of our native land for the wealth and promise of America, and not everyone is supportive of his neighbor.

"I need money for food," I lied. "I need money for clothing. Please help."

Eventually we acquired enough money to secure a second interview. I prayed and fasted for twenty-four hours prior to the appointment, in the hope of improving my chances. I barely slept the night before. I was so nervous, and I felt instinctively that this would be my last chance. In the morning I put on the same jeans and T-shirt I had worn to the first interview, and fell to my knees beside my bed, so that I could ask for God's guidance on the most important day of my life.

Sitting in the embassy, waiting for my name to be called, I could barely contain my anxiety. My pulse was pounding. I felt queasy. This was the crucial moment, when I could almost see my dream coming true, and know that one day I'd be able to help my mother and grand-mother. I silently said another prayer, this one more practical in nature.

Please, God, let me do well. And don't let it be the same woman conduct-ing the interview.

My prayers were answered.. This time I was interviewed by an older woman with far more experience, which gave me hope, but the line of questioning was exactly the same. I told her I planned to attend school in America. She asked if I was aware that classes would be taught in En-glish. I explained that I was aware of this fact and that my school would be providing extra support because French was my native language.

"Are you sure of this?" she asked.

I showed her the documentation to prove it. She nodded approvingly.

"What is your main goal after you get an education in the United States?" she asked. Her tone was deadly serious. I could tell it was an important question, and that my answer might determine the outcome of the interview. I paused for a very long time before speaking, in order to get my thoughts straight.

"America is a place of great wealth and promise," I explained. "It is a place where I can pursue my dreams of getting an education and playing professional basketball."

I paused and looked at her, to see if she approved. Her expression did not change.

"And then I hope I can come back here, to my country, and help my people," I continued. "The Congo is my home."

She smiled. This, clearly, was what she wanted to hear. It was also the truth.

"Good luck, young man," she said. And with that she handed over my visa. I thanked her profusely and ran out of the building. And I kept running, all the way home, a distance of roughly ten miles. I burst through the front door, waving my visa. My mother wrapped her arms around me and started crying.

"Thank God!" she sobbed. "My boy is going to America!"

My happiness was tempered by the realization that I would be going alone—that my friend Christian would not be getting a visa. Part of me was angry with him for not trying a second time, but I understood his situation. Like me, Christian came from a poor family. To each of us, $150 was a princely sum, the acquisition of which required sacrifice, solicitation, and a stretching of the truth. I was willing to do anything to get a second interview. Christian was not, and I cannot blame him for that.

We kept this news to ourselves for a while, as we knew there was always the possibility of further complications. This turned out to be prescient, for while I had possession of the proper legal documents to leave the country and attend a prep school in America, and a scholarship from that school, there was something we hadn't considered:

How was I going to get to America?

I mean, obviously I understood that there would be a very long and expensive trip involved, but for some reason it hadn't occurred to me that I would be expected to pay the fare. I was young and naive, so when Dr. Lissa informed me that the plane trip to America would cost nearly $2,000, I didn't know what to say. *Two thousand dollars?* My family had been compelled to sell off our furniture and beg to neighbors just to come up with the $150 visa fee. How in the world could we possibly get two thousand dollars? This was an unfathomable sum, more than my mother earned in a year.

"I do not understand," I said to Dr. Lissa. "Why doesn't the school that is giving me a scholarship also pay for my plane ticket? They know we don't have that kind of money."

Dr. Lissa seemed perplexed, as well. "I guess they're not allowed to do that. They can only pay for your education, and your room and board. But not your transportation."

I did not understand any of this. It seemed illogical that a school would offer me a scholarship, which implied that my family was impoverished, but somehow expect us to pay such an extraordinary amount for a plane ticket.

"What do we do, then?" I expected Dr. Lissa to have the answer, as he always had in the past. But the truth was, this was merely a hobby of his. He was a friendly man who loved sports and had helped a few kids from the Congo get to school in America, but he was hardly an expert. He fell quiet while formulating a response. Finally, after a long pause, he said, "I'm not sure. But don't give up hope."

The clock was ticking. The embassy had given me one month to leave the Congo. If I had not secured transportation by then, my visa would be revoked. Each day that passed, I felt the crush of anxiety and the ticking clock. Can you imagine? I had been dreaming of this moment for years— since the first time I touched a basketball. I had been insulted, bullied, kicked out of pickup games because I wasn't good enough; walked miles in 110-degree heat to get to basketball practice; threatened with dismissal because I didn't want to be part of my teammates' pagan rituals before games; trained all night by myself to improve; been beaten up by soldiers while walking home after pickup games. I had given buckets of blood, sweat, and tears to become a better basketball player, in the hope that the game would somehow take me to America. And now I had to come up with an astronomical amount of money to pay for transportation. It seemed impossible.

With less than four days before the visa was to be revoked, we still had no answers. The worst part was hearing my mother cry almost every single night of that month. There was nothing she or I could do to come up with $2,000, the reality of which brought tears of despair and incessant prayers. "Oh, Lord I believe in you!" she would wail. "I believe you can turn impossible into possible. I believe in your name and in your power. The same God that protected me and my children throughout the journey of civil war, through the jungle of the Congo—I believe the same God will come through. My family and I trust in you!"

I prayed, as well, though in the quiet of my room: "God, I want to be a miracle. When the world sees me, I want them not to see me, but I want the world to see your glory through me. I know with all my heart that you will come through at this moment in my life. When you start something, God, you always finish it, and I'm asking you today to finish what you started with me. Please . . ."

With only three days remaining until the deadline, and no prospect of acquiring $2,000, Uncle Joseph walked into my room. I was lying on the bed, so depressed and nervous that I could not eat. I didn't even want to go to Foyer Social, because playing basketball reminded me of my dream, and how it seemed to be sleeping away.

"What is it, Uncle?" I said. Slowly, his face formed a smile.

"The Lord never lets down his child," he said.

I sat up. "What do you mean?"

"Dr. Lissa just called. You have a plane ticket to America. You should start getting ready to leave."

I was so shocked that I didn't know what to say.

"But how is this possible, Uncle? What happened?"

"You have a cousin named Patrick in America," he explained. "He lives in Houston, Texas, and he paid for your ticket, and he will meet you when you arrive."

I couldn't believe my good fortune! I did not even know that I had a cousin in the U.S. And now he was paying for my trip to America? It was almost too good to be true. But then, we were family. And maybe he had become a rich man, like everyone else in America.

"There is one change," my uncle said. "You're no longer going to Golding Academy."

"Where am I going?"

"Dr. Lissa said you are going to a school in Phoenix, Arizona."

This seemed strange. "Why am I going to Arizona if my cousin lives in Texas?"

My uncle shrugged. "I don't know. It is better to not ask too many questions. Just be grateful."

It all seemed a little mysterious, but in some weird sort of way it also made sense. If Patrick paid for the ticket, then he must have had a good reason for wanting to change the plans. And I figured that wherever I was going, I'd be living in a dorm room. I assumed that this new school in Arizona was also a boarding school. Frankly, I did not care. I would have gone to any town or city, and attended any school. All I heard was this word, the one that had sustained me for years:

America!

The next day I went to Foyer Social one last time, just to say goodbye to some friends, and to look around one last time at the place that had been both a boon and a bane to my existence. It was here that I was first taunted and insulted, and chased away from the court, and told that I would never amount to anything; it was here that they called me *Mulayi ya busoba,* Stupid Tall Man.

But it was also here that I fell in love with basketball, and found a way to pursue my dream. It was here that I proved the naysayers wrong and made some of the best friends I have ever known. It was here that I became "ShakaFly."

Now, I was about to live out the dream of millions of young Africans.

With all of these conflicting emotions swirling around me, I walked from one end of the court to the other. I jumped up and grabbed the rim with one hand, and hung there for a precious moment, taking it all in. Then I let go and fell gently to the ground, my eyes filling with tears that bubbled up from my heart

Yes! *I am going to America!*

CHAPTER 10

S tanding in the kitchen of our home on that late-summer morning, waiting for my uncle Joseph and my mother to take me to the airport in Kinshasa, I felt a strange mix of sadness and joy.

The day before I had hugged my sister and told her how much I loved her. She smiled and said, "I love you, too, brother." But I did not explain why I held her just a little tighter, or why I had a lump in my throat. To the very end, until I had disappeared, my sister was kept in the dark.

That was hard, but necessary.

The next part was even harder.

You see, before leaving the house, I had to say goodbye to my grandmother. I was going so far away, to such a strange and wondrous land. I had no idea when I would return, or how much time would pass. There is something final about leaving a grandparent, the implication being that age and time make very real the possibility that you might never see that person again. This was especially true in the Congo, where nothing is certain, most of all the prospect of good health and the longevity that naturally comes with it.

I bent over to give my grandmother a hug and a kiss. It seemed like not so long ago that she would wrap me in her arms, and tell me that everything would be okay. Now it was my turn to reassure her, and to tell her how much I loved her, and what she meant to me. My grandmother was one of the strongest women I have ever known, but she seemed in this moment to be so small and frail and sad.

"Thank you for everything you have done for me, Grandma," I said. "Thank you for the love that you showed me. I promise you that you will live your life in peace because I will take care of you."

My grandmother pulled me tight and kissed me on the cheek. I could feel her tears against my skin, and the soft rhythm of her sobs against my chest.

"It's okay," I said. "I am going to America. I have a goal and I will not stop until I reach my goal. I will become a great basketball player and I will make you proud. I love you, Grandma."

I turned and walked away, leaving behind the woman who had spent so much of her life raising me, feeding me, making sure that my clothes were clean and that I had a safe place to sleep at night. My mother had protected me and my sister in the jungle, and she had worked herself to the bone traveling in the Congo to provide for her family from a financial standpoint. She had risked her own health and well-being, and had forfeited much of the time and interaction with her children that so many mothers cherish. She did it because it was necessary for our survival, and I understood this on some level (I understand it even more now, of course), but the fact is, I missed that time with my mother. And it was my grandmother who filled in the gaps with her firm but boundless and unwavering love.

I cried all the way to the airport. In fact, by the time I bid farewell to my mother and my uncle, I was all cried out.

"Be brave, work hard, and never forget where you come from," my mother said, pressing her hand against my heart. "I love you."

"I love you too, Mama."

Uncle Joseph seemed at once proud and sad. Normally stoic, he shook my hand, then pulled me in for a hug. "Blondy, you know that if we had money, we would send you to America with lots of nice things."

"I know, Uncle." The truth is, I did not care. I was thrilled and grateful to be going at all; that I had no material possessions to take with me was irrelevant. I had always been poor; what difference did it make now?

"But we don't," he continued. "So this is all I can give you. It's the most important thing, anyway." He handed me a Bible, its cover worn but not tattered, as if the book had been well-read and cared for. "Read this every night," he continued. "If you are feeling lonely or sad, you will find hope in its pages. When things don't go your way, let God be your guide."

We sat in the terminal for a little while, until we heard the announcer calling my flight number, and instructing everyone to head to the checkpoint. I got up, shaking, still in disbelief that I was about to board a plane for the first time in my life—and a plane bound for the United States, of all places! It felt almost like a dream. But it wasn't. It was real.

I gave my mother a huge hug and told her again, "I love you." Tears were pouring out of her eyes. I gently wiped her face and gave her a kiss.

"He has to leave," Uncle Joseph said. But my mother would not let my hand go. Finally, my uncle stepped in and separated us.

"Please take care of your sister and your mother," I said to him. "I'm going away, but I will always be there with you guys in my heart. And I will help as much as possible when I start making money."

Uncle Joseph—who was really the only father I had ever known—simply smiled. "Don't worry too much about us; we will be okay. Take care of yourself out there. You are a grown man now. You are not a boy anymore."

Uncle Joseph then reminded me that my cousin Patrick would be my guardian in the U.S. "He is a successful businessman there. Listen to him and trust in him. He guarantees me he will take care of you."

"Okay, Uncle," I replied.

I started to walk away toward the checkpoint. I stopped and looked back at my mother for the final time. I saw a woman of faith, a woman who fought to keep me safe, a woman who held my hand through the jungle of the Congo. A woman who sacrificed all she had to put food in my mouth, and who sold everything she had to see my dream come true. I could not go on. I turned back and ran to her and held her in my arms, crying so hard that I could barely breathe.

"You are my hero," I said before pulling away.

By the time I took my seat on the plane (and my goodness how big this machine was!), melancholy had been replaced by a feeling of anticipation, an excitement so palpable I could barely sit still. I had never been on an airplane before. I had never been out of the Congo. And now I was on my way to America! Soon, I thought, I won't have to walk miles just to use a computer that will let me look at video clips of NBA players. I can watch games live on television. Maybe I will go to one of those magnificent arenas, where the great players perform in front of thousands of fans. Maybe I will meet my idols. Maybe I will play against them one day!

Anything was possible.

★

THE TRIP ITSELF WAS arduous. I was the proverbial fish out of water. We left Kinshasa at 1 p.m. and made the first of several stops, Addis Ababa, Ethiopia, roughly seven hours later. There, I had to change planes for the second leg of the journey, which would take me to Rome. To say I was confused would be a dramatic understatement. Suddenly I was in a foreign land, where everyone spoke either Amharic or English, neither of which I understood. I did not know where to go, and I could not ask for directions.

The airport itself was the most beautiful place I had ever seen, yet I wasn't even in the U.S. yet. I asked myself, "If Ethiopia can look this beautiful, what about the United States?" I couldn't stop looking around. And for the first time, I was walking alongside scores of white people.

Is this really happening? I wondered. In my entire life I had seen perhaps a handful of white people. They were to me like ghosts: unreal, unapproachable, mysterious. Yet suddenly they were everywhere.

I wandered around the airport, staring at monitors that made no sense, looking for someone who appeared kind enough to give me some guidance. I saw two white people walk by and I wanted to ask for help, but fear got the best of me and I bit my tongue. I had never spoken to a white person before. A moment later I stopped a friendly-looking black girl; using hand signals, since I did not speak her language, I asked for help. She smiled and took my ticket from my hand, and then explained as best she could where I was supposed to go, pointing to a long line of people standing at a gate. I did not understand protocol and I was worried that I would miss my flight, so I ran up to the crowd and took a spot close to the door—in the process, cutting ahead of at least a hundred people. What can I say? I was ignorant. I did not know that in Western culture you have to wait in line for your turn. I just wanted to jump on the plane and get to the U.S., before someone decided that this was all a big mistake. Some of the other passengers stared angrily at me. A few of them made comments. I was embarrassed and unsure what I had done wrong, but it occurred to me later that many of these people were probably afraid of me. After all, I was a very tall young man.

On this flight, which was to Rome, I settled into my seat and tried to relax. After a short time, one of the flight attendants offered me something to eat. I could not believe my good fortune. And then I realized that everyone was being fed. A full meal. Was this normal? Was this what life was like in Western culture? More food than I could imagine, even on an airplane? I did not even recognize most of what was served, but I ate it anyway, in quick, ravenous gulps. I ate bags and bags of peanuts and crackers and pretzels, washing it all down with several cups of cola. Inevitably, after perhaps an hour or two, my stomach began to protest. The combination of strange food, excessive sugar, and persistent turbulence left me in a state of gastric distress I hadn't known since I was a little boy. Compounding matters was the embarrassment that comes with experiencing that sensation while in a claustrophobic environment. On the flight to Rome I must have used the bathroom a dozen times, each time excusing myself in a language my seatmate did not understand, and then unfolding myself as quickly and unobtrusively as possible before shuffling down the aisle, terrified that I would have an accident along the way.

Eventually, after a long layover, I landed in the United States of America, specifically at Dulles Airport in Washington, D.C. Our flight landed at 8 a.m. on September 4, leaving me with another nine hours to kill before the final leg of my trip, which would take me to Phoenix. By noontime my stomach had settled and I was growing hungry, but I had no money at all, and did not speak the language. I wandered around a bit, never straying far from my departure gate. I was befriended at the airport by a young traveler named Sam, who spoke Amharic and English. We bonded as Africans in a foreign land, and Sam's ability to speak English, coupled with his innate generosity, allowed me to gain a measure of comfort right away; we spoke through hand signals and facial expressions. He asked me what I wanted to drink and I responded, "Milk, milk." Because milk was so expensive in the Congo and I dreamed of drinking as much milk as possible after leaving. Sam bought me some milk and food because he knew I had no money. This was my first experience with the charitable influence that America could have on people.

When I landed in Phoenix and made my way through the airport, I had no idea what to expect. But the disorientation did nothing to quell my excitement. I kept saying to myself, "I am in the United States of America! I have made it!" I knew only that a cousin I had never met was supposed to be waiting for me. I did not know what he looked like; I presume he did not know what I looked like. But at the same time, how difficult could it be for him to find me? He knew my flight number and it had arrived on time. How many 6-foot-8 basketball players from the Congo were on that flight? I'll tell you how many: exactly one.

As I exited the terminal's restricted area and entered a larger area where hundreds of people waited for loved ones, I scanned the crowd, looking for . . . well, I'm not exactly sure what I was looking for. I had no way of identifying Patrick, so I guess I was looking for a tall black man who might be African, and that if our eyes met he would recognize me as a relative. As if the blood of our ancestors was some sort of transcendent link that could reach out across a great divide. In fact, it was not even my cousin who spotted me first. I saw him in the crowd, with three white people, and noticed his eyes darting back and forth, looking for someone familiar. But while he scanned the room, the woman next to him, a smiling, pleasant-looking middle-aged woman, pointed in my direction.

I had no idea who any of these people were, but upon introduction they seemed warm and friendly. Patrick stepped forward after the woman had pointed me out and extended a hand for me to shake. He smiled and welcomed me to America. His demeanor seemed somewhat odd and stiff, but I didn't think much of it. After all, while we might have been cousins, we also were complete strangers. But Patrick was polite and clearly in charge of the proceedings. He introduced me to each of the people in his little entourage. The woman's name was Laurie Blitz. The man beside her, smiling warmly, was, as I suspected, her husband. His name was Terry Blitz. The third person was a younger man, perhaps a few years older than me. His name was Brandon Blitz, and he was their son.

Although Patrick was obviously Americanized, I was not. In the Congo, it is customary upon meeting someone to offer a gentle kiss on the cheek, which is what I tried to do. At the same time, Terry and Brandon extended their hands, while Laurie tried to wrap me in a hug. All of this resulted in a very awkward and funny little dance that left all of us smiling and laughing.

"You're going to be living with the Blitzes," Patrick explained. "And Brandon works at the high school you will be attending. He'll be one of your basketball coaches."

This all sounded fine to me, although I wondered if perhaps there was something wrong with the dorms at the high school. I had no expectations beyond meeting my cousin and doing whatever he told me I was supposed to do.

Brandon smiled. He seemed like a nice guy, very easygoing.

"Pleased to meet you, Blondy," he said (my cousin translated for me, speaking Lingala, an African dialect). "I've heard a lot about you. I'm looking forward to working with you."

As the Blitzes led us toward the baggage claim area, Terry asked Patrick to ask me how many bags I brought with me. Patrick relayed the message in Lingala, and with a big smile on my face I explained to him I had nothing. "It's just me and my backpack. Uncle Joseph told me you will take care of me, so I gave away all my clothes to my friends before I left the Congo."

Patrick nodded, but his facial expression betrayed a hint of embarrassment. Indeed, I had carried with me only a small backpack that contained nothing more than my Bible and a bottle of water. The only clothes I owned were on my body: a pair of sweatpants that were totally inappropriate for the wilting heat of an Arizona summer, a tattered polo shirt and sandals. Patrick turned to Laurie and explained that there was no need to stop by the baggage carousel. She gave me a quick and sympathetic glance, but turned away so as not to cause me any embarrassment. I liked her very much right away and could tell that she was a good person.

"Well, then, let's go home," she said.

As we walked out into the Arizona air, I was struck by the intensity of the heat. It must have been a hundred degrees, even though it was early evening. And the air . . . it was like nothing I had experienced. So dry that I could barely breathe. The Congo is hot, but it is also humid. This arid environment was foreign to me, and totally disorienting.

"I thought it was cold in America," I said to Patrick.

He laughed. "In some parts of the country, yes. But we live in Arizona. It's the desert. You'll get used to it."

There were a couple other things I had in my bag, including one of my championship basketball belts, and a simple T-shirt bearing the Congo flag. The latter I presented as a gift to Patrick, who seemed grateful, and the Blitzes appeared to approve. On the ride to their home, the car was filled with nonstop chatter, as I told Patrick of my journey and my hopes and aspirations, and tried to answer questions from the Blitzes with Patrick serving as translator. I felt such warmth from these people and though I could not really understand why or how they had decided to take me in as part of their family, I wanted to do my best to assimilate as quickly as possible.

On the drive from the airport, I couldn't stop looking out the window. The city had so many lights, like nothing I had seen before. There wasn't a bump on the road. It was one of the most perfect rides I had ever experienced. In the Congo, after all, the roads are in terrible condition. Terry rolled down the window for me. I put my head out and felt the fresh air of America. Growing up in the Congo we were told that American air has the power to make your skin fresh again, like a baby, so I wanted to feel that fresh air.

"I am going to work hard in school and play basketball," I told everyone. "I am going to learn English in a couple of months so that we can all talk together. I will make everyone proud."

Terry and Laurie smiled as Patrick explained to them what I had said.

"Two months?" Terry repeated, his tone betraying both amusement and admiration. "Well, okay."

Later on, I pulled out my championship belt and showed it to everyone in the car. I said, "Me champion. Congo champion." They all cheered for me. It was a great feeling.

It took us less than an hour to get to the Blitzes' home in Mesa. It was a nice suburban home, relatively normal by American standards, which meant it seemed like a palace to me. It was located in by far the nicest neighborhood I had ever seen.

I am going to live here now? I thought to myself. In this house? It was so big!

I smiled at the wonder of it all, the way people took in strangers and made them part of their family. America was amazing!

When I first walked into the Blitzes' house, I was welcomed by two dogs, which I later learned were named Shady and AJ. They ran toward me enthusiastically, and I ran in the other direction and tried to hide behind Patrick. In the Congo, you see, most dogs are not at all friendly toward strangers; I presumed that Shady and AJ were going to attack me. But the Blitzes explained that both dogs were friendly, and pretty soon I found myself patting them both on the head.

Inside, I was given a quick tour of the house and shown to a bedroom.

"This is yours, Blondy," Mrs. Blitz said warmly. "Please think of it as home."

I nodded appreciatively. To be perfectly honest, I had no idea what was happening. A week earlier I had been told that I was going to a prep school in the American Northeast and that I would be living on campus. Now, suddenly, I was in Arizona, living with a white American family whom I had never met, but whose generosity and kindness seemed extraordinary.

"What is going on, ?" I asked when we had a moment alone. "Why am I living here if you are in Texas?"

Patrick shook his head. "I don't live in Texas. I will be here, with you."

"But Uncle Joseph said you live in Houston."

Patrick made a disapproving face. "This is where we will be living now, you and me. Don't worry about Houston. Don't worry about that other school. The only thing that matters is that we have a place to stay together. We will take care of each other. I will find a job and support you, one hundred percent."

He held out his hand and I took it in mine. "Okay, cousin. Thank you for being in my life."

"No problem, Blondy. Remember, we are blood."

Where I come from, such a proclamation means everything, and its impact is felt even more dramatically when you are thousands of miles from home, in a strange land, where you don't speak the language or understand the customs.

But the truth is, blood is not always thicker than water. Sometimes blood means nothing; it can be the weakest of links. And the most likely to be exploited.

CHAPTER 11

A lot happened before I came to America, discussions and barter-
ing that took place without my knowledge, and the substance of
which I learned in small pieces over the next several months, as the impact on my life—and that of my new family—became apparent.

It is true I had a cousin who lived in Houston. I knew nothing
about him except that he was twenty-six years old and supposedly had
been a pretty good basketball player who came to the United States to
play ball and get an education. But as I would discover, there was much
more to the story.

Unbeknownst to anyone in my Congolese family, Patrick, I would
come to believe, had begun plotting a path to use me for his own benefit as soon as he got wind of the news that I was bound for America
to play basketball. Patrick had likely heard about my impending arrival at Golding from a man named Sam Greer, an American scout
and agent who sometimes helped young student athletes from Africa
secure scholarships to American prep schools by acting as an intermediary. Sam had been one of Dr. Lissa's contacts in the United States.
Sam also knew Patrick through basketball channels, so he may have
reached out to Patrick about helping with his cousin's transition to
a new land. I believe Sam and Dr. Lissa merely thought Patrick, as

"family," might be able to help with paperwork and other logistics; they did not expect that he would become so deeply involved in my life, or that he would try to use me for his own benefit.

Once informed, Patrick took over. He called my mother and my uncle Joseph. He told them a beautifully tailored story in which he was portrayed as a successful businessman in the United States, one who would surely be able to help a young man—a cousin, no less!—new to the country and the culture. A man who would look out for his family. My mother believed Patrick's promises that he would look out for me in the glorious but complex new world and care for me as if I were his own child. He asked my mother and uncle to turn over guardianship to him (since I was not yet a legal adult), which they had done. But I would soon come to believe that what Patrick was all about was not looking out for his family, but having his family—specifically, me—be his his ticket to a better life.

My cousin maneuvered almost from the outset. He called Golding Academy and made it clear that he was my official guardian and authorized to represent my interests in all matters. The first order of business, Patrick explained, was that Golding would have to provide travel and living expenses for him so that he could join me at the school. The school refused to honor my cousin's request. His demands were patently ridiculous, so the school predictably chose not to negotiate with him. In response, my cousin decided that I would not be going to Golding, after all. Instead, he made arrangements for me to fly to Arizona in an attempt to place me in a high school program there.

How did this happen? Well, he engaged in negotiations with multiple high school coaches, all the while keeping me and my family in the dark. We sat at home in the Congo, wondering what was happening and presuming Patrick knew what he was doing. As I said, my family knew little about Patrick's life in America beyond what he told them. He was family so they took it at face value. And I was told almost nothing.

So when he called and said, "Blondy will come live with me in Arizona. Everything will be fine," they trusted that he was operating in my best interest. Blinded by the urge to escape the Congo, without any idea of Patrick's true nature, I boarded a plane and headed for my new life, one that, at first at least, was not exactly what I anticipated.

Through later conversations with the Blitzes, I came to believe Patrick had manipulated everyone within his gravitational pull.

His efforts began a couple months before I arrived. Brandon Blitz, the assistant head coach of basketball at Mesa High School, revealed to his parents during a dinner visit that Mesa had an inside track on getting two young kids from the Congo for the basketball team. Terry later told me that he laughed when Brandon first shared this news. Terry, you see, was a former college and professional athlete who had recently semiretired from his job as a public school teacher; he understood the complexities of the education system in America, and the challenges associated with recruiting international student athletes.

"Recruiting" is the right word, even though it is technically not allowed in the public school realm. Private schools can recruit athletes, but public schools like Mesa High School have a different mission: to educate the children who reside within the borders of the school district, and to provide extracurricular activities (art, music, athletics) as warranted by the needs and desires of the people who pay taxes within the district. Coaches are strongly discouraged from pursuing students from other districts; practically speaking, transfer is difficult, as the student must establish residency within the new district. But it happens, even if the student's family never moves. An uncle or guardian can be found, for example. Or a grandparent. Complicated residency arrangements are sometimes made in order to allow a talented, but almost always impoverished, student athlete to get an education and to play sports at a particular school. Sometimes the motives are noble, sometimes not. Regardless, running afoul of eligibility standards imposed by state and local school districts or athletic associations can have serious consequences for both the school and student athlete. Therefore, the majority of talented international athletes end up at private boarding schools, where the regulations are more permissive. By simply being accepted and enrolling, the student is generally eligible to play interscholastic sports.

This was the path Dr. Lissa had tried to arrange for me, but the interference of my cousin changed everything.

"Don't get your hopes up," Terry had told his son. "It'll probably never happen."

But, somehow, through basketball channels, my cousin had gotten to know Shane Burcar, the head basketball coach at Mesa High School. He had told Coach Burcar that he was the legal guardian of two boys from the Congo, which was also his native land, and that he was planning on moving to Arizona and bringing one of the boys with him. That boy, as it turned out, was me. His cousin. But there was a catch: Patrick's relocation, and the delivery of a 6-foot-8 basketball player, was dependent on someone providing him with a job and a place to live. It looked like he was shopping me to the highest bidder, and that bid would have to include compensation for my guardian.

Coach Burcar informed Patrick that such an arrangement would not be possible. It was both unethical and likely a violation of the rules governing high school sports and eligibility in the state of Arizona.

Undeterred, my cousin came to Arizona anyway in early August, a few weeks before I arrived, without telling anyone. He had no place to stay and no job. When he arrived, he called Coach Burcar. Unsure of what to do, Shane dispatched his assistant, Brandon, to meet with Patrick. I believe Coach Burcar was worried about my cousin and wanted to help; I do not think he was motivated by greed or even the desire to have a great basketball team. He was simply put in a difficult position. In that meeting my cousin told Brandon that he had enrolled in classes at a local community college. His deposit, he said, had been paid for by a girlfriend. Patrick immediately asked the school if it would be okay for him to share the room with a younger cousin who was coming to America from the Congo. The school not surprisingly declined his request. But Patrick could be a very smooth and charming man. He made a good first impression, and people generally wanted to help him. Certainly, this was the case with the Blitz family. When Patrick decided to withdraw from school because he would not be allowed to share a room with his cousin, he essentially became homeless. All of this happened very quickly. Coach Burcar arranged for Patrick to stay with a family in town for a few days, but that family had several children and did not have the space or flexibility to take in a grown man with no job or money. But the Blitzes were not similarly restricted. Their children were grown. They had three bedrooms, and only one in use. Most important of all, they had an enormous capacity for compassion.

Brandon spent some time with Patrick, reported back to his parents that he seemed like a thoughtful and engaging young man who had basically suffered a few unfortunate setbacks but would soon be on his feet. Maybe, he said, they should offer Patrick some support.

Is it possible that Patrick's link to Congolese basketball players played a role in their generosity? I really don't think so; I believe they wanted to help a person in need, and my cousin exploited that characteristic. Brandon brought him to dinner at his parents' house one night, and Patrick made a strong and dramatic impact with stories of his homeland, and promises to take advantage of any opportunity that came his way. He talked about growing up in the Congo, and how his father had been a powerful man who had been murdered during a violent coup. Patrick had escaped to America, where he sought political asylum. It was a compelling tale, enhanced by the scars Patrick showed them—long, jagged lines supposedly hacked into his skin by machete blades.

How much of this was true? I don't know. And it doesn't matter to me, for I assume Patrick's real purpose in relating the story was merely to curry sympathy from the family. It worked beautifully. The Blitzes offered Patrick a place in their home, but they were smart enough to attach some conditions to the arrangement. Terry and Laurie had raised three boys, after all, and all of them were self-sufficient. They told Patrick he would have to spend his days looking for a job; they would not charge him rent, but would ask him to contribute a small amount of money to the family's finances, essentially to help out with meals.

"He was very engaging," Laurie Blitz later told me. "We wanted to help him. But we didn't want to encourage him to rely entirely on others. We thought he would be out on his own within a few months."

For several weeks, Terry and Laurie drove their new houseguest all over the area to search for work. They would pick up applications, bring them home, and believed Patrick was following up. Whatever his true efforts, he certainly was not successful. In late August, Patrick approached Terry and Laurie with a story about his cousin Blondy. Until that point the Blitzes knew only that Patrick supposedly had connections to one or more boys from the Congo who might be coming to America. They had never heard of me specifically. He explained that I had a visa to leave the country and a scholarship offer from an American prep school. But the school, Patrick said, catered exclusively to students with special needs and therefore was a bad fit for me (this was not true of the school, and was beside the point anyway; Patrick's decision to reroute me to Arizona I believe was based purely on selfishness). As a result, I had no way to pay for my transportation to the U.S. And the situation in my hometown, Patrick said, was desperate and dangerous.

"He needs to leave immediately," my cousin explained. "But he doesn't have the money. Can you help him out?"

Terry was so moved by the story and convinced of Patrick's sincerity that he agreed to help.

The Blitzes later found out that Golding Academy was in fact going to pay my airfare (because of course that is typically part of the deal when recruiting international student athletes), but had rebuffed Patrick's attempt to secure room and board for himself as part of the arrangement. Patrick, who by now had been granted guardian status by my family, and thus became the primary line of communication regarding my future in America, responded by telling the school that there was a problem with my visa and I would not be coming to America after all.

It seems he wanted to make a better deal for himself. In the end, Terry Blitz gave Patrick $1,800 to pay for my plane ticket to America. (This represented the roughly two-thousand-dollar miracle that Uncle Joseph referred to when he said that my cousin had paid for my plane fare. My uncle, of course, had no idea that Patrick had already set in motion a plan to steer me away from prep school and to another location; I do not even think that Dr. Lissa knew what was happening.) When I found out about this, I felt both guilt and gratitude. That a family in America was willing to help a complete stranger seemed like a miracle; at the same time, the information that prompted their generosity was mostly untrue. The Blitzes never expressed any bitterness, at least not toward me. Terry had been an athlete himself; a baseball scholarship had helped fund his education. He said often that he had enjoyed a good life, and that sports had helped make all of that possible. While $1,800 represented a lot of money to Terry and Laurie, they were willing to make the sacrifice to help someone who might benefit in a similar way. The understanding was that the money was not a gift, but a loan, and that Patrick would pay them back over time after he got a job.

So that's how I ended up at Mesa High School, in Mesa, Arizona, living in the home of a wonderful and generous middle-aged couple. Initially, I believed they accepted me and gave me a place to live primarily to help their son's basketball team, and in so doing help his career. But I was wrong. This was not their primary motivation. Terry and Laurie, I soon found out, were also people of faith who believe in helping those less fortunate.

On my very first night in Mesa, after we had dinner (there was so much food! More food than I had ever seen!), Brandon asked me if I would like to visit my new school. Patrick translated and I replied enthusiastically, "Yeah!" Mesa High School I now recognize as a perfectly nice, large public high school, the kind you can find in almost any comfortable suburb in the southwestern United States. But to me, on that first night, it felt like a castle. It was so big and clean, the classrooms neatly outfitted with all manner of equipment and technology. I could not believe that this was what public education was like in the United States. Where I came from, after all, even the very best private schools had meager resources; the public schools were abysmal.

We wandered the dark and empty hallways for a while before Brandon showed me the gym. As we walked through the doors and he flipped on the lights. I felt my jaw drop.

Oh, my goodness! This can't be real.

The gym was so big and beautiful, with a glistening hardwood floor that appeared never to have been scuffed by anything other than the highest-quality sneakers. Bleachers stretched from courtside high up into the rafters, from baseline to baseline. How many people could this place seat? A couple thousand, at least. Was it possible they filled the place for high school games? Would I be playing here, in front of so many people? I could barely get my head around the concept. I had grown up playing on dirt courts, or asphalt courts that heaved and cracked under the African heat. Two days earlier I had been in Kinshasa. Now I was here, in the comfort of an American high school. It seemed too good to be true.

"This is where I will be playing basketball?" I asked my cousin.

He looked at Brandon, then smiled at me. "Yes, Blondy. Right here."

Brandon tossed me a basketball so that I could take a few shots. The ball was slick and shiny, almost brand-new. I can honestly say that I had never played with a ball in such pristine condition. I dribbled a couple times and nearly lost control because it was so slippery. Then I walked closer to the basket, pounded the ball twice, and jumped off two feet. With both hands on the ball I pulled it back behind my head to gain momentum and then threw down a dunk as hard as I could. I let out a yelp of delight that echoed through the empty gym as the ball hit the floor.

At the edge of the court, Brandon looked at me and smiled. My cousin said something to him in English that I did not understand. Whatever it was, it made both of them laugh. Brandon then pulled out his cell phone and called Coach Burcar to let him know how good

I was, based on what he had seen so far. Brandon was clearly excited. I shot around for about ten or fifteen minutes, then we closed up the gym and drove back to my new home.

That night I was introduced for the first time to the concept of an American shower. It was unlike anything in the Congo, where I typically washed outdoors in an open area. Mrs. Blitz gave me some towels, pointed to the tub, and left me alone. I know she was merely trying to respect my privacy, but a tutorial of some sort might have been in order. Too embarrassed to ask for help, I tried to figure out on my own precisely how the shower worked. It took me a minute or two to get the water running and turn on the shower. It felt so good to stand in the spray—it was the warmest and strongest shower I had ever experienced. Indeed, the pleasure was so intoxicating that I stayed there for what seemed like an hour, letting the water soak my skin, then soaping up and rinsing off, and doing it all over again. Multiple times. Finally, when I had begun to look like a prune, I turned off the water and stepped out of the tub. It was only then that I realized what a colossal mistake I had made. I had wondered why there was a curtain hanging from a rod above the tub. I guess I figured it was purely decorative, so that people wouldn't have to look at an open shower or tub when they used the bathroom. I had never seen anything like it before and didn't really give it much thought. I just pushed it aside and took my shower.

A very long . . . wet . . . shower.

As I stepped out of the tub, I discovered to my horror that the bathroom floor was covered with water—nearly an inch deep, from wall to wall. I might as well have stood outside the tub and taken my shower; the effect would have been no worse.

"*Mama nakufiye, bako bomanga lobi na tongo!*" I whispered out loud. (Translation: "Mama, I am going to die. They're going to kill me in the morning!") I believed this, too. In Africa, you see, the stereotype of white America is one of intolerance and selfishness. I thought for sure that the Blitzes would cast me out of their house on the very first night for being such an ignorant fool. I frantically began scooping water with my hands, throwing it into the toilet or back into the tub. I did this for the longest time, until the water started to abate, and then I used every towel I could find to soak up whatever was left. Then I put on my clothes—the same sweatpants and shirt I had been wearing for days—and walked sheepishly into my bedroom, where Patrick was waiting. I told him what had happened.

"I have flooded their house. They will kick me out for sure."

Patrick waved a hand dismissively. "Don't worry, Blondy. We all expected something like this might happen. You will adjust. Relax."

I had hardly slept at all in the previous two days, and I was suffering from terrible jet lag. My new bedroom was cool and comfortable—everything looked and smelled so clean. But I could not sleep. I tossed and turned all night, thinking about how I must have been the luckiest kid on the planet. That same night I walked outside the house with a huge bowl of ice cream that had been sitting in the refrigerator. I stood under the dark sky with a big smile on my face, eating ice cream and quietly singing an African song so that I wouldn't wake anyone else. I looked around the neighborhood and sat down in the driveway, shaking my head in disbelief. I still couldn't get over the fact that I was in America!

The next morning, I woke up early and checked the bathroom to see if the floor was dry. It wasn't; there were still puddles of water all over. All I could think of was, "These white people will kill me when they see this." As I was leaving the bathroom I met Terry and Laurie coming out of their bedroom. I tried to stand between them and the bathroom door, but Laurie realized that something was wrong: there was water leaking out into the hallway. I started shaking. She walked into the bathroom, stood there for a moment, and then came out and said something to Terry. I could not understand what she was saying, but I presumed it had something to do with the mess I had created. She looked at me sympathetically and tried to explain how to use the bathroom.

"Blondy," she said, leading me into the bathroom. "Curtain." She pinched the shower curtain with two fingers and repeated the word. "Curtain."

I still didn't know what she meant. The words were gibberish to me. For some reason I pulled up my Mesa T-shirt that had been given to me and started saying, "Mesa, Mesa, Mesa," with great pride. As if this had anything to do with the situation.

"No Mesa," Laurie said. "Use the curtain."

"Mesa! Mesa!" I shouted.

Terry just stood nearby smiling, as if he was watching a comedy show.

Finally, Laurie laughed and walked away.

"Don't worry," Terry said, patting me on the back reassuredly. "We'll fix it."

That morning, Terry cheerfully showed me the proper way to safely operate an American shower. My flooding days were over. Then Laurie and Patrick took me to a nearby shopping mall to buy some clothes. When I think back on this now, I am overwhelmed by their unquestioning kindness. I had nothing—no money, no clothes, no ability to speak the language. The Blitzes knew neither me nor my cousin, and yet they opened their home and their hearts to both of us.

As we walked from store to store, filling bags with T-shirts and polo shirts and pants and shorts and shoes and socks, I marveled not just at Laurie's generosity, but her ability to pay for it all. A swipe of the plastic, and off we went. Is it like this for everyone in America, I wondered? Does everyone have a stack of cards in their wallets, with an unending line of credit? Is everyone rich, as I had been led to believe when I was growing up? I did not know what to think. Everything was happening so quickly, and so seamlessly, and yet it was all beyond my comprehension.

Another funny thing about that first shopping excursion: I was shocked by the sight of so many women, some of them as old as my grandmother, wearing what appeared to be very skimpy shorts. In America, of course, this is perfectly normal, especially in the desert Southwest. But to me it was startling.

Why are these older women wearing tiny shorts? Do they have no dignity, no self-respect? Do they not understand that this is unacceptable?

In African culture, adult women did not dress in this manner, and I understood for the first time why my grandmother used to say that the devil lives in America, because women do not know how to dress.

"Why are these women exposing their bodies?" I whispered to Patrick. "Do they not know any better?"

He laughed. Many years later, I can only smile at my naïveté.

The shopping itself was equally overwhelming. "What am I supposed to choose?" I had asked Patrick when we first arrived at the mall.

He shrugged. "Whatever you want."

I walked through a sporting goods store and picked out three or four pairs of sweatpants. "That is enough," I said.

Patrick showed them to Laurie, who laughed. They talked for a moment, and then Patrick translated.

"You can't just wear sweatpants," my cousin explained. "It's a hundred degrees here every day. You need some shorts, as well."

I looked at Laurie, seeking her approval. She smiled and nodded.

That's the way we went about our lives for much of the next month, communicating often through my cousin, or using hand signals and facial expressions. It is truly amazing what people of different cultures can accomplish if they are working from a foundation of love and respect, as was clearly the case with the Blitz family. I was scared and excited and disoriented and happy—all at the same time—and the Blitzes somehow understood all of this and made me feel welcome.

It was a miracle.

When we got home from our shopping trip, my cousin made what seemed like an unusual request. He wanted me to stand on a bathroom scale. I was very tall and rail thin, and I wasn't sure why my weight was of any concern to Patrick, but he explained that Terry and Laurie were concerned that I wasn't just skinny, but perhaps malnourished. I stepped onto the scale and watched impassively as it registered my weight: 155 pounds. Patrick merely smiled, but Laurie seemed shocked.

"She is worried that you are too skinny," Patrick said.

"No, please tell her I am fine." I smiled and tightened my hands into fists and flexed my slender muscles. "I am strong!" This wasn't just an attempt to deflect Laurie's concern. I believed it. In the Congo, it is not unusual to be tall and lean. Genetics, environment, and poor diet combine to create a rather different standard than in Western culture. Admittedly, I had lost a few pounds in the previous week due to travel, anxiety, gastric issues, and a general shortage of food, but in those days, even under the best of circumstances, I was extremely thin.

Laurie patted me on the back and said something to Patrick. Again, he laughed.

"She says we are going to put some meat on those bones."

I wasn't quite sure what this meant, but I liked the sound of it.

'd been in town only a few days when it was time to start school. On the first day I was both nervous and excited. I woke early and took a shower (without flooding the bathroom!), then put on some of the new clothes that Laurie had bought for me. At breakfast my stomach rumbled from both hunger and anxiety. I wasn't scared—I'd been through far too much to be frightened of going to school, even in a strange land where I did not speak the language—but I was certainly apprehensive. What would the other students be like? What would they think of me? On the ride to school, Laurie and Patrick both told me to relax.

"Everything will be fine, cousin," Patrick said. "Do not worry."

Since I was living with the Blitzes and Patrick was my guardian, they both accompanied me to help with the registration and enrollment process. Everything about the process was confusing. There was so much happening at the school, so many people running around preparing for a new school year. (And so many pretty girls!) Everyone was talking and moving, but I couldn't understand a word; it passed through my ears like the humming of a fan, or the buzz of a motorway: ceaseless, rhythmic, impenetrable.

When Coach Burcar walked into the main office, he shook hands with Laurie and Patrick. For two days, my cousin had been instructing me on how to behave and respond during this introduction, so that I would make a good impression on my new coach. I was supposed to stand erect and firmly shake Coach Burcar's hand; that much I knew instinctively. But it was Patrick's idea to teach me a single line of English, to be uttered proudly and emphatically when I met Coach Burcar.

"Repeat after me," Patrick said. " 'I am a soldier.' "

I said it first in Lingala, and then in English: "I am a soldier."

"Good," Patrick said. "Keep practicing. He will respect you for knowing some English, and for what it means."

I had no idea whether Patrick was right or wrong. I mean, I wasn't a soldier. I was a seventeen-year-old boy. But I guess the idea was to be portrayed as a survivor, a fighter (which was certainly true), and to let the coach know that I would bring that same spirit and intensity to the basketball court. When Coach Burcar walked into the office and introduced himself, and immediately made a joke about my slender physique, I stood up, extended my hand, and proclaimed, rather loudly, "I am a soldier!"

The entire office fell silent. Everyone stared at me, including Coach Burcar. With a confused look on his face, he turned to Patrick. They talked for a moment, and it soon became apparent that Coach Burcar had not understood what I had said.

"He is saying that he is a soldier," Patrick stated.

Coach Burcar smiled and nodded. Then he turned to me.

"I am a soldier!" I repeated. And then again, even louder, as if by shouting my diction would become clearer. "I AM A SOLDIER!"

By now, people in the office were beginning to laugh, which made me laugh, too.

"I AM A SOLDIER!" I repeated. "I AM A SOLDIER!!!!"

Coach Burcar held out a hand, palm down, a universal signal for, "Okay, calm down, son. I get it."

After registering for classes I had to see a doctor for a physical examination and multiple immunizations. This was an unpleasant surprise for two reasons: I thought I had already received all the necessary vaccinations before leaving the Congo, and I hated needles. Apparently, some of the medical paperwork had been lost or never transmitted; either that, or someone in the Congo did not realize the extent of immunization requirements for a student in the U.S. Regardless, I soon found myself getting poked with one needle after another. Each time I protested and cried like a child, my whining so loud that it could be heard in the waiting room. When I walked out, everyone was staring at me in disbelief.

Was this giant man really responsible for all that whining?

Good thing Coach Burcar could not hear me. I sounded more like a baby than a soldier.

The school administration was not sure what to do with me. They had transcripts of my academic record, but these were of limited value thanks to my language deficiencies and the extreme differences between American and Congolese schools. I found out later that they considered enrolling me as a sophomore, which would have given me more time to catch up academically, along with three years of high school athletic eligibility. But because of my age (I was seventeen), it was decided that eleventh grade was a more appropriate designation.

To say that I was a novelty at Mesa High School would be an understatement. I was the tallest person in every class. Despite being enrolled in the English Language Learning program (an intensely immersive program that requires students who speak English as a second language to spend at least four hours a day in classes where only English is spoken), I was slow to acquire skills in the native tongue. I was not alone in this, of course. Mesa had a fair share of Hispanic students who spoke little or no English, but most of them blended in with the rest of the student body. This was not possible for me. My body was too big, my skin too dark, my story too dramatic and well-known. Very quickly people came to know me as "the African basketball player." For better or worse, I was an instant celebrity.

The workload was hard, there is no denying that, but I did my best to keep up and prove myself worthy of the Blitzes' generosity. It helped that I was able to start playing basketball right away. We had informal workouts most days, even though basketball season was a couple of months off. The very first time I walked into the locker room to get ready to play, Coach Burcar showed me my locker stall. I opened the door and inside was a new pair of basketball shoes—silky smooth Nikes, just like the pros might wear. Or so it seemed to me. I had never owned a pair of shoes like this, and the sight of them made my heart beat faster.

"Me?" I said, pointing a finger at my own chest.

"Yes," Coach Burcar said. "They're for you, Blondy."

All I could think of was how different they looked compared to the basketball shoes that I had worn back in the Congo. I was accustomed to beat-up old shoes, and now I was about to rock these new Nikes?

Thank you, Lord!

My teammates accepted me unconditionally. The first to open his arms, and his heart, was a kid named Donte Medder, the team captain. He walked me to classes, and to practice, and introduced me to many people. So did a pair of boys named Lorenzo and Adrian, both of whom were Mexican. On my first day of school, Lorenzo and Adrian took me to lunch. I was bewildered by the spectacle of it all, and ignorant of protocol. There was a long line stretching from the front of the cafeteria out into the hallway. The smell of the food made me ravenous, and I was tempted to just walk past everyone; I had no idea what the rules were, but I remembered the response I had provoked by butting in line at the airport, and decided instead to follow Lorenzo and Adrian, and to do whatever they did.

As we made our way through the line, I picked out an assortment of things to eat. Finally, we got to the end, where a woman sat at a cash register. Adrian paid for his lunch. Lorenzo paid for his lunch. Then it was my turn. The woman looked at me blankly. I understood what she wanted, but I had no money. In the confusion that day, neither my cousin nor my host family had remembered to give me lunch money. It was an honest mistake. But what was I to do now? I thought that I had been invited to lunch as a guest of Adrian and Lorenzo. In the Congo, when someone took you to lunch, they paid. I did not understand that this was different, that lunch was part of the everyday school experience, and that I would have to pay for it.

Lorenzo and Adrian tried to explain to me what was happening. I shrugged and turned out my pockets, to show them that I had no money. They both laughed. Then Lorenzo said something that sounded like "It's okay." He took out his wallet, removed a couple bills, and paid for my lunch. I nodded appreciatively. Lorenzo waved a hand, as if to say, "Don't worry about it." After that, and even to this day, Lorenzo and Adrian would joke that I still owe them money for lunch.

Another of my teammates, a boy named Leon, found out that I spoke French, as well as Lingala, and volunteered to translate much of what I was saying from French into English, so that people would understand me, and I could understand them. This was incredibly nice of him, and made it much easier for me to assimilate. Indeed, I couldn't believe my good fortune. People were so welcoming that I barely felt any homesickness. There was even a story about me in one of the local newspapers, telling about my journey to America from the Congo, and describing me as a potential Division I basketball player. Patrick translated the story for me and seemed impressed. But he also warned me that the publicity might cause a backlash among my new friends.

"Be careful," he said. "They are your teammates, but they are your enemies, too."

"What do you mean?"

"They are American and you are from Africa. You are different. You are also a better basketball player than them, so they will be jealous."

I didn't like hearing this, but inside I felt there might be some truth to it. Every team experiences some degree of infighting and envy, often directed at new players. I had been through it in the Congo. But this team seemed different, and I did not want to listen to Patrick's toxic negativity.

"I am not worried," I said. "They are my friends."

"No," Patrick said. "They are competing with you for playing time and exposure. Don't trust them." He paused. "Especially Donte. He was the best player on the team. Because of you, that is no longer true. Believe me—I have been here long enough to know the way Americans really are. He will try to trick you. He only cares about himself."

I did not know what to say. I didn't want to believe Patrick, but he was my guardian and my cousin; he was an African, like me. He was older and presumably wiser. He would know the truth . . . wouldn't he?

For a few days after this conversation I withdrew somewhat from my friends and teammates, but they were not easily dissuaded. I think they probably just felt I was homesick and as a result they tried even harder to make me feel welcome. Donte taught me how to lift weights with proper technique (for someone 6-foot-8, I was very weak).

Then Coach Burcar introduced me to a man named Joe Ward, an African American former professional player who ran a local AAU club (AAU teams are like club teams and are not affiliated with a particular high school; they play games in the off-season and often provide the primary recruiting avenue for aspiring college athletes). Coach Ward held clinics for younger kids in the evening at Taylor Middle School, but when Coach Burcar told him about me, Coach Ward asked him to bring me along. I worked out for Coach Ward, not realizing at the time that it was basically a tryout for his AAU team.

I did not know what to think of Coach Ward. He pushed me hard, and he yelled a lot. It seemed like every other word out of his mouth was "motherfucker." I did not know what this word meant. At some point during training, I approached Patrick on the side and asked him in Lingala, "What does 'motherfucker' mean?" He laughed and translated it for me. Now I got the meaning of this new word I had been hearing in the last few hours. Then I asked Patrick with a big smile on my face because I thought it was funny, "Am I a motherfucker?"

Patrick laughed harder. "No, no, no. Coach just likes to use the word."

My cousin and Coach Burcar both attended that workout; afterward,

Coach Ward asked me to practice with his AAU team. I played very well. I ran as hard as I could, blocked a ton of shots and grabbed almost every rebound that came close to me. When practice ended, Coach Ward came up to me, smiling and nodding his head. He tapped me affectionately in the chest.

"Motherfucker, you're playing with us."

"Okay," I said with a laugh. I thought Coach Ward was the coolest person.

CHAPTER 13

E verything went pretty well, until it didn't.

Patrick and I shared a room with two beds. I was thrilled to have a comfortable mattress, plenty of food to eat, and a legitimate chance to fulfill my dreams and aspirations. I went to school all day, practiced basketball in the afternoon, and worked hard to learn a new language and fit in. I suppose I was somewhat blind to what was actually happening around me.

From the first day of school, Terry and Laurie did their best to organize routines for everyone. This could not have been easy for them. They had settled into a comfortable and quiet life as empty nesters, and now suddenly they had two very large young men living in their home. There were massive cultural and language barriers, but all of these the Blitzes figured they could handle through patience and diligence, and by logically imposing accountability upon their guests. In other words, they expected from me the same things they had expected of their sons: hard work and good behavior. Patrick was in a slightly different category because of his age and the fact that he already had assimilated into American culture. Combined with his apparent easygoing manner and general likability, this led Terry and Laurie to assume that Patrick would need little oversight, and that indeed he would help his younger cousin adapt and adjust to life in America.

The focus of my schedule was school and basketball. I was supposed to get up at 7 a.m. and get to the bus stop, located a few blocks away. Terry and Laurie assigned Patrick the task of making sure that I was up on time, showered and dressed, and that I was ready to eat breakfast (which Laurie prepared for everyone). Patrick almost immediately balked at this assignment.

"Blondy is a big boy; he can take care of himself."

He had a point. I was a big boy—literally and figuratively—and certainly I had faced far more daunting challenges than getting to school in the morning. But being in a new country, where I neither spoke the language nor understood customs and mores (to say nothing of geography), did make the first few weeks rather difficult. I could have used Patrick's help. More importantly, the Blitzes had asked Patrick to be my mentor in this regard. It was hardly an unreasonable request, given that they were providing both of us with food and shelter and money. To me, Patrick's obstinacy was both selfish and disrespectful (it was also a sign of things to come). Rather than depending on the bus, Laurie quickly assumed the responsibility for dropping me off at school every morning before she went to work. Terry would drive me home every afternoon.

My cousin had promised the Blitzes that he would contribute $40 a week to help with expenses, but even this meager amount went unpaid. Moreover, he failed to secure employment as he had promised, and after a while did not even seem to bother to look for work. Terry and Laurie resented his attitude, and tensions predictably arose between them. I would come home from school or practice and find them arguing, and immediately be caught in the middle. I did not yet understand how my cousin had manipulated his way into his role as my guardian, so when he began making claims about the integrity of our hosts, I wasn't sure what to believe. It didn't help that I barely spoke English and was unable to even track the course of their disagreements. I had to rely on my cousin's interpretation of events, which proved to be self-serving and unreliable.

"Don't trust these white people," he would tell me. "Don't think because they're buying you food and clothes that means they love you. They don't love you. They have an agenda. They're writing down everything they do for you, so that whenever you make it to the NBA, they're going to expect you to pay it back—with interest!"

In reality, it was Patrick who expected to be repaid. Eventually I began to feel that the relationship was mercenary. He did not love me or care about me, but for a while I was too scared and confused to do anything about it. Laurie would cook dinner for me and help me with my homework. Meanwhile, my cousin would just sit there and watch TV or go out and party. But he was family, right? And you don't turn your back on family.

I tried to keep my head down and do what was expected of me. I went to school every day and worked hard to improve as a basketball player. After a month or so, Jared Blitz, one of Laurie and Terry's sons, moved back into the house for a while. Like Brandon, he was a very nice young man who even offered to help me with my homework and to tutor me in English. I noticed that as I became more comfortable and independent, my cousin grew increasingly irritable. If Brandon wanted to take me out to the mall or to get something to eat, Patrick would ask to tag along, so that he could listen to our conversations. In time, I felt that he was worried about losing control.

With the help of the Blitzes, Patrick was twice able to secure employment, but neither time did the job last very long. He worked with a construction crew and quit after the first day. His job was menial and simple: tossing tree branches into a shredder. Patrick came home exhausted and angry and announced that he would not be going back the next day.

"It's too dangerous," he said.

Laurie then got him a job picking up trash at Arizona State University after football games, but Patrick somehow managed to fail a written safety test that was a requirement of the job. The Blitzes found it rather astonishing that a twenty-six-year-old man who had been in the U.S. for seven years could not pass a rudimentary exam to ensure that he was capable of picking up trash without getting hurt. They suspected that Patrick had deliberately failed the exam to avoid getting the job, and they were probably right. I mean, it wasn't like Patrick was unintelligent.

Patrick was ineligible for a great many jobs because he said he did not have a driver's license, so Terry took it upon himself to help Patrick learn how to drive. They bought him manuals so he could study and practice taking the written test. Three times he attempted the test, and three times he failed. Terry would take my cousin to an empty parking lot on weekend mornings so that he could practice driving in safety and seclusion. He would notice that Patrick appeared comfortable behind the wheel—like someone who wasn't entirely unfamiliar with how to operate a vehicle; in fact, he was almost too comfortable. Patrick would slump down in the front seat and drive with one hand on the wheel, or with only a thumb on the bottom, like someone who had been driving for years. This both perplexed and infuriated Terry, who assured Patrick that exhibiting such nonchalance during a road test would result in immediate failure. It all seemed so strange.

It also made perfect sense, as the Blitzes learned, when they were introduced to Sam Greer. Terry told Greer of his frustration with my cousin, and of how he had tried to teach him how to drive. Greer, who had known my cousin for years and in fact had helped him come to America, as well, seemed surprised.

"Really?" Greer had said. "When I first brought Patrick here he worked as a cab driver in Philadelphia."

There was so much more to the story. My cousin had graduated from a high school in Pennsylvania, where he also played basketball, before attending a junior college in Texas on a basketball scholarship. Patrick had told Terry and Laurie that he had quit the team because he was unhappy with his lack of playing time. He had subsequently quit school. Greer explained that Patrick had only modest skill as a player, but that he had secured him a place on the team as a favor to Patrick's father, who was a family friend. Greer hoped that Patrick would make the most of this opportunity for a free education, regardless of whether he received any playing time. Unfortunately, Patrick grew disgruntled and wound up leaving school. I cannot attest to whether my cousin applied any effort to his academic effort; I can only say that I saw no ambition when we lived together with the Blitz family, and that he certainly was not much of a basketball player (we worked out together many times).

Patrick's increasingly antagonistic behavior weighed heavily on all of us. At night, he would keep me up by listening to music or talking on his phone, and sometimes complaining about Terry and Laurie. I did not know how to handle any of this. I just wanted to go to school and play basketball. I had come to like my new life in America, and I didn't want to do anything to jeopardize my standing, or to disappoint my new family. At the same time, I was constricted by tradition and culture. In the Congo, a young man is expected to be respectful and obedient to his elders, especially if one of those elders is a family member. Patrick was only nine years older than me, but he was still family, and he was my legal guardian, so I felt compelled to be obedient and respectful toward him, even if he did not deserve it.

I don't mean to imply that my behavior was perfect. It was not. Sometimes homesickness would set in, which affected both my mood and focus. Sometimes I would get frustrated with my inability to speak or understand the language clearly. In general, these were internal issues that I tried to handle on my own, but sometimes they led to problematic interactions with a teacher or coach. Coach Burcar called Terry Blitz after a workout session in which I did not follow instructions properly and then walked away when Coach confronted me. This was my fault entirely; I had been immature and self-pitying, and Coach Burcar was right to report this behavior. There was just one problem: Terry Blitz wasn't my guardian (though he was certainly better suited for the job).

"Why are you telling me this?" Terry asked Coach Burcar.

"Because you're kind of like his dad now, and maybe you can do something about it."

"I've known Blondy less than a month and we don't even speak the same language," Terry said. "And I am not his legal guardian."

All of this was true, so Terry did the only thing he could do: he spoke to Patrick and asked him to intervene. Patrick subsequently did nothing, except to reiterate his opinion that I should be wary of the white people in my life, and to remind me that I could trust only him.

A few weeks later I felt a sharp pain in the bottom of my foot while playing ball. I thought nothing of it at first, as the pain went away quickly. But then it returned. Again and again. It became relentless, interfering not just with my ability to practice, but to walk or even sleep. Laurie insisted I visit a podiatrist. The doctor pressed his hand into the ball of my foot, which hurt so much that I let out a loud yelp.

"Let's get an X-ray," he said. "He could have a fracture."

There was no fracture. Instead, the X-ray revealed something embedded beneath the skin in the bottom of my foot. Whatever it was, it needed to come out, the doctor explained. It was a very minor surgical procedure, but it was surgery nonetheless. I did not have proper health insurance, so the bill would be close to a thousand dollars. Terry and Laurie naturally felt this was Patrick's responsibility, since he was my guardian, but of course he did not have the money to pay for the procedure. So the Blitzes agreed to pay for the surgery, with the understanding that Patrick would repay them when he got a job. For his part, Patrick seemed unconcerned about my health. He just wanted to know how quickly I'd be back on the basketball court.

There were no complications with the surgery, although the doctor did seem surprised at what he discovered: a large piece of plastic—shaped like a toothpick—buried in my foot. In all likelihood, he said, it had been there for some time, perhaps even years. Why it suddenly began to cause problems was anyone's guess. As was the reason for its existence. It could have happened during one of my barefoot pickup basketball games in the Congo; it could even have happened years earlier, when I was trekking through the jungle. There was just no way of knowing. For whatever reason, it had made itself at home in my body. But now the eviction notice had been served.

The doctor advised against playing basketball or any other activity involving heavy impact for at least two months, but I ignored his advice. How many miles had I walked barefoot in the Congo? How many times had I played basketball shoeless or with shoes that were falling apart? Was I going to let surgery stop me from playing basketball? No way! I was back on the court within a couple weeks. Yes, I returned with some pain in my foot, which probably wasn't the smartest thing to do, but it seemed like a minor nuisance compared to what I had experienced as a boy. By comparison, this was not a big deal. I'd put on my Nikes and feel like my feet were wrapped in pillows.

Laurie was worried that I would cause lasting damage to my foot, but she also understood that playing basketball was important to my happiness and my attempt to feel comfortable in America. I was just starting to get back in shape when another long-ignored issue began to cause problems, this one involving my teeth.

Like most poor children in the Congo, I had received virtually no professional dental care while growing up. I did not consume much sugar and tried to clean my teeth often, but this was not a substitute for the sort of dental hygiene that is customary in the U.S. At dinner one evening I noticed a vague pain in the back of my mouth. It grew worse over a period of days, exacerbated by cold or hot substances, or if I happened to chew on something hard. After a week or so I stopped eating altogether. My friends and teammates noticed I was only sipping juice at lunch and asked me what was wrong.

"I don't have money for lunch," I lied.

They offered to buy lunch for me, but I declined. Eventually my face began to swell; it looked like someone had punched me in the jaw. Unable to hide the problem any longer, I revealed my condition to Laurie.

As usual, she was sympathetic and motherly, and insisted on taking me to a dentist right away. There were more X-rays, which revealed an abscess, followed by oral surgery, which immediately relieved the pain but which further depleted the Blitzes' savings account. Again, they told my cousin that they would cover expenses for which they should not have been responsible, and again he agreed to repay them as soon as he found employment.

Neither of these things ever happened.

Slowly and without expressing to me any of the resentment they naturally felt toward Patrick, the Blitz family began assuming more and more responsibility for me, and treating me like their son. Although Patrick might have been my official guardian, it was Terry and Laurie who stepped in to fill that role. They gave me five dollars every day so that I could buy lunch at school. Often when Terry would pick me up after classes, he would take me to Burger King and let me order whatever I wanted. In the evening, Laurie and Jared would both help me with my homework. At the evening dinner table, we would all sit together and try our best to communicate. Sometimes the conversations would devolve hopelessly into laughter as we conversed with a mix of English, French, and impromptu sign language. I loved these meals and the way we connected. I felt at home.

One night after I told the Blitzes another of the sad stories about my youth in the Congo, Terry smiled. I don't remember exactly which story it was, as I did this quite often. The stories usually reflected my happiness at having escaped the Congo, but also betrayed the homesickness I sometimes felt, and the distance from my family.

"Blondy, you have a family here, too," Terry said. "And we will love you and support you one hundred percent. All we ask is that you do your best and be grateful for the opportunity to chase your dream."

"Thank you," I said. These were words that came easily to me now, and I said them often.

★

PATRICK WOULD SOMETIMES TAKE me to a local playground and work with me on rebounding and shooting. He would implore me to be strong. He would encourage me and assure me, and tell me that soon I would be in the NBA. I liked hearing these things; it made me feel good. But then we would go home, and I could sense tension between my cousin and my new family.

One day in November, shortly after preseason practices had begun, Brandon Blitz pulled me aside. Using Google Translate, he typed out a message.

"Blondy, I have to ask you something," he said. It seemed very serious.

"Okay, Coach."

"Do you know what's going on between your cousin and my parents?"

I told him I did not. I knew only that they appeared to be distant and unhappy with each other, and that my cousin had not gotten a job, as he had promised.

"There's a lot you don't know," Brandon explained. He then proceeded to tell me what the Blitzes now believed about Patrick's background, of his failed attempt at school, and how he had brokered a deal to bring me to Arizona, and how the Blitzes had taken him in because he was homeless. The arrangement was supposed to be temporary, but to the dismay of the Blitzes, it now appeared permanent. Terry and Laurie did not know what to do. And I was caught in the middle.

As the details of the story unfolded on Google Translate—including the fact that Patrick had gotten the Blitzes to pay for my plane ticket—I felt a surge of anger toward my cousin, and shame for the situation I was in. I felt guilty about accepting the Blitzes' generosity when it had been established through my cousin's failures. I didn't know what to do or say. I looked at Brandon and shook my head.

"I'm sorry," I said feebly.

"It's okay, Blondy," he said. "I just thought you should know."

After that, I tried not to be a burden to anyone. I simply kept my head down and tried to do my work. But I felt totally out of place.

Basketball was my refuge. I loved playing, and I loved hanging out with my teammates, especially Donte, who was my closest friend. Regardless of what my cousin had said, I trusted Donte and I respected his ability as a basketball player. Like everyone else on the team, he seemed happy that I had joined their ranks.

We all thought it would be a great season. It certainly started out that way. In the first game I played for Mesa, I was astounded to see such a big crowd, with so many screaming people. Our student section chanted my name, which helped alleviate some of my nervousness. In the locker room I was so excited that I couldn't sit still. I paced around the room, exchanging high fives with my teammates. It had been a long time since I had played a real basketball game, and many of the old emotions that fueled my play back in the Congo—the anger and the need to prove myself—began bubbling up inside. I took a deep breath, tried to calm myself. When it came time to run out onto the court for warmups, though, the anger subsided, and in its place was pure joy. I looked into the stands, and there I saw students not only cheering, but also holding up signs, some of which said, "Welcome to Mesa High, the Congo Kid."

I smiled and waved. Maybe this was home, after all.

We won that game and I played pretty well: eight points, five blocked shots, and more than ten rebounds. I was a little rougher around the edges than some of the other guys, but I was also bigger and more athletic, which I used to my advantage. After the game, when we got home, my cousin took me straight to our room. He congratulated me on the way I had played, but also turned the night into something negative.

"Yeah, brother, they told me you were no good . . . a waste . . . but you just proved these people wrong," he said, gesturing toward the bedroom door (and presumably the people on the other side). "They don't believe in you. I do. And together we're going to make it."

By the middle of December things were going really well at school and on the basketball court. Our team was winning games and I was playing well and having a lot of fun. Donte was our senior star and getting some Division I offers, which didn't bother me in the least. He had earned it. Moreover, he never let it go to his head.

"Bro, next year I'll be gone and everything is going to be in your hands," he said to me. "And then maybe we can play together again in college."

This was my dream; unfortunately, reality interfered, as the situation at home continued to deteriorate. Based on what I saw and some of the things that Patrick said, I believe my cousin felt a sense of entitlement for bringing me to Arizona; he considered my services as a basketball player to be a commodity worthy of compensation—and he was the one to be compensated. In exchange for delivering a 6-foot-8 African basketball player to the Blitzes, Patrick seemed to expect free room and board and, eventually, a piece of whatever I might earn.

I had even heard Patrick telling his girlfriend on Skype that he had given the Blitzes a good player, and it was their job—not his—to take care of me.

After several months of tension, if not outright fighting, Terry gave my cousin an ultimatum: get a job or get out of the house. He chose to leave.

"And I'm taking Blondy with me," he said.

I was not present at the time. I was at school getting ready for a game against Hamilton High. But Terry and Laurie told me everything later. Terry had argued with Patrick, mainly because he was worried about me. Terry knew that Patrick had no place to go, and was worried about what would become of me if I left with him.

"Blondy is staying here," Terry said. "He's doing well in school and with basketball. He has friends and he is like our son. He belongs in this house."

But Patrick was not easily dissuaded.

"You should remember something," he said. Then he left the room for a moment, before returning with my guardianship papers. "He is my cousin and I am his guardian and I am taking him with me," Patrick said, waving the papers in Terry's face. "And you can't do anything about it."

That night, while I was sitting in the stands watching the junior varsity game with my teammates, getting psyched up to play, Patrick called me on my cell phone and told me that we were getting kicked out of the house, and that we'd need to look for another place to live. I was shocked and devastated. I went into the locker room and started crying, thinking about the possibility of being homeless again. I'd known that feeling in the Congo; I thought it would never happen in America. Especially after I had been taken in by such a wonderful family.

After the game Coach Brandon took me home. It was a rainy night. I was so nervous. One thought kept going through my head on the way home: do I rebel against my cousin or my new family? I didn't know what to do.

Patrick was my guardian, so there wasn't much anyone could do. I could barely understand what was happening and had to rely on my cousin's interpretation, which basically boiled down to this: "They don't want us here anymore."

The night we moved out I cried like a child. This family had been so kind to me: Why would they be kicking us out? It made no sense. I was particularly confused by the way the Blitzes acted as Patrick and I packed our gear and prepared to leave. They didn't seem angry; they were filled with sadness. Terry said almost nothing, but his eyes were red and swollen. And Laurie? As I walked into the living room with my bags—bags filled with clothing the Blitzes had bought for me—Laurie wrapped her arms around me and pulled me close. With her voice catching and her eyes filled with tears, she held me tightly, just like my mother used to do.

"I love you, Blondy," she whispered.

"I love you, too, Laurie."

I wanted to be strong, but I was filled with self-pity and confusion. Why couldn't they work things out, my African family and my American family? Why did it have to end this way? I did not want to leave, but I had no choice but to follow my cousin. I was seventeen years old; in a very real sense, he owned me.

I later found out that Terry had given Patrick $300 shortly before we left, in case we needed a hotel room for a day or two. But Patrick had already made arrangements. He had reached out to Joe Ward, my AAU coach, and given him a very one-sided version of why and how things had deteriorated with the Blitzes. Coach Ward was both sympathetic to my plight and angry with both my cousin and the Blitzes. Like me, I guess, he just wanted everyone to get along. Coach Ward had less room than the Blitzes, but he said we could stay with him for as long as we needed—presumably, until Patrick finally landed that elusive job that would allow him to rent an apartment for the two of us. That night, as Patrick and I settled into a small room that once belonged to Coach Ward's daughter, I got a text message from Terry Blitz.

"I know it is hard for you to leave us right now," he wrote. "It's hard for us, too. I did not have any choice but to let you go. But please . . . I am asking you to be strong and to go to school tomorrow."

I texted back with a single word: "Okay."

Coach Ward opened his home to us, but that arrangement also went sour almost immediately, as Patrick's fondness for staying up late and sleeping all day—and even inviting friends over to the house without asking permission—irritated Mr. Ward enormously. There was only one spare bed, and of course Patrick took it. He made me sleep on the floor despite the fact that he had no obligations in the morning, while I had school and basketball practice. Very quickly, Mr. Ward, who took shit from nobody, came to understand why the Blitzes had grown so frustrated.

Thankfully, Coach Ward knew that I was not the problem, so he called Terry and Laurie Blitz and asked them to take me back in. They agreed, under one condition: Patrick could not be part of the deal. I also spoke with Terry and Laurie. I told them I wanted to come home (and indeed, I had come to think of their home as my home, and of their family as my family). With or without my cousin.

I told Patrick what was happening, and surprisingly, he agreed to these terms, albeit with a tone of sarcasm, if not tyranny.

"Okay, go live with them," he said. "But you won't be there long. I'm going to get a job and an apartment, and then you will come and live with me, where you belong."

I did not want to fight with him. I just wanted to go home.

"Fine, Patrick," I said. "Whatever you say."

In late December, shortly before Christmas, I returned to the Blitz home, where I was welcomed once again with warmth and kindness, and I began to realize with utter clarity the truth of the situation. These were good people; my cousin was the problem.

Periodically, Patrick would call the administration at Mesa and threaten to prevent me from playing on the basketball team. I did not understand how or why he would do this, but apparently, as my guardian, it was within his power. Eventually he relented and agreed not to get in the way of my basketball career, so I was allowed to play. Patrick even showed up at my games, which was extremely awkward and confusing. The first time I played after he had agreed to stop threatening the coaches and administration, Patrick was sitting in the stands, cheering and applauding like everyone else. As I went through warmups, I looked up at him. Our eyes met. He nodded and tapped his heart, as if to say, "I love you." I nodded and pointed back at him. "I love you, too."

And I did love him. It was all just so . . . *complicated*. I will always appreciate that Patrick tried to help me, even if his motives were suspect and his methods questionable. He did want me to be successful; and maybe, on some level, he really did believe all that nonsense about only being able to trust a blood relative. But the thing is, he was wrong. Dead wrong. It just took me a while to figure it out.

★

A SHORT TIME LATER, in early January of 2009, just as Mesa High was getting into the thick of its conference basketball season, and I was beginning to get some interest from college coaches, Patrick called me on the phone. I was surprised to hear from him. And apprehensive. After some initial sadness and guilt, especially during the Christmas season, I had begun to feel comfortable with the separation from my cousin. He was no longer micromanaging my life, nor infuriating everyone around us with his laziness and lack of ambition. Did I feel sorry for him? Of course I did. But he was a grown man and I was just a high school student; I could neither protect him nor make excuses for him; nor should that have been an expectation on his part. I hoped that Patrick would find his way in the world, but I had to detach from him emotionally to concentrate on my own responsibilities.

It was painful, it was sad, but it was necessary.

By the time he called me, I had grown accustomed to the idea that Patrick would no longer control my every move. I had cut the cord. But he had other ideas.

"Blondy, I need to talk to you," he said. "I'm at the park. Can you come over?"

Against my better judgment—and because I felt sorry for him—I agreed.

So we met, and Patrick immediately behaving true to form.

"Man, I love you," he said. "You're the only blood I have in America. We've got to stick together no matter what."

"I'm sorry, Patrick, but I'm not leaving the Blitzes. That's my home now. I like where I am."

Patrick smiled. "I've got something better," he said. And then he proceeded to tell me that he had brokered a deal with another school.

"The head coach will give me five thousand dollars and employment if you transfer."

I was disgusted. First of all, I did not know whether Patrick was lying. Second, regardless of what Patrick seemed to believe, I was not a commodity to be traded or sold to the highest bidder. Not anymore. The only people I trusted in America were the Blitz family and the people associated with the Mesa basketball program. I wasn't about to just walk away from them now, after all they had done for me, just to rescue my cousin.

Still, I wasn't sure how to respond. Even though he had lied and manipulated everything about my situation so that it would benefit him, I felt both pity for Patrick, and a sense of responsibility to our shared bloodline. Also, I will admit, I was afraid of him. But I had spent too much of my life in fear; I had spent too much time running and hiding and trying desperately to survive. It was time to stand my ground, consequences be damned. From somewhere deep within, I summoned the courage to confront my cousin. I was bigger and stronger than Patrick, but he was not a small man by any stretch of the imagination (he was about 6-foot-4), and he was older than me. I was intimidated by him despite my physical advantage.

"Patrick, did you do this for my benefit, or for your own benefit?"

He seemed taken aback by this response, at first expressing surprise, and then hurt.

"Blondy, what are you talking about? We are brothers. I told you I would fix this situation, and now we are good."

"Cousin, I love you to death," I said. " But it's not fair for you to go behind my back trying to sell me to other schools."

Patrick stared at me. Rather than let him speak, I continued.

"You are the only blood family I have here in America. But I just cannot do this. I love my teammates, my coaches, my new family, and my school, so I really cannot leave for something unsure. I had a very hard time moving from place to place with you. I was embarrassed going to school for a while. Now my situation is stabilized and you want me to leave again? No! I cannot! If you really care about me, you would let me stay with the Blitzes so that I can get my education and hopefully go to college."

Patrick said nothing. He just glared at me, his eyes narrowing as he took it all in. I could see the anger rising; I could almost feel his blood boiling. Suddenly, without saying a word, he lunged forward and punched me in the face. I had no time to react or sidestep the blow in any way. I fell to one knee as blood gushed from my nose and the lights flickered in my brain. I stayed on the ground, stunned and disoriented, waiting for everything to come back into focus.

Patrick took another step forward and stood over me.

"You're going to trust these white people over me?" he shouted. "I'm your guardian. I brought you to America! You will do what I tell you to do!"

I looked up at him, saw his hands balled into fists, his jaw clenched in fury. He looked like he wanted to kill me. Rather than allow him to beat me without a fight, I slowly rose to my feet. I tried to make myself as big as possible, like an animal in the wild, and then I looked right into his eyes. They were the eyes of a coward . . . a bully.

"No," I said. "I am not your dog. You cannot tell me what to do."

Patrick's arms dropped to his side. He eyes softened into something less menacing, something almost fearful. Finally, he laughed.

"We'll see," he said, and then he turned and walked away.

I did not know, as his silhouette faded into the night, if I would ever see him again. And frankly, I hoped that I would not.

CHAPTER 14

Patrick was nothing if not relentless. Two days later he showed up at school and tried unsuccessfully to have me removed under his supervision, even though my mother and my uncle had gotten involved from the Congo and told Patrick to leave me alone since I was happy with my new family. And the school administration had determined that since I was almost a legal adult anyway, there was no benefit to disrupting everything and forcing me into a living arrangement that would be short-lived.

While Patrick was at the school office trying to take me out of school, Coach Brandon came to my class to alert me as to what was going on. I was so angry that I wanted to see Patrick and possibly knock him out. I walked to the school offices and went straight to the athletic director's office, where Patrick was waiting. My facial expression said it all. I was ready for anything. I interrupted their conversation as soon I walked into the office, shouting in broken English, "I am not leaving the school no matter what, Patrick! You are not my father or my mother. You fucking leave me alone!"

Understandably, the athletic director became concerned that a violent confrontation was about to commence. He got between me and Patrick and tried to pull me out of the office, but I refused to leave.

"Yes, Blondy, you are leaving this school!" Patrick yelled. "I am your guardian here in the U.S. I brought you here. I paid your ticket to get here." He said it with a smile on his face, too. Patrick did not know that I had been told the whole story. Or maybe he just didn't care. Either way, his arrogance and selfishness was repulsive to me, and it made my blood boil.

With perhaps ten feet separating us, I rushed at Patrick, prepared to do great bodily damage. I am lucky (and Patrick is even luckier) that Coach Brandon and one of the school security officers held me back.

"Let me go, I want to knock his ass out!" I yelled as they dragged me out of the office. Everyone at the office stared at me. They knew me as a happy and lighthearted boy. But right then, I was out of control. "You are not my father or mother. I will kill you!"

★

WHILE THAT WAS THE end of the custody battle, it was far from the end of my tribulations, as Patrick, like a jilted lover, devoted extraordinary time and energy to exacting a measure of revenge, and to controlling my life from afar.

A few days before my eighteenth birthday, in the middle of my junior year, Patrick told a newspaper reporter inaccurately that Coach Burcar had actively recruited me, before my coming to America, which would have been a violation of rules set forth by the organization that oversees high school athletics. This led to an investigation by the Arizona Interscholastic Association (AIA), the results of which hinged largely on the fact that I was living with the parents of my assistant basketball coach. Now, this was not a surprise to anyone, and in fact I had already been granted a hardship waiver by the AIA. But because of the story that appeared in the newspaper, my case was reevaluated, and in the end, it was determined that Mesa's handling of the situation could be interpreted as a recruiting violation.

I received the news on January 12, 2009: the day before my birthday. I was shooting around before practice, joking with my teammates, talking about the big game against Mountain View the following night. I was turning eighteen and we were playing our biggest rival, so I was excited and happy on both counts. Everyone had been talking about Mountain View since the day I arrived in Mesa, so I couldn't wait for this game. On my first night in the Blitzes' home, Coach Brandon had played some tape of the previous year's game between the two teams, just to show me how exciting it was. The gym was packed and the fans were wild. It was so intense! And now, finally, I was going to play in that game, in that kind of atmosphere.

Suddenly the principal and athletic director walked into the gym. They summoned Coach Burcar to the end of the court, and the three of them began talking. I suspected right away that something was wrong, as they all wore grave expressions. The principal and athletic director did most of the talking; Coach Burcar mostly just nodded grimly. A few minutes later the two administrators left the gym. Coach Burcar went straight to the middle of the court and called everyone to join him. We did. Everyone was happy. Until he started talking.

"Guys, I have some bad news." He looked me in the eyes and said, "I'm sorry, but Blondy, you can't play tomorrow." Everyone was shocked. Some of my teammates thought it was a joke. "Unfortunately, I'm serious," Coach went on. "I just heard from the school principal that based on the newspaper story about Blondy and his cousin, the AIA has decided to suspend Blondy. He is no longer eligible to play high school basketball in the state of Arizona."

That was only part of it, and in a strange way, maybe not even the worst of it. Additionally, since I was now considered an ineligible player, the AIA ruled that Mesa would have to forfeit every game in which I had appeared. So we became, at this point, a winless team; and a team that had just lost one of its best players. It was a crushing blow not just to me, but to the entire program, one that dashed our hopes for a state championship and caused embarrassment to the whole team; to the whole school!

This news hit everyone hard. Some of my teammates collapsed on the floor. They just couldn't believe this was happening the night before our big game. I was in shock. I began to cry without saying a single word. I just stood there in front of everyone, shaking and crying.

"I'm sorry," Coach Burcar said, and while I know he meant it, the words did nothing to ease the pain. I walked toward the locker room with my head down, reluctant to make eye contact with any of my teammates, although I could feel them all staring at me. At the edge of the court I grabbed a cage filled with basketballs and flipped it over, sending balls all over the gym. Once in the locker room, my anger spilled forth like a raging river. I cried and yelled. I cursed at the top of my lungs, and began punching lockers until my knuckles started to bleed.

"Patrick!" I shouted to no one in particular. "Why, Patrick?" I kept pounding at the lockers, screaming my cousin's name in anger. Over and over. "Patrick! Patrick! Patrick! Go to hell, my cousin!" In that moment, to me, my cousin seemed as evil as the rebels back home who had killed so indiscriminately.

Coach Burcar followed me into the locker room. After watching me act out for a few minutes, he walked over and wrapped his arms around me. I could feel him crying against my shoulder as I slumped to the floor.

"I know it's not fair, Blondy," he said. "I'm so sorry."

I didn't want to hear any of it. I was inconsolable. What had I done wrong? What had Mesa High School done wrong? Or Coach Burcar? Or the Blitz family? It seemed cruel that everyone was being punished for simply trying to help a refugee who was trying to make a new life for himself by playing a game that he loved.

In retrospect, I understand the rules that are in place, and how they are intended to protect both the integrity of the educational process, and to prevent the exploitation of unwitting and often desperate student athletes. At this moment, however, I saw only the flaws in a system that had arbitrarily taken basketball away from me.

I pulled away from Coach Burcar and ran out of the locker room and into the gym, where Terry and Laurie were now waiting to take me home. It was one of the saddest days of my life, and the pain was compounded by the fact that its source had been my flesh and blood. I had fallen in love with basketball and was actually quite good at it, but now, just halfway through my first season, I had apparently been banned from ever playing high school basketball again in the state of Arizona; it felt like a lifetime sentence. How could I fulfill my dream of playing in college (let alone the NBA) if I did not even play high school ball? At that moment I was too sad and overwhelmed to even consider the possibility of playing somewhere else. And I didn't want to leave, anyway. I loved my new home and my new family.

That night I cried until deep into the early morning hours. A young man's eighteenth birthday is supposed to be one of the most important days of his life: a celebration of impending adulthood, and the freedom and responsibility that comes with it. But for me it was a nightmare. I just wanted to be happy and play basketball; I couldn't understand how things had gone so very wrong. At a little after three in the morning, Laurie came into my bedroom; she had heard me crying and was worried. Laurie talked to me for a while and told me everything would be okay.

"Try to get some sleep," she said.

It wasn't possible. And while I know she meant well, Laurie's words provided little solace. I didn't want to hear that everything would be okay. I wanted to play basketball. Now! I had struggled most of my life and I thought that coming to America would bring peace and joy; but it was beginning to feel like just another jungle to endure.

The following night, before the game against Mountain View, I stayed at my house, still crying in my room, feeling sorry for myself. I did not want to go to the game. I simply wanted to drown in my own misery.

At around 5 p.m. I heard a chorus of horns honking outside the house. I jumped off my bed and looked out my bedroom window. To my amazement, there were more than a dozen cars lined up outside, filled with friends and classmates and teammates, all calling for me. Some of our neighbors had come out of their homes to see what was going on. I threw on some clothes and walked out of the house. My friends began shouting even louder. A few ran over and they all began crowding around me, giving me hugs and high fives. It was overwhelming. Their support and friendship cut through the sadness and made me smile.

"Let's go!" they shouted. "Jump in!"

They insisted that I join them and drive to the game, even if I would be only a fan. What could I say? Their love made me realize that I was being selfish and immature. I had been through worse. Somehow, I would survive this. And anyway, I owed it to my teammates to be there with them, helping in any way possible.

The parking lot was packed when we arrived. I walked through the lobby and could hear the music playing during pregame warmups. I went into Coach Burcar's office to wish him luck. He seemed to be more concerned about me than he was about the game.

"Are you okay, Blondy?" he asked.

"Yes, Coach. Don't worry."

"I'm really sorry about this," he said. "I know it's not fair. But you are still a part of this team, and we need you on the bench. Things will work out."

I nodded. "Thank you, Coach."

When I walked into the gym in street clothes, the most amazing thing happened: the entire crowd started chanting.

"BLON-DY!"

"BLON-DY!"

"BLON-DY!"

The chorus echoed over the whole gymnasium.

Nearly overcome with emotion, my eyes filled with tears, I walked toward my teammates on the other side of the court and started high-fiving each one of them. I knew at that moment it wasn't about me anymore. It was about my team, and they needed my support. I could see on their faces that some of them didn't want to play that game without me. Like me, they were disappointed and angry, but none of us could do anything to change the situation.

It was an ugly, painful game to watch, especially for me. I squirmed on the bench. I peeked nervously through my fingers, overwhelmed by the helplessness that comes with seeing your teammates fall behind by as many as twenty-five points. I stood and cheered. I tried to offer encouragement, but mostly I just felt sad and useless. I felt like I had let my team down in some way. I wanted to be out there with them, fighting and sweating against our rival. Instead, all I could do was watch them lose.

But then something miraculous happened, and it had nothing to do with the score of the game. As I followed my teammates into the locker room at halftime, a group of kids from the Mesa student section stopped me at the edge of the court and pulled me aside.

"We have something for you, Blondy," one of them said.

They led me to the center of the court as the crowd stood and cheered. Then they presented me with a bunch of balloons and a huge birthday card, as the whole student section led the crowd in a spirited rendition version of "Happy Birthday." Afterward, as the crowd applauded, I broke into tears once again. It seemed like I spent a lot of my time in those days crying. But at least on this occasion, they were tears of happiness, for I could not believe my good fortune. To have so many friends and so many people who cared about me, even in my darkest moments, was truly a blessing.

The next day at school, during lunch with my friends and teammates, I decided to call Patrick from a different number, because I knew he would probably ignore a call from my number. He picked up the phone.

"This is Blondy," I said. "I just wanted to thank you for the trouble you have brought to my life. You have ruined my dreams—something that I have worked so hard for my entire life." I paused for a moment and thought about the lessons I had learned while growing up—the faith that had been instilled in me by my mother and grandmother. What would they have wanted me to do in this situation? What would God have wanted?

"I am angry with you, Patrick," I continued. "But I forgive you."

This was an incredibly difficult and emotional thing for me to do, but it felt right. I don't know what sort of response I expected, but the one that came should not have surprised me.

"Blondy, I told you to listen to me," he said. "But you chose to listen to these white people." He laughed into the phone. "This is what you get, Blondy. Remember—I am your king here."

Even for Patrick this seemed extreme. I was so shocked that I did not know what to say. After a moment's silence, I said "Thank you" and ended the call.

These were the last words I ever said to him.

CHAPTER 15

Although I missed basketball, I decided to move on from the situation and try to be happy. I asked our school volleyball coach if I could participate in some of their practices. He was more than happy to give me a chance—after all, we didn't have a lot of 6-foot-8 guys on the volleyball team. Unfortunately, I was a rather terrible volleyball player. And I didn't improve much with practice. Still, it was kind of fun to give it a try.

One morning in late February, a school security officer summoned me from class.

"Blondy is needed in the main office," he explained. The teacher let me go, and I followed the officer through the hallways. He did not say why I had been called. As soon as I entered the office, I got a bad feeling. Terry was there waiting for me.

"Come on, Blondy," he said. "We're going home."

At the house, Terry and Laurie sat me down and said they had some news to share. By the looks on their faces, I knew that it was not good news. I began to panic. My heart started racing and I broke out in a cold sweat.

"What is it?" I asked. "Am I in trouble? Did I do something wrong?"

"No," Terry said. "You didn't do anything wrong. But there is a problem that we have to address."

He proceeded to tell me that representatives from Golding Academy, the school that had originally recruited me, had inquired about my whereabouts. They were surprised to learn that I was in Arizona, when they were the ones who had recruited me, and Patrick had told them I had never left the Congo. So, naturally, they were upset to learn otherwise. They said that my visa had been written specifically for me to attend Golding, so technically I was in the country illegally.

"They want you there within twenty-four hours," Terry explained. "Or they will call immigration and you will be deported."

"Deported?" I said, repeating a word that was among the most frightening in my limited English vocabulary. "For real?"

Terry nodded. "I'm afraid so."

The thought of going back to the Congo was terrifying. In my mind, I would rather have been sent to jail than return to the Congo. At least in jail I would be fed and clothed. In the Congo there was no guarantee of either of these things.

"It will be okay," Terry said, trying to sound reassuring. "The coach says you'll be able to finish your junior year up there, and they will take good care of you."

Terry also said that if my visa issues were straightened out, then maybe I could return to Arizona for my senior year. As it turned out, only some of this story was true. Terry and Laurie had massaged some of it in order to make it more palatable to me, and to protect me from some of the scarier parts. In fact, here is what actually happened.

I couldn't play basketball at Mesa High and I needed to play basketball to get a scholarship to attend college because I only had one more year left of high school. Terry and Laurie felt terrible for me, and wanted to help, so they reached out to Golding Academy to investigate the possibility of my going to school there. It was a logical choice, since Golding had recruited me. But in contacting the school, Terry and Laurie inadvertently set in motion the wheels of immigration protocol. They quickly found out that Golding had no idea I was still in the U.S., and that in fact I was deemed an illegal immigrant. Not only that, but school officials threatened Terry and Laurie for essentially harboring someone who had broken the law. Now we all were in trouble.

As I said, though, Terry and Laurie did not tell me all of this at that time. They tried to put a positive spin on the story, so that I would be more willing to go. I was far from eager, but I also realized I had no other option. My bags had already been packed and a plane ticket purchased. I did not even have time to say goodbye to my friends in person; I had to catch the next available flight to the Northeast.

Less than an hour after I got home, I was on my way to the airport. I cried all the way there.

Although I was sad to be leaving, on some level I felt relieved that Golding still wanted me, and that I would have a chance to play basketball. But the fact that the school's offer was shaded by threats of deportation (there was anger, not entirely unjustified, about my having landed in Arizona when my cousin had lied and informed the school that I had remained in Africa) made me feel uncomfortable and apprehensive. As much as I missed basketball, I still loved Mesa High School and my home with the Blitzes. You see, I was no longer just a basketball player at Mesa. I was a friend and teammate, regardless of whether I wore the uniform. I was so happy and comfortable in Mesa that I might have stayed even without basketball—if that had been a possibility. But it wasn't. My choice, it seemed, was simple: enroll at Golding Academy, or return to the Congo.

It wasn't really a choice at all.

Before leaving I called Donte and told him what was happening. We talked about how maybe someday we would still play against each other in college. Maybe going to Golding would make that possible.

"We will see each other again, my brother," I said to Donte.

"Yes," he replied. "Be strong, Blondy."

★

GOLDING, AT THAT TIME, was a school with a mediocre basketball program and more than a few international students. While the campus was not unattractive, I felt an immediate sense of displacement and unease. For one thing, it was so cold! I had grown up in the Congo and been living in Arizona. By comparison, the Northeast in February felt like Antarctica. But that wasn't the real problem. I simply did not want to be there. I wanted to be home, sleeping in my own bed, having dinner with my mom and dad (which is the way I thought of Terry and Laurie). I wanted to be walking the halls of Mesa High School, attending class with teachers I knew and liked, and making my friends laugh in the cafeteria.

Simply put, I was profoundly and instantly homesick; in some ways, the homesickness was even worse than when I first arrived in America. At least then I had moved by choice. I wanted to leave the Congo behind. But now? I had been uprooted because of circumstances beyond my control, and the anxiety this produced was so severe that I couldn't even think straight, let alone concentrate on basketball.

I arrived on campus around 9 p.m., and went straight to the gym, where the basketball team was having practice. Everyone stared at me when I walked into the building. A lot of people introduced themselves to me, including my new teammates, three of whom were from Africa (two from Nigeria and one from Cameroon). They seemed happy to see me, and one of them even spoke French, so we conversed right away in a more fluid manner than I had been able to converse with almost anyone at Mesa. And yet, still I felt out of place.

My body was in the Northeast, but my mind was back in Arizona.

Because there were no remaining spots in the dorm, and because I had not yet registered for classes, I moved in with the basketball coach, thinking he had my best interests at heart, but in fact he treated me in a strange and almost abusive manner from the very beginning. I had never met Coach Moreland prior to my arrival on campus; we had never even spoken with each other by phone, so I had no idea what to expect from him. I had played for a number of different coaches in my career, and I knew that some were more demanding than others, so it wasn't like I was unaccustomed to discipline. But this was like nothing I had ever experienced. The coach behaved as though I was an unwanted guest that had been foisted upon him. And I suppose, by this point, that's exactly what I was.

Coach Moreland's house had three bedrooms, but I was instructed to sleep in the living room—on the floor, no less, not even on the sofa. I did not complain because, frankly, I reasoned that sleeping on the floor was preferable to being sent back to Africa. I had slept under worse conditions, and I tried to remind myself that in the grand scheme of things, I was still fortunate to have been given a chance for a new life in America—even if it wasn't as comfortable as the life I had been leading in Arizona.

But then things got worse and my ability to put a positive spin on my circumstances faltered. Less than one week after I arrived, during an AAU tournament in Chicago (the school season was over by this point, and since it was an AAU tournament, I was allowed to play even though I hadn't yet enrolled in classes at Golding), I sprained my ankle and was only able to play a few short minutes. I limped to the sideline and sat down on the bench, with a bag of ice on my ankle, fighting back tears. It seemed like nothing was going right.

Because I continued to live at Coach Moreland's house and was not officially enrolled in school, I did not feel like a true member of the campus community; indeed, after about three weeks, I began to wonder when I would start taking classes. This made me anxious, as I wanted to finish my junior year and graduate the following year. I had trouble communicating my concerns to Coach Moreland, but eventually I asked him when I would start school.

"You'll go to class when the time comes," he said gruffly. I could not figure out why he always seemed to be so annoyed with me. I believe now he simply resented my presence because of my history with the school (he viewed me as untrustworthy), and made no effort to hide his feelings. He would berate me constantly, usually with the threat that I could be sent back to Africa. He would wake me at five o'clock on a winter morning and order me to go to the gym to work out. There was often no food. A couple guys on the team used to sneak food out of the cafeteria for me. I don't know why it went on this way; my guess is that because I had not yet enrolled in classes, I was not technically a student, so I couldn't live in the dorms or eat in the dining hall.

A month and a half went by, and still I had not enrolled in classes. This stemmed largely, I believe, from the team's desire to have me enroll as a sophomore, so that I would still have two years of basketball eligibility. I found this inexplicable and inappropriate. I was eighteen years old! How could I be a tenth grader? Looking back on it, I understand their point of view. I was supposed to have been a student athlete at Golding for two years; thanks to my cousin's behavior, I had lost a year of eligibility. By reclassifying as a sophomore, I would still be able to play two years of basketball, and make progress from an academic and language standpoint. Of course, this meant I would have been twenty years old by the time I graduated from high school, which, while not unheard of in the world of prep school athletics, seemed crazy to me.

The truth is, I was so miserable that I could not look at any of this clearly. I was homesick and unhappy, and I wanted my time in prep school to end as quickly as possible. I couldn't understand why the coach would want me on his team for two years when he seemed to be angry with me all the time.

I tried explaining what was happening to Terry and Laurie Blitz. They felt sorry for me, but told me to be patient and strong. As time went on, however, and I still hadn't enrolled in classes (all I did was hang out at the house or go to the gym and play basketball), Terry and Laurie became concerned. I later found out they had several heated conversations with Coach Moreland, during which he explained that the school was trying to make the appropriate adjustments to my visa after my time in Arizona, after which I would start school. But he also told the Blitzes that my attitude was poor and that I was being difficult, and that if I didn't start behaving differently, there would be consequences.

Serious consequences.

Terry did not tell me this until much later, but the coach used words like "deportation" and "illegal." Terry considered me to be like a son, so he viewed this as a threat against his family. Their conversations became more frequent and more acrimonious. Not one to be bullied, Terry at one point told the coach that he believed the basketball program should be investigated for the way it was handling my situation. Again, I did not know about this until much later, but I am proud of Terry for sticking up for me. Unfortunately, I don't imagine that it helped endear me to the coach.

Eventually Coach Moreland let me sleep in one of the bedrooms, but still I did not have enough food or water. I got sick and he took me to the doctor but berated me the entire time because he would have to pay the bill.

During this time, I felt helpless and alone, but not abandoned, because I knew that God was by my side. I would lock myself in a room, fall to my knees, and cry for hours on end, clutching the Bible that Uncle Joseph had given me to my heart. All the while proclaiming my trust and faith in the Lord.

I know you have a plan for me. I know you will not leave me.

After a month and a half of feeling like a prisoner, I broke, and everything came to a head. The argument began around ten o'clock at night, when I asked the coach for my phone. He would routinely confiscate my cell phone for the slightest infraction. Sometimes he would take it away just because he was mad at me. On this night, I was particularly sad and lonely and wanted to call my friends and family back in Arizona.

"You want your phone back?" he said.

"Yes, it is my phone. You do not pay for it, and you have no right to keep it. I don't care what you do. Send me back to Africa. I don't care."

Coach Moreland walked over to a drawer and withdrew my phone. He had an angry look on his face.

"Here, take it," he said. And with that, he threw the phone at me. It bounced off my chest and landed on the floor with a thud. I was stunned, but I was also worried that my phone had been broken, which would have cut off all communication with the outside world. I went to one knee and scooped it up. And as I did so, the anger rose in my throat. I could feel my skin becoming hot. It was just like the time I confronted Patrick in the park, and in the Mesa High School office.

I had reached the breaking point.

I stood up and began screaming at the coach. I cursed at him and threatened him. And finally, I picked up the flat-screen television in his living room and threw it to the ground, smashing the screen in the process.

I was completely out of control.

As soon as the TV hit the floor, I knew that I had crossed a line. Coach's face went blank. He was beyond angry. He was resolute.

"Take your phone and everything else, and get the fuck out of my house," he said. He didn't really yell. He just stated it as an order, which only underscored the seriousness of things. I was accustomed to hearing him yell and shout. I was not accustomed to stoicism.

Suddenly I regretted what I had done. I was shocked. I hated Coach Moreland, but I had nowhere else to go. I knew I had screwed up, and I was ashamed of my behavior.

"It's cold outside," I pleaded. "What will I do?"

"I don't care," he said. "You don't listen to me, you don't do what you're told, so you're not going to live in my house."

He took a couple steps toward me, until we were separated by only inches, and shoved me in the chest so hard that I lost my balance and fell down. I was much bigger and stronger than the coach, but I did not even consider fighting back. We had pushed each other to the brink, but he was an adult. He was my coach.

"Get out," he said again, this time with even greater animosity. "Now!"

The coach stood in the bedroom doorway as I cried while packing my meager belongings. He opened the front door and stood stoically as I walked past him, out into the chill of a Northeastern night. It had snowed the previous day, so the ground was still covered with white, even though it was almost April. And it was so cold—below freezing, for sure. Normal for that time of year, but I was still accustomed to the desert Southwest.

I did not say anything to Coach Moreland as I walked away, but I could hear him shout at me from behind.

"Leave the campus," he said. "If you try to stay with any other student, I will report you."

I believed him. This man seemed to me then to exhibit the same sort of cruel demeanor I had witnessed in the rebel soldiers in my homeland. I wanted to get as far away from him as I could. There was just one problem: I had no money and no resources. I could have called Terry and Laurie, but I was ashamed of myself, and I worried that my failure would have disappointed them.

I didn't know what to do, so I wandered around for several hours, until my toes went numb and I could barely walk. I kept pulling clothes out of my bag and adding layer upon layer. I had no hat or gloves, so I used socks to keep my hands warm. I felt completely lost and hopeless. Eventually the cold became too much to bear, and the discomfort outweighed my pride. I still couldn't bring myself to call Terry or Laurie, so instead I texted Thomas, one of my African friends on the Golding basketball team. I told him I had been kicked out of the coach's house and that I had been wandering around outside for hours.

"I think I am going to freeze to death," I told him.

"Come to my room," he replied. "You will be safe."

I told Thomas that the coach had warned me against trying to stay in the dorms, but Thomas did not care. He, too, disliked the coach's tyrannical ways, and obviously he felt a connection based on our African roots.

Speaking in our common language of French, I said to Thomas, "I appreciate this, brother, but I don't want you to get in trouble. As soon as I get warm, I will leave."

Thomas waved a hand dismissively. "Fuck that," he said. "And fuck the coach. You can stay with me as long as you like. I won't tell anyone."

This was a warm and courageous gesture on Thomas's part, but it was impractical to say the least. One cannot hide for long in a prep school dorm without being discovered. But we gave it our best shot. I stayed with Thomas for a couple days. He brought me food, talked with me like a good friend, and offered to do whatever he could to help. I worried that if my presence was revealed, Thomas would lose his scholarship and be thrown out of school, so I decided it was best to leave.

"Where will you go?" he asked.

"I don't know. I just have to get away."

Then I did something that brought me a good deal of shame. I asked Thomas if he had any money that I could borrow, because I was broke. My plan was to buy a bus ticket out of town. And that was the extent of it. I had no destination in mind.

"Of course," Thomas said, peeling off a few bills and pressing them into my palm.

"I will pay you back someday," I promised.

Thomas shook his head. "Don't worry about it, my friend. Just be safe."

Because he was much more fluent in English than I was, Thomas called a taxi on my behalf. Before getting in the car, I walked down the street to the coach's house, which was only a few doors from Thomas's dorm. I don't know why, but for some reason I felt compelled to say goodbye to him before I left. Even though I despised him, and he had been mean to me, I sought his respect and approval. He answered the door and stared at me blankly.

"What do you want?"

"I am leaving, Coach. I wanted to say thank you for giving me a chance."

His demeanor was oddly calm. He did not seem the slightest bit surprised to see me. I realized then that the coach must have known I was staying in Thomas's room, but did nothing to stop me from squatting. "I am sorry about everything that happened," I said, apologizing for something I did not even understand. "But I can't say here."

The coach shrugged. "I don't care if you leave. Goodbye."

He turned and went back into the house as I walked away and got into the waiting cab. But then a funny thing happened: as the cab pulled away, I saw Coach Moreland walk out of his house again and take a few quick steps toward the cab. He raised a hand as if to flag the vehicle down, but the driver did not see him and sped away.

By the time I got to the bus station, Coach had called me several times. I did not answer any of the calls, but in his messages, he said repeatedly that he wanted me to return to school, and that we could work things out. Instead of calling, I responded with a text.

"I will come back if you are nice to me. That's all I want."

"Okay," he responded. "I will be nice to you."

I do not know if the coach was lying but I do know that I was lying. I had no intention of returning to campus. I was just stalling for time, because I reasoned that Coach's sudden attempt to negotiate would invariably lead to someone—a school representative, the police, agents from the Department of Homeland Security—trying to track me down. I trusted no one. I was frightened and lonely, and more than a little paranoid. Shortly after I finished texting with Coach Moreland, I got a text from Terry. It was obvious the coach had called him. As usual, Terry was calm and supportive. I told him I was at the bus station, and that I was safe. He urged me to return to school, and explained that the best way to preserve my visa and my legal status was to continue at Golding until everything was straightened out.

"Then you can transfer," he said.

I lied to Terry, as well. I told him I would do as he asked and return to school. Instead, I walked up to the ticket window at the Greyhound station and placed my money on the counter.

"Where to, son?" the agent asked.

I scanned the board. Some cities I recognized, others I did not. There was a map nearby, so I looked at that as well, and then tried to pair up the name of a city on the board with one on the map that appeared to be the furthest from where I was. That city was Jackson, Mississippi. I had no friends or family there; what I did have was the name of a contact, someone I knew from basketball circles—a coach from Jackson who had recruited and coached several international players, including some from Africa. As the situation at Golding had deteriorated to the point of intolerability, I reached out to the coach.

"If I come to Mississippi, will you help me?" I had asked.

This was an unfair question, one that put the coach in a compromising position. Technically, a coach from one private school is not supposed to discuss transfer options with a student who is currently enrolled in another school. Then again, I wasn't really enrolled. I was in some sort of athletic and academic limbo. And I couldn't take it any longer.

"I will do what I can," the coach said.

So I called him before boarding a bus for Jackson, Mississippi; I gave him my ticket information and he said he would meet me at the station. I was putting a lot of faith in someone I did not even know, but I figured that at the very worst, Jackson would be warmer than the Northeast. I also knew that by the time I got there, I would have a big head start on all the people who were trying to track me down and send me back to the Congo.

In short, I had no idea what I was doing.

If I have one major regret about the way I handled this entire affair, it is in the pain and hardship that I caused the Blitz family. Not only were they worried about my safety, but they also had to endure threats against their own reputation and good standing. As soon as I left, Terry received calls from school representatives that the issues surrounding my visa remained unresolved, and that by leaving the school I was in violation. I was, in their estimation, an illegal immigrant. Moreover, since I had been living with the Blitzes, it was supposedly their responsibility to report me to Homeland Security. Failure to do so could have legal ramifications for Terry and Laurie.

When I think about this now, years later, it still makes me cringe with shame. Terry was sixty-three years old and preparing to settle into peaceful retirement. Then I came into his home, along with my cousin, and brought chaos to his life. It wasn't my fault, but I certainly didn't make things easier for him or Laurie by running away from the prep school, and I would not have blamed Terry for calling Homeland Security and turning me in. But he didn't. He later explained to me that he wasn't really worried about being arrested; he was far more concerned about what might happen to me if it was determined that I was an illegal immigrant. Terry and Laurie were in a very difficult position—trying to protect me and help me when I was a panic-stricken and painfully homesick teen.

"Go back to school," Terry urged once more, when he called me a second time. "We will figure everything out."

It was much too late for that. I was already on the bus, with a plan that did not go beyond getting as far away as possible, and trying to find a benevolent coach, one who would understand my plight and might be able to offer assistance. But if not? I was on a bus to nowhere.

For two days, along endless highways, stopping at seemingly every little town along the way, I rode the bus, hunched over in my seat with a hoodie pulled over my head to hide the shame and fear that was etched upon my face (and to disguise myself from law enforcement and federal agents whom I presumed to be in hot pursuit). I had no money and no food. I had only a backpack with some clothes in it, along with my Bible.

After many, many hours, the bus stopped in Memphis. Everyone got off, while I remained in my seat, just as I had at every other stop. I figured we'd be on the road again shortly, but that was not the case. When the driver noticed that I had not departed, he approached me and asked for my ticket. I showed it to him, and he explained, very patiently, that my connection would not be leaving until the next morning. It took a long time for him to get this point across through our language differences, but eventually I figured it out. As the other passengers left the bus station to go home or to find a hotel room, I wandered around for a while, until I was asked to leave.

That night I slept outdoors, in a parking garage, huddled against a wall, hoping no one would see me and that I would not be arrested for vagrancy. I was tormented by thoughts of all the people I had hurt and disappointed. Terry and Laurie were worried sick about me; and what of my family back in the Congo? I thought about the day I left, and how happy I had been. I was going to work hard and become successful, which would make everyone proud. I was going to be a professional basketball player and make so much money that I could bring my entire family to America, and buy them all houses in which to live. That was the dream.

Instead, here I was: homeless and penniless, sleeping in a parking garage—an illegal immigrant who could not even last two months at prep school.

I felt weak and ashamed. And utterly terrified.

At 6:30 the next morning, I boarded another bus. Roughly four hours later, after several more stops, we arrived in Jackson, Mississippi. Although lonely and disoriented, and painfully hungry after two days without food, I was relieved to feel the comparative warmth upon my skin. But it was still April, and even in Jackson that is not a good time of year to be without shelter or food. I reached into my backpack and pulled out my phone. I thought about calling Terry and asking him to come and get me. I would apologize for being so soft and stupid, and I would do whatever he thought was best—including going back to Golding. Maybe I could make things right with the coach. I had friends there, at least—other Africans who understood the challenges of adapting to a new culture and a new school. Perhaps I had been too quick to run away.

I stared at the screen of my phone. It was black. I tried to turn it on. No response.

Oh, no . . . the battery.

Suddenly things had gone from bad to bleak. Not only had I exhausted the charge on my phone, but I had left without a power cord. And I had no money to buy a new one. This was not good. Suddenly I was completely untethered. I had only a minor grasp of the language and no concept of local geography or custom. I had no place to sleep and no way to acquire food.

But then, from across the bus terminal lobby, I saw someone staring at me. He was a black man, perhaps fifty years of age. He began to walk toward me, as if he knew who I was, and as he drew near, a smile came across his face.

"Blondy?"

"Yes, sir."

"I'm Audie Norris. How was your trip?"

It occurred to me at that moment that I did not even know Coach Norris's first name.

"Fine, thank you."

There was a moment of awkward silence before Coach Norris finally said, "Well, let's go home."

I nodded. "Yes, sir."

We walked out into the parking lot. As he opened the car door for me, all I could say was "Thank you."

"No need," he said. And then we drove away.

Twenty minutes passed, during which we didn't talk much. I was in the car with a complete stranger—a man I had never met in my life—in a town I had never visited. What if he was not who he said he was? What if his motives were less noble? What would have happened to me? All these years later, I still sometimes ask myself these questions. Was I merely lucky, or was God watching out for me? Eventually we arrived at the man's house. He pulled into the driveway, turned off the engine, and asked me to wait in the car.

"Gotta tell the wife we have company," he explained with a smile.

A short time later he and his wife both came out to the car. She was just as friendly as her husband, and invited me into the house.

"Are you hungry?" she asked.

"Yes," I replied. "I am very hungry, thank you."

That afternoon, over lunch, I did my best to convey to Coach Norris and his wife the story of my journey, and how I had somehow traveled from the Congo to Jackson, Mississippi, with many stops along the way. He kept nodding and occasionally turning to his wife to say something. After a while it became clear that they had a rather intimate understanding of my circumstances, even though I had not told him much in advance.

As both an AAU and prep school coach in a metropolitan area, Coach Norris had a lot of experience dealing with players who came from impoverished backgrounds or had educational difficulties. A lot of his players, he explained, had received college scholarships, sometimes with a year or two of prep school along the way. He also said that he had worked with some international players and was familiar with immigration laws and regulations. Some of this I already knew through my contacts, but I did not realize the depth of Coach Norris's experience.

"I know what you're going through," he said. "I think I can help."

Coach Norris and his wife were incredibly sweet and generous. They even offered me the bedroom where their son slept. The son was about my age, but Coach Norris explained what I had been through and asked the boy to sleep in the living room for a couple of weeks while they tried to sort out my rather complicated situation. He was a nice kid and he didn't mind. We got along great.

The day after I arrived, Coach Norris took me to a local high school to play some pickup ball.

"These are pretty good games," he warned. "Big guys. Grown men. Don't let them push you around."

"Don't worry. I won't."

I felt comfortable as we walked into the school, which reminded me a little of Mesa High. But I was clearly an outsider, which the other players let me know with some pregame trash talk. As I walked onto the court, one of the other guys made a joke about my appearance. I was so tall and skinny, and so obviously not an American. I was embarrassed but also angry, and over the next couple hours I took out my frustration on my fellow competitors. Aside from a few practices at Golding, when my ankle wasn't too sore to keep me on the sideline, I hadn't played competitive ball in a couple of months. I had almost forgotten what it was like to play in a game where someone is keeping score. Even a pickup game is different from practice.

On this night I played with ferocity. I was so mad! I was blocking almost every shot. I was trying to dunk everything. And people were like "Who the fuck is this guy? He doesn't even speak English." They had no idea what I had been through or where I had been. Growing up in Africa, I had a vision of America as a place where everything is easy. I had heard about Hollywood and Las Vegas. The glitter of New York and Miami. There was abundant wealth in America. All you had to do was find a way to get here and then seize the opportunities that would be laid at your feet. But what I discovered was something else entirely. I was as poor and desperate in the United States as I had been in the Congo. And I was so very angry about it.

I was lucky to have found Coach Norris. He and his wife fed me and cared for me, and ultimately reached out to Terry and Laurie Blitz on my behalf. Coach Norris explained how his family had taken me in. Mainly, he just wanted the Blitzes to know that I was safe. Terry explained my situation in far greater detail, and with much more clarity than I was capable of providing.

Coach Norris explained to them that he could help fix my visa, as he had experience in these matters, along with contacts in the Student and Exchange Visitor System (SEVIS), a division of U.S Citizenship and Immigration Services (USCIS), under the umbrella of Homeland Security. These were exactly the people I feared; but with an ally in their ranks, helping to clear up a mess that was created by my self-serving cousin, then perhaps everything would be all right. I couldn't believe my good fortune. Not only did they open their home and their hearts, but Coach Norris also took me to the gym almost every day so that I could continue to play basketball.

Coach Norris talked with the Blitzes, and together they decided that at least for the time being, I should go back to Arizona. So, within a few weeks I was on my way home to Mesa, to the people I now considered family, and whom I referred to as my parents. I wasn't sure what the future would hold. Since I was still ineligible to play in Arizona, Coach Norris wanted me to return to Mississippi in the fall to attend Genesis One Christian School, a prep school in Mendenhall, Mississippi, where he was basketball coach. There, he said, I could finish high school and have access to academic support and college recruiting. In the meantime, he said, he would continue to work on fixing my visa situation.

By now it was nearly May, so there was no point in trying to take any classes at Mesa. It was too close to the end of the school year and I was too far behind. Regardless of whether I would be transferring to Genesis One or reenrolling at Mesa (even though I was ineligible to play basketball), it made sense to wait until the following fall and the start of a new school year.

That spring and summer, I returned to my old AAU team, where I got to play for Coach Ward again. I was so happy to be with my old teammates and living in my old house with Terry and Laurie. Everything was going great. A large contingent of college coaches attended our first AAU tournament. Despite not having worn a uniform since January, I played very well. I don't know how to explain it. I should have been rusty and apprehensive, but instead I felt comfortable and relaxed. My fitness was pretty good considering I'd only been practicing a few weeks. Coach Ward seemed to bring out the best in me. He was a challenging but encouraging coach, and I loved playing for him. In that first tournament, I grabbed every rebound that came within reach, and blocked shots all over the gym. My shot was not terribly inaccurate, so I settled mostly for dunks and layups on offense. My goal was to have a tireless motor, and to play with great and demonstrable passion.

Apparently, it worked, because college coaches immediately began reaching out to Coach Ward. I was something of an enigma, because my entire high school career to that point had consisted of only a handful of games. For most Division I prospects, the recruiting process starts in ninth or tenth grade; by the summer after junior year, they've whittled down the list of suitors to a handful or already made their decisions. I was eighteen years old and not even sure what grade I was in (although by making up classes I was told that I would still be able to graduate the following summer, despite having missed much of the second semester in my junior year). I had no basketball record to speak of; no sparkling statistical output, no championships or awards, no flashy video with highlights.

Nothing.

I was a complete unknown.

But with each tournament I continued to perform well on what is commonly referred to as the "eye test." This is exactly what it sounds like: I looked good on the court. I was tall and fast, and I played very hard. Oddly enough, my relative lack of experience was seen not as a hindrance, but an attribute. Coaches liked the fact that I played hard and seemed to have a good attitude (I got along with my teammates, didn't argue with my coach, and never behaved disrespectfully toward the officials). And they liked my physical characteristics, of course. But what really piqued their interest was the idea that I hadn't come close to reaching my potential. I was one of the best players on the floor in every game that summer, despite having little experience or coaching in the American style of play. I was considered raw and unpolished—a diamond in the rough. Sometimes a coach will look at a recruit and decide he has already peaked, either physically or in terms of skill. Coaches looked at me and saw a player who would continue to improve throughout his college career.

A number of Division I programs began recruiting me, but I decided very early that I wanted to attend the University of Tulsa, because that was where my friend Donte would be going to school and playing basketball. Like I said, Donte and I had talked often about reuniting in college and playing on the same team, and now we had a chance to make it happen.

"I want to go to Tulsa," I told Coach Ward. "I don't want to think about anyplace else."

Coach Ward just nodded and told me to be patient and to keep my options open. He had been around the recruiting game a long time and understood that things could change quickly. But my mind was made up. In July, during a long bus ride on the way back from an AAU tournament in California, I spoke on the phone with Doug Wojcik, the head coach at Tulsa.

"Blondy, we'd like you to come to Tulsa, and we'd like to offer you a scholarship," he said.

At first, I said nothing. I just sat there with a big grin on my face, barely able to process what I had heard.

"Blondy?" he repeated. "Are you okay?"

"Yes, Coach. Yes. . . I am very okay."

"So what do you think?"

"I think I cannot believe it. Yes, I would like to go to school at Tulsa. Thank you very much, Coach."

I told everyone on the bus, and we celebrated on the ride home. I called Terry and Laurie and told them. And then I called Donte and shared the good news.

"Bro, you won't believe it," I said. "We're going to play together in college. You and me, back together."

To say we had beaten the odds would be a dramatic understatement. Less than 1 percent of all high school basketball players in the United States go on to play at the Division I level. And now there were two of us on one team who would be receiving scholarships. On so many levels it was remarkable. . . . We talked for a while and started making plans. Finally, everything was falling into place. It seemed almost too good to be true.

CHAPTER 16

The summer of 2009 was the first time in my life when I felt like a normal, happy high school kid. An American kid! I played a ton of basketball, hung out with my friends, had dinner every night with my family, and generally just allowed myself to relax and feel safe. The upcoming school year was going to be hard. I'd have to take extra classes in order to graduate on time, along with an SAT prep course because my language deficiencies were sure to make any standardized test more challenging. Without a decent score on the SAT, I would be ineligible to play basketball in college.

But none of these things felt like an insurmountable obstacle. There were so many people in my corner, helping out and trying to ensure that I could chase my dream, that I felt completely confident. At least once a week I called Coach Norris to talk about basketball and school. He said he was still working on my visa issues, but that everything would be okay. He reiterated his belief that I would do well in prep school and eventually have even more offers from which to choose.

"I don't want more offers," I said. "I want to go to Tulsa."

Coach Norris laughed. "Well, that's fine, too."

Terry Blitz stayed in contact with Coach Norris throughout the summer, sending paperwork and discussing what needed to be done to acquire a valid student visa that would allow me to attend school in Mississippi. By late July, however, when the visa still had not been approved, Terry became concerned. Like any father, Terry hid this from me for a while, preferring instead to shoulder the burden himself (along with Laurie). Adding to his concern were phone calls from various college coaches who expressed reservations about my plans for the upcoming year.

Genesis One, apparently, had come under scrutiny for what can best be termed a distinct lack of academic rigor. In a span of just a few short years, the school had expanded from serving a small primary school population to grades kindergarten through thirteen, the latter being a postgraduate year that is intended primarily for athletes who need a year of maturation or academic support in order to meet college entrance requirements. This is common at prep schools, including even the best of the traditional elite boarding schools, but Genesis One, like some other institutions, had been described by critics as being nothing more than a "diploma mill," where much of the high school student body was comprised of future college athletes who struggled badly in the classroom.

There is nothing wrong with a school providing academic support and guidance—indeed, it should be part of the package if you grant a scholarship to a student athlete who, for whatever reason, clearly has demonstrated academic shortcomings. I did not know it at the time, but a small industry had erupted around the recruiting and supposed educating of disadvantaged students who had great promise on the basketball court but significant struggles in the classroom. Some of these schools came and went within just a few years, pumping out Division I athletes and winning championships before suddenly going out of business for financial or accreditation reasons. When media reports in the mid- to late 2000s began highlighting the struggles of some of these graduates after they reached college, or when they graduated but failed to achieve the necessary score on the SAT, the diploma mills came under fire and began to disappear from the landscape. Those that remained were viewed with increasing skepticism by college coaches.

Unbeknownst to me and my family, Genesis One fell into this category. Soon enough, it became apparent that moving back to Mississippi and attending Genesis One might cause more problems than it solved. I knew nothing about this while the drama unfolded. Terry and Laurie handled everything, with help from Coach Ward and Coach Burcar. They all wanted me to focus on basketball and school and friendships; they knew what I had already been through and did not want me to worry or suffer. But each time Terry spoke with a college coach, the issue of eligibility was front and center. Whenever Terry mentioned Genesis One, the coach would fall briefly silent, and then gently try to convey his concern.

"Oh . . . are you sure that's a good idea?"

"Well, if he doesn't go there, he won't be able to play high school basketball," Terry would explain. But this did nothing to influence the coach's decision.

"Doesn't matter," one of the Tulsa coaches told Terry. "Let him stay home, finish school, and play AAU ball. He can sit out his senior season and it won't make any difference to us. He'll be fine. We know Blondy can play."

In the end, Terry came to believe that it was not a good idea to return to Mississippi. Like the coaches who recruited me, he was worried that a year at Genesis One would worsen, rather than enhance, my academic profile. He worried that the school might go out of business, or that a lack of accreditation would result in my being declared ineligible. Although we all liked Coach Norris and appreciated him coming to my rescue, there was just too much risk associated with transferring to Genesis One.

What really solidified the decision in Terry's mind was the fact that my visa problems remained, even as the summer deepened and fall appeared on the horizon. The primary reason for going back to Mississippi was because my new, corrected (and legal!) visa would stipulate those terms, as I was going to be a student at Genesis One. But if I enrolled at Genesis One, without a valid visa, then my situation would be just as precarious as it was now in Arizona. And at least in Arizona

I would have the love and support of the Blitz family; I would have my friends and teammates, my teachers and coaches. But ultimately it would be my decision to make.

One night in early August, Terry and Laurie summoned me from my room and asked me to sit at the kitchen table. Instantly I became nervous and apprehensive—in the past, whenever I was told to sit down for a serious conservation, some terrible, life-altering event usually followed: leaving home with my cousin, going to prep school. Tentatively, I pulled up a chair.

"Relax," Terry said. "It's nothing bad."

He proceeded to explain everything that had happened related to my visa and my recruitment. He put a positive spin on everything, but ultimately left the choice up to me. After all, I was an adult.

"You can stay home and graduate with your friends," Terry said. "You probably won't be able to play basketball at Mesa this year, but you'll have your scholarship to Tulsa and you can play AAU and work out every day." He paused. "Or you can go back to Mississippi. You might be able to play there, or you might not be able to play. It's risky. If something happens, we won't be there to help you."

I felt terribly conflicted. I really liked Coach Norris as both a coach and a person. A cynic might say that he helped me only because I could play basketball, but that is not the impression I got from him and his family. They took me in when I had nowhere else to go. They treated me with compassion and warmth and generosity. Coach Norris never pressured me to play at Genesis One, and did not try to prevent me from going back to Arizona for the summer. I mean, he was a basketball coach and probably felt like a gift from heaven had presented itself when a 6-foot-8 African kid walked into his gym and began kicking butt in pickup games. But he didn't act that way. He was kind and gentle. I believe he simply wanted to help me.

And I wanted to play for him.

But I trusted Terry and Laurie to know what was best, and to steer me in the right direction. I'd been to prep school once and hated it; while I felt reasonably confident that Genesis One would be a different experience, especially with Coach Norris there, I liked the idea of staying at home. There was safety in Mesa. There was comfort. There were people I loved and trusted. All of that, I decided, was worth more than a single basketball season. God willing, there would be more games to play in college.

The decision became easier when we found out that Genesis One was closing its high school division. Coach Norris would be moving to a new school and a new program, and I certainly could have tried to join him. It all seemed too risky and nebulous, though, especially with the uncertainty over my visa status. I talked with Terry and Laurie a lot, and in the end decided to take their advice and remain in Mesa. I called Coach Norris and thanked him for everything he had done for me; I hoped he wouldn't be too angry or think I was ungrateful. I just had to do what was best for me under the circumstances. He said he understood and that he wished me the best. There are predators and sycophants and generally bad people in the world, and no shortage of flesh peddlers in the orbit of Division I sports. I know that. I also know there are good people, and Coach Norris is one of them.

But he was not a miracle worker, and since I was no longer going to return to Mississippi, there was only so much we could expect him to do about my visa. As the start of a new school year approached, we had heard nothing. Technically, I was in violation of my visa; while it was possible that U.S. Citizenship and Immigration Services might not catch up to me before the end of the school year, which meant I would be able to graduate, there was no way I would be able to enter a U.S. college without a valid student visa. My offer from the University of Tulsa remained on the table, but unless something changed, I would never get an opportunity to matriculate or play basketball.

This was yet another staggering obstacle, and I had no clue as to how to go about trying to overcome it. Thankfully, once again, I had Terry and Laurie in my corner, offering guidance and support and unconditional love, as well as the financial resources that I obviously did not possess. They suggested that we hire an immigration lawyer and file for political asylum in the United States, a daunting process that I was warned had little chance for success.

"It's a long shot," Terry said to me. "But don't lose hope. We're going to do everything we can."

Think about this for a moment, as I have on numerous occasions over the years. Think about what this family did for me—the emotional and financial support they offered, and the unconditional love that went with it. For me, a poor African kid who was not part of their bloodline, and whose sudden appearance in their lives (with so much baggage) could not have been easy. Terry Blitz became the father I never had—a man of strong faith and conviction, he never wavered in his support, offering guidance and stability and love just as if I were his very own son. Laurie Blitz also treated me like her own flesh and blood. No one will ever replace my mother, of course; my strength and endurance came from her and my grandmother, and I was in touch with them throughout my entire journey (although I did not share with them the details of my hardship; this I told only Uncle Joseph, who felt it was best to spare my mother and grandmother the anguish they surely would have felt). But Laurie Blitz is like a second mother to me, and I will be forever grateful that she came into my life . . . and welcomed me into hers.

I had been told that less than one percent of applications for asylum in the state of Arizona are approved, but I was so moved by the love and support of my new family that I couldn't help but feel confident.

"Don't worry, Dad," I said to Terry with a smile on my face. "I got this. I know who I am. I know God is with me. I didn't come this far just to be turned away. I'm going to go to college in America."

This may have been naive, but in my mind I was thinking that if I could survive the bloodshed in the Congo, nothing could stop me from getting asylum. The odds were less than one percent? Fine. I knew I needed only one tenth of one percent to be successful. As my mother had always said, "When things get hard, turn your eyes to the Lord, and he will be there for you."

Terry smiled. "All right, Blondy."

Terry and Laurie began the painstaking process of putting together a detailed history of my life, so that an attorney could make a strong case for my application. This was a daunting task for the Blitzes, for they knew only an overview of my story—anecdotes I had shared and some that had been provided by Patrick. In seeking political asylum, a candidate must demonstrate clearly that his health and well-being are in danger if he is deported to his native country. A detailed timeline of events is required—documented evidence supporting the candidate's request. Compiling all this information was challenging, in part because of my shortcomings with the English language, but also because Terry and Laurie were reluctant to ask me to talk about my childhood in the Congo. They knew the basic outline of my story, but not the gruesome details, and they worried that the sharing of this painful journey, in all its bloody sadness, would be a devastating emotional experience. And, frankly, I'm sure I had blotted some of it from my memory as a simple act of self-preservation.

But we were all in this together, so I told Terry and Laurie as much of the story as I could. I also wrote to my uncle Joseph and asked him to fill in some of the gaps, especially from my early childhood. Using every tool at our disposal, we crafted what we all felt was a compelling argument for my being granted political asylum.

We met first with an immigration attorney from a large firm in Phoenix. The lawyer had a good reputation, but the meeting did make any of us feel confident. Terry and Laurie told him my story, and he responded by mapping out his case—a plan that could take many years and multiple appeals, and drain every penny from the Blitzes' savings and retirement accounts. I did not particularly like this attorney—he was very young and seemed arrogant; he also failed to make an emotional connection with any of us. He actually recommended to Terry that I be sent back to Golding Academy, because he believed that represented my best chance to get a new visa. This, he said, was a far more likely path to victory than seeking asylum in the state of Arizona. Thankfully, Terry and Laurie rejected his suggestion. Now, I understand that you don't hire an attorney based on personality, but this was an intensely personal situation for me and the Blitz family. We all wanted to believe that our attorney was willing to fight for us with everything he had; we needed to feel as though he believed in us, and understood what we had been through. None of us felt that that attorney did.

Terry and Laurie decided to seek out another attorney, one who was more personable, confident, and perhaps a little less expensive. Terry chose from a directory a female attorney with a name that sounded as though she was of Asian descent. She had solid credentials, to be sure, but Terry also figured a woman might be more naturally sympathetic to my plight; he also thought that, given her name, maybe she wasn't several generations removed from a personal connection to the immigrant experience in America. All of this was merely a hunch on Terry's part, but it proved right.

The attorney, as it turned out, was from China. Her name was Joy Huang, and she spoke fluent English, but with enough of an accent that our first meeting was challenging. Terry's and Laurie's first language was English; mine was French; the attorney's was Chinese. With all of these dialects flying around the room, it took great patience for all of us to arrive at the same level of understanding. I was somewhat lost, but Terry and Laurie remained calm and reassuring throughout the process, and then relayed the details when we got home.

After hearing the story, the attorney said that I should not seek political asylum. This surprised Terry and Laurie.

"Why not?" they asked.

"Because you have no chance of winning," Joy responded. "Not because Blondy doesn't have a good case, but simply because it's almost impossible to receive political asylum." She reiterated some of the depressing statistics we had already heard: less than one percent of cases approved, an endless and overwhelmingly expensive journey that would likely end in failure and deportation.

We all hung our heads.

"Then what do we do?" Terry asked.

The attorney advised us to forget about political asylum and instead focus on a much more attainable goal: fixing my visa. This involved applying for a new and updated Form I-20, a document more formally known as the Certificate of Eligibility for Nonimmigrant Student Status. I already had an I-20, but by traveling to Arizona when I first came to America, I had inadvertently violated its terms. The best course of action now, Joy explained, was to apply for a new I-20 in the hope of reinstating my student status. We had a far greater likelihood of success with this approach, she said, and if the I-20 was approved, not only would I be allowed to finish school at Mesa High School, but I would be able to attend the University of Tulsa, as well.

I was encouraged by this meeting; Terry and Laurie, not so much. They had spent the better part of the previous four months working with Coach Norris while he tried to expedite a new I-20 application on my behalf. Even with his connections, there had been little to no progress. The Blitzes were naturally pessimistic that an attorney would be able to accomplish this task, but they deferred to her judgment. Unfortunately, their doubt was confirmed a short time later when Joy reported that obtaining a new I-20 was unlikely, if not impossible. So, we came full circle, with our attorney telling us that my only chance to remain in the country legally was to apply for political asylum. Disappointing as it was to hear this news, we all respected her honesty.

"Nothing has changed," Joy said. "It's a long shot. But it's the only chance we have."

Unlike our previous attorney, she did not map out a questionable plan of attack that would take years and cost my family every penny they had. She would charge a flat fee that would cover all expenses, including court dates and appeals; the meter would not simply run forever. It was still a lot of money—approximately $6,000—but Terry and Laurie said they could handle the expense.

"Don't worry, Blondy," they said. "You just concentrate on school and basketball."

I wanted to cry when they told me this; the combination of guilt and gratitude that their generosity provoked was overwhelming. Someday, I promised myself, I would pay them back. In the meantime, I had an obligation to hold up my end of the bargain, and I embraced it with a full heart. I had received no academic credit for the second semester of my junior year, but I still hoped to graduate in June of 2010 with my class at Mesa High School. That way, if my visa situation was somehow corrected, I'd be eligible to enroll at Tulsa.

The administration at Mesa graciously accommodated this request, but they made it clear that the schedule would be daunting, to say the least. In addition to taking seven classes each day in school (one more than the usual load), for two semesters, I would also have to register for one online class each semester. The possibility of a summer school session loomed, as well. All of this was a bit intimidating, especially for someone still struggling to master the English language, but I wasn't about to complain. If my family was willing to fight for me, then I had to fight alongside them.

The days were long: up at 5:45, home around four in the afternoon, dinner at five, work online for a couple hours, and then go to basketball practice or training with Coach Ward until 9:30 or 10:00. This was the daily routine in the fall of my senior year. There wasn't a lot of time for socializing, which was sometimes frustrating, but ultimately unimportant. I had my eye on a bigger prize.

After working on it for several months, we completed a narrative of my life story, which would be the centerpiece of my appeal for political asylum. The goal was to gain an appearance with an immigration officer who would listen to my story and then either act on the request for asylum or refer it to the court system. If it went to the courts, as was usually the case, we would likely be fighting for many months, with little chance for victory. As I understood it, the interview would be demanding; the officer's job was to poke holes in my story, to separate fact from fiction. Many people request political asylum in the United States. Some of them have a legitimate fear of reprisal if they are deported. Others have fled because life in their home country is so dangerous. Some are merely seeking a better life in America, which may be perfectly understandable but is not sufficient reason to be granted political asylum.

Life in the Congo was dangerous. I had escaped death a multitude of times while growing up, and the situation in my homeland remained volatile. As a somewhat prominent athlete who had left the country and sought asylum in the U.S., I faced the prospect of being targeted upon returning to the Congo. There was no doubt about this. The challenge was to convince a USCIS officer of the veracity of my story.

In early October we found out that we had cleared the first hurdle. My case would be heard by an immigration official. I would have a chance to tell my story. In person. I was excited and hopeful about this opportunity, but quite anxious, as well.

"We have another month to get ready," Terry said. "But don't worry. You're going to be great. We're all going to help."

After that, I went to bed every night thinking about the interview, replaying the narrative in my head, the monologue coming out in a jumble of English and French. But always the message was clear.

If I go back to the Congo, I will die. If you let me stay, I will live. I will be grateful. And I will make you proud.

All of this was serious business, and it should have been enough to occupy my mind. But as basketball season approached, I found myself growing sad and distracted. I was working out with Coach Ward and playing pickup ball with my Mesa teammates. It was fun, and I was playing very well. I had come to terms with the notion that I would not play competitive basketball again until I got to Tulsa—assuming I got to Tulsa—but the more time I spent in the gym with my teammates, bonding and talking about the upcoming season, the more I wanted to play. And not just pickup ball. I wanted to wear a Mesa High School uniform. I knew in my heart that this was not an important matter—not in comparison to the larger issue of gaining political asylum—but I couldn't stop thinking about it. One day, I asked Terry if we could talk. I even steered him toward the dinner table, the way he and Laurie always did to me when a serious topic was at hand. And, like me, Terry responded apprehensively.

"What's on your mind?"

"I miss playing basketball," I said. "And I was wondering if there is any way for me to play this season."

Terry waited a long time before answering. I could tell he did not want to hurt my feelings. But Terry is an honest man, and he wasn't going to give me false hope.

"As far as I can tell, no," he said. "There is no way for you to play at Mesa. Or anywhere else. Not until you get to college."

He paused and looked me hard in the eye. "I'm sorry, Blondy. This isn't your fault. I wish there was something I could do."

Short of hiring another attorney, which he could not afford, and which I did not expect him to do, there was little Terry could offer aside from sympathy; he and Laurie had already done enough for me. They understood how much I loved basketball, and how hard it would be for me to sit on the sideline all winter while my friends and teammates played. Nevertheless, it was important to keep my eye on the prize: political asylum and the right to pursue my education in America. Coach Wojcik had repeatedly assured us that if I was in the country legally, my scholarship was safe, and that I would play for the University of Tulsa the following year. They saw no problem with me sitting out my senior year. But I did, and with each passing day, the pain grew worse.

But wait! There was another angel looking over me, for the news of my story had traveled far and wide, resulting in an offer from another lawyer who wanted to fight the lifetime ban that had been imposed upon me by the Arizona Interscholastic Association. His name was Charles Riekena.

"I don't like the way this young man has been treated," Charles said in an email to Terry. "It's not right. And I would like to represent him."

Mr. Riekena told Terry that he wanted to fight on my behalf. Terry later admitted to me that he started sweating during this exchange, as he immediately began thinking of the financial implications.

"Don't worry," Mr. Riekena said. "I'll do it for free."

I tried not to get my hopes up, but the attorney seemed confident. Even better, he seemed angry—like he felt personally offended by the AIA decision. I took this as a good sign: if someone is going to plead your case, you want that person to believe in your cause. And what other motivation was there? After all, he wasn't getting paid.

Fortunately, I was much too busy to obsess about my appeal to the AIA. In addition to juggling a heavy load of classes and homework, I continued to study intensely for my upcoming interview with U.S. Citizenship and Immigration Services.. You would think that I would have known my own life and story well enough to communicate it effectively to anyone, but it wasn't that simple. For one thing, I was extraordinarily nervous about the interview and the impact on my life. I worried that the interrogator would be wily and treacherous—that his (or her) intent would be to make me so anxious and confused that I would mess up or otherwise seem unconvincing. The entire Blitz family rallied together in this cause. Terry, Laurie, and Jared all read my story many times; then they took turns interviewing me, peppering me with questions, sometimes in an antagonistic manner. They tried to fool me. They tried to make me uncomfortable. But each time I answered the questions correctly.

"I am going to get political asylum on the first interview," I told Terry.

"I hope you're right," he said. But Terry was a pragmatist, and every so often he would remind me of the odds. "Remember, less than one percent of applicants for political asylum are successful on the first attempt, Blondy. It's not going to be easy."

CHAPTER 17

I did not expect it to be easy. But I did believe that God was watching over me. Just as he had carried me through civil war and delivered me to America, he would help me win this struggle, as well. I believed this in my heart. I had come too far to fail. The thing that concerned me most was the possibility that I would not understand some of the questions because of my deficiencies with English. But our lawyer assured us that communication would not be a problem, as a translator would be present in the room during the interview. I could give my responses in French. This made the process less terrifying, although it remained intimidating.

The interview took place in early November, in Phoenix, at the offices of U.S. Citizenship and Immigration Services. My whole family came with me: Terry, Laurie, Brandon, Jared, and Travis (the oldest Blitz son, who wasn't around much because he had such a busy work schedule, but who showed up to support me nevertheless). We sat together in the waiting room, making small talk the way families do, and reassuring each other that everything would be okay.

"Mr. Baruti?"

Standing in the doorway was a pleasant-looking woman. She held a folder in her hand. In that moment, neatly dressed, with a big smile on her face, she seemed benign.

I stood up. So, did Terry and Laurie. I gave each of them a big hug.

They seemed even more nervous than I did. I guess that's the way it is with parents: nothing hurts more than seeing one of your children go through a difficult time. And while I was obviously not part of the Blitz bloodline, I was in many ways their fourth son.

"Do not worry," I whispered to them. "Everything will be all right."

Four of us disappeared into a room: me, the immigration officer, my lawyer, Joy Huang, and the translator. For the first few minutes I was very nervous. The woman remained just as friendly as she had seemed upon introduction, but the process was inherently traumatic. There was so much at stake! Despite the presence of the translator, the immigration officer never took her eyes off me. She would look right at me—right through me, it seemed—as she formulated long and complicated questions in English. I would return her gaze, but then break away as the translator put her words into French. It was such a long and laborious way to conduct a conversation—I worried with each question and answer that something was getting lost in translation, but I did my best to remain calm and provide accurate information. I didn't want to lie or even embellish my story; indeed, any deviation from the truth as she already knew it would only have hurt my application for asylum.

It was interesting to watch her response as I spoke. She would look me first in the eye, and then as my response wore on, she would lower her gaze—to my lips, my hands, my feet. I had been told this would happen, that immigration officers who conducted these interviews were skilled at ferreting out fabricators not just by listening to their words, but by examining their body language. I had been advised to sit tall and proud, and to not avert my gaze. I had been told to keep my hands on the armrests of my chair, or on the desk in front of me, so as not to appear uneasy.

Don't squirm.

Don't fidget.

Don't scratch yourself or clear your throat.

All of these things, I was told, are indicative of trying to hide something. Of course, they also represent a perfectly reasonable human response to an extraordinarily stressful situation. But that was beside the point. It wasn't enough to avoid lying; I had to avoid the *appearance* of lying, which is a far more difficult thing.

The interview went on for nearly four hours. I became more comfortable with the line of questioning, more confident that I was effectively relating the tale of my journey from the Congo to Arizona. Nevertheless, it was an exhausting experience. At the end, the immigration officer thanked me for my time and complimented me on my presentation.

"Do you have anything else you'd like to add," she said.

In fact, yes, there was something I wanted to add. From a folder I withdrew a sheaf of papers—my written scholarship offer from the University of Tulsa. I handed it to the officer and let her look it over for a moment.

"I want to go to school and get my education," I said, this time using fractured English to get the point across: that I was determined to assimilate. "I want to be a citizen here in America. I want to be a citizen—just like you. And I want to have a family here in America, and also help my people in the Congo."

She smiled and nodded, thanked me for my time, and then we left the room. Outside, Terry and Laurie were nervously waiting. We all walked to the parking lot together, and on the way Joy informed the Blitzes that the interview had gone very well. It was still a long shot that asylum would be granted based on a single interview, she said, but anything was possible. She also stressed that patience would be necessary.

"They never give an answer right away," she explained. "It'll probably be a few months."

Around this same time, I was granted a meeting with the AIA in regard to my athletic eligibility status in Arizona. My attorney, Mr. Reikena, had been dogged in his pursuit of reinstatement. Rather than beg forgiveness on my behalf, he went on the offensive, pressuring the AIA for answers and information, and arguing persuasively that I had done nothing wrong. There had been no proof of recruitment by anyone associated with the Mesa High School basketball program, and while there might have been mistakes in protocol, they occurred without my knowledge or approval, and were entirely orchestrated by a third party—specifically, my cousin Patrick. The lawyer argued that it was grossly unfair to punish me for something I knew nothing about. He also stated that in handing down a lifetime suspension, the AIA had violated my right to due process.

Basically, Mr. Reikena took a sledgehammer to an organization that routinely made draconian decisions affecting people's lives, and yet rarely was compelled to defend those decisions. Hardly anyone challenged the AIA; the organization was simply too powerful, and a fight was too costly for the average person. But I was blessed to have an attorney fiercely devoted to the cause, and not only willing to work for free, but also shrewd and talented.

Although both Terry and Mr. Reikena felt we had a strong case, they were careful to caution against being overly optimistic. The AIA was a large and influential bureaucratic organization. Even if its leaders determined that my case had been mishandled, and justice meted out unfairly, they would likely still feel a need to save face.

"What we are really hoping for," Mr. Reikena explained, "is some sort of compromise."

The meeting with the AIA was intense. My attorney was well prepared and filled with passion. I was moved almost to the point of tears as he pleaded my case and accused the AIA of behaving in a rash and inappropriate manner. I could not understand everything they were saying, of course, but the message came through loud and clear:

This young man is a victim. He did nothing wrong.

Finally, as with the immigration interview, at the end of the meeting one of the members of the AIA asked me if I would like to speak. We thought this would probably happen, so I wasn't caught off guard. I was planning to say just a couple of words, but after watching Mr. Reikena fight so bravely for my cause, I was inspired to do the same. I stood up, took a deep breath, and began to speak in my broken but impassioned English.

"I am one of the luckiest people in this world. There are so many kids who would give anything to be in my position right now, and I am so grateful for it. My heart and my mind have been hurt by bad memories, but God is here for me now. I can see that. Leaving the Congo and coming to Arizona was the biggest dream that any kid in Africa could have. Why would I put myself in a bad position here? I did not know anything about what was going on before I came here. I just wanted to work hard every day to accomplish my dreams, which is to become a professional basketball player. My family back in the Congo and I trusted my cousin. We didn't know any better. But I am grateful for what I have today. I grew up very poor until these people, Terry and Laurie, took me into their house and gave me food, clothes, and water; they were there for me anytime I was in need. They do not see me as a kid from Africa; they see me as their own son. They love me and I love them, so no matter what happens here today, they will always be my family."

I paused to take a deep breath and a drink of water. There was so much more to say. I looked at them, one by one, staring into their eyes so they would know how I really felt.

"You guys took my joy away from me. You suspended me for something I did not do. The people who put me in this situation were not punished. But what about me? I had to leave my teammates and go somewhere else. I had to run away from people who mistreated me. I slept outside in the cold. I was sick and I did not have medicine. I cried every single night, begging God to rescue me. I ran away from people at Golding who mistreated me, and I wound up in Jackson, Mississippi, because I had to go somewhere that I thought would be safe. All of this happened because a few people made decisions about my life for their own benefit. I love my Mesa teammates to death. I would have done anything to be on the court with them in the second half of my junior year, but I was not. I watched them lose again and again, and I could not help."

I paused again. It was possible that I was saying too much. I looked at my lawyer. He nodded subtly, as if to say, "Go on . . ." And so I did.

"I want to be part of my team once again before I attend college. I want to wear my jersey again, and win games with my teammates. Please, I ask you—give me that opportunity."

I thanked the committee for their time and sat down. The room was very quiet. Mr. Riekena leaned toward me and whispered, with a smile, "Maybe you should think about becoming a lawyer." I tried not to laugh.

A few days later, the committee offered us a deal, just as Mr. Riekena had predicted. The AIA was in a difficult position. If the organization had rescinded its ruling completely, it would have faced a credibility problem. Moreover, while I had no control over the circumstances that led me to Arizona instead of the Northeast, it is true that rules were broken; I suppose someone had to be held accountable. Since the AIA held no jurisdiction over my cousin, the burden of responsibility fell mostly on me, and, to a lesser extent, on Mesa High School. Mesa had served its time by forfeiting the games in which I had played the previous season. But I was serving a lifetime sentence. It just didn't seem fair. In the end, the AIA agreed, handing down a partial reversal that would uphold the forfeiture of the previous games, along with a suspension. The good news, however, was that the lifetime ban was lifted; I would have to sit out the first fifteen games of the 2009–10 season. Then I would be eligible.

When I first heard about the offer, I was conflicted, for I had hoped for a complete exoneration, despite the fact that my attorney had said that was unlikely. I wanted to get out on the basketball court immediately, with my friends.

"What happens if we don't take the deal?" I asked.

"Then we go to court," Mr. Riekena explained. "It could take a long time—probably more than fifteen games—and we still might lose."

"Okay," I said. "Let's do it."

Within a couple of days the AIA announced its decision, and there were stories in the local newspapers. Although I had to sit out the first fifteen games, I was nevertheless a member of the team and thus allowed to participate in practice. Game nights, of course, were tough. I wanted to be out there, helping my teammates, swatting shots into the bleachers and running up and down the floor. But at least as I was practicing. I worked on my game every day, tried to be a strong and supportive teammate, and maintained a positive attitude. Before each game, I would gather the whole team beneath the basket. We would form a circle, with me in the middle.

"WHO'S NEXT?" I would shout, as the circle rocked in rhythm.

"WE NEXT!" came the response.

What did this mean? Well, it referred to a sign on the wall of the Mesa gym. The team had won many state championships, the most recent coming six years earlier, 2004. Next to a banner denoting this accomplishment was a sign with the words "Who's next?" (To win a state title.)

"WE NEXT!"

I had a lot of fun leading this chant every game, and if it wasn't quite like playing at least it made me feel like a valuable member of the team. The team was doing well, too, which made me even more excited about playing. After fifteen games, our record was 12–3.

My first game was January 8, 2010, at Tucson High School. Tucson was almost an hour and a half from Mesa, but a lot of our fans made the trip. I was so pumped up that I could barely get through warmups before the game. My hands were slippery, my mouth dry. But everyone was encouraging. I was not about to let them down by playing badly.

I did not start the game, but four minutes into the first quarter, Coach Burcar called my name.

"Blondy! Let's go."

I stood up, took off my warmups, and began to walk toward the scorer's table. The gym was nearly packed—it seemed like Mesa had almost as many fans as Tucson. Everyone stood and clapped as I knelt at the scorer's table. Then they began to chant.

"BLON-DY! BLON-DY!"

It took only a few seconds to get my first touch—a nice pass from Jahii Carson. I grabbed it, turned to face the basket, and threw down a monstrous dunk with as much force as I could. I'd been waiting almost a year to dunk the ball in a real game, and in that single play I was able to release all of the anger and frustration; in an instant they were replaced by something closer to joy.

"All day, my boy," Jahii said as we ran up the court together. "All day."

I was a little rusty, but I played all right and we won the game. Three days later, on January 12 (the day before my nineteenth birthday), I played a home game for the first time since my suspension. Eaxctly one year earlier my hopes and dreams, along with my basketball career, had been shattered. So much had happened since then. Now there was light again, after all the darkness.

As I took my place at the center circle for the opening jump, the crowd went crazy, chanting my name in unison.

"BLON-DY! BLON-DY! BLON-DY!"

This time it wasn't just the student section. As I looked up into the crowd, I could see others chanting, as well: grown men and women, parents with their children. Emotion swelled in my heart. I thought for a moment I might start crying right there in the middle of the floor, before the game even started.

I lowered my head and took several short, shallow breaths. Then I looked into the crowd again and gently tapped a fist against my chest.

"I love you," I said, though I'm sure they couldn't hear me.

We won that game, as well. I had eleven points and seven rebounds, felt a little more comfortable on the floor. But the biggest regular-season game of the year was January 18, in the Martin Luther King Classic at Arizona State University. Our opponent was Mountain View, our big rival. I'd been dreaming of this game for a year. Last year, after all, I'd been suspended right before the game. As happy as I was, I sometimes felt waves of anxiety over the possibility that something could still go wrong and take basketball from me again. Part of this was due to the fact that we still hadn't gotten a response on my petition for asylum.

"Don't worry," Brandon said to me one day after practice. "This year, you're playing against Mountain View. Hope you're ready."

Oh, I was ready, all right. And so were our fans. A few days before the game, Laurie's brother (I referred to him as Uncle Brad) sent us more than one hundred blue T-shirts emblazoned with the words "Blondy's Bombshells." A few people, including Jared Blitz, wore blond wigs along with the T-shirt. It was quite a sight.

Quite a game, too, very intense and well played. It went into overtime. With just seconds to go in OT Mountain View was trailing by two, 54–52, and called timeout. When play resumed they ran a nice play that screened a defender and freed one of their guys to drive to the basket. It wasn't my man, but part of my job as the tallest player on the court, and a defensive specialist, was to protect the basket and help my teammates.

With seconds to spare, I saw him rise for the shot, and slid over to block it. If I had been even a fraction of a second late, he would have had a layup and Mountain View would have tied the game. But I got there just in time. Leaping between the player and the basket, I reached out and swatted the ball away as the buzzer sounded, preserving a Mesa victory.

The crowd went wild! The entire team danced around, screaming and celebrating on the court. It felt like we had won the state championship. For me, personally, it was one of the highlights of my basketball career. I remember feeling so happy as my teammates swarmed around me. I raised my right index finger into the air and waved it back and forth, shouting "No, no, no!" like Dikembe Mutombo. And then we fell into a pile on the floor, hugging each other and laughing.

This, I thought to myself, is why I love basketball.

★

WE HAD A MUCH better season than anyone expected; it's funny how things work out that way sometimes. In my junior year, when Donte and I played together—a pair of Division I recruits—Mesa was supposed to be one of the best teams in the state. But everything fell apart when I got suspended and the team was forced to forfeit some of its games.

This year, with Donte gone and my status uncertain, expectations were low. By sectional time, though, we were practically unbeatable, and we entered the state tournament as the favorite. Unfortunately, we lost to St. Mary's, 65–62, at home, in the quarterfinals.

When the game ended I was filled with sadness and disappointment. I have always hated losing, but there was something about this loss that was particularly painful—the sting of uncertainty and the possibility that I had played not just my last high school game, but my last game ever in America. It was bad enough knowing I would never wear a Mesa High School uniform again, or play with any of my friends and classmates. But what if I never wore any uniform again? What if my application for asylum was rejected? I thought about this in the locker room, fighting back tears as I peeled off my jersey for the last time.

The uncertainty ended just a couple of days later, when an envelope arrived in the mail at the Blitz house. According to the return address, it came from U.S. Citizenship and Immigration Services. I was in my room doing homework when Laurie yelled from the living room.

"Blondy! Come out here."

When I walked out, Laurie was holding the envelope in her hand. She was smiling nervously. Terry and Jared were also in the room.

"Is that it?" I asked.

Laurie nodded and handed me the envelope. "Open it," she said.

I did, but I didn't read it. Not right away. I was too nervous about what it would say, and fearful that I might not understand. Instead, I handed the letter back to Laurie. Her hands shook as she read it silently, although I could see her moving her lips. After a few short moments, a smile crossed her face. She lowered the letter and looked at me, her eyes wide.

"Yay! Blondy!" Laurie shouted. "You did it!" She waved the paper furiously as she turned to face Terry and Jared. "He's been granted political asylum!"

Terry looked absolutely shocked. He took the letter from Laurie's hands, read it for a moment, and then smiled.

He showed me the letter. At the very top, in boldface letters, underlined for emphasis, were the following words:

ASYLUM APPROVAL

The first few sentences told us everything we needed to know:

Dear Mr. Baruti:

This letter refers to your request for asylum in the United States filed on Form I-589.

It has been determined that you are eligible for asylum in the United States. Attached please find a completed Form I-94, Arrival-Departure Record, indicating that you have been granted asylum status pursuant to 208(a) of the Immigration and Nationality Act (INA) as of 12/09/09.

I looked at Terry and smiled. He nodded approvingly and then said loudly, "Blondy, you are a warrior!"

Hearing those words from Terry, a man I admired so deeply, and to whom I owed so much, was almost more than I could bear. I began to weep, softly at first, and then uncontrollably. I wrapped him in a bear hug and held him tight. And then I did the same to Laurie, as we all cried together.

"Thank you," I said to them both. "I love you."

That very day I called home to give the news to my family. Well, that isn't quite true. I actually spoke only with my uncle Joseph. As I said, when I first began having problems in America, I sometimes confided in my uncle. At his suggestion, though, I said nothing to anyone else back home. My mother and grandmother worried about me incessantly, and Uncle Joseph felt it would be best to spare them the details of my struggle. So while I spoke with my mother or grandmother roughly once a week, or every other week, I never shared with them any disturbing news. It was better, Uncle Joseph said, to simply pretend that everything was okay.

I agreed.

That night, when I called home, and the phone rang across ten thousand miles, I felt both happy and homesick.

"Uncle Joseph, I have been granted asylum in America!" I said.

"That is good, Blondy," he said. There was a long pause. "This means you cannot come home."

This was true, of course. I had sought political asylum based on the likelihood that I would face persecution or even death if I returned to the Congo. Now, having won my case in part by publicly describing the horrors and atrocities of my homeland, I had made that likelihood a certainty. I could never go home. The risk was simply too great.

"Yes, Uncle, I know." I was so emotional that I decided not to speak at all with my mother or grandmother; I might have been tempted to share the good news, which to them wouldn't have been good at all, but instead an alarming resolution to a mystery they did not even know existed. It would have been hard for me, as well, knowing that while I had been granted my greatest wish, it came at a price: I might never see my family again. So I spoke only with Uncle Joseph. I just wanted him to know that I was safe and sound. He would take care of the rest.

"Please tell Mama I love her," I said.

CHAPTER 18

After so much uncertainty and turbulence, it felt great to be a normal high school senior. My course load was heavier than most, but I didn't mind because I enjoyed spending time in school, with my friends, and I knew that soon all the hard work would pay off. I no longer had to worry about being deported or losing my scholarship to Tulsa. For the first time, there was very little anxiety in my life. I was safe. I was happy. There was only one thing missing.

Something every high school senior needs.

A driver's license!

Yes, like every other adolescent male in America, I dreamed of having the freedom that comes with a driver's license. I would no longer have to ask Terry or Laurie to chauffeur me everywhere I needed to go. I could drive myself to the gym, or to the movies, or to the mall. Best of all, I would be able to spend more time with girls without Terry and Laurie knowing exactly what I was doing. What can I say? I was becoming, in many ways, just a typical American boy.

I studied the manual and committed to memory most of the rules of the road before I ever sat behind the wheel. I had taken only a single short lesson by early springtime, when Jared showed up at the house while we were all standing outside in the driveway. Jared, knowing that

I was eager to learn how to drive, pulled along the curb at the end of the driveway, got out of the car, and left the engine running.

"Blondy, would you like to park the car for me?"

What happened next, I can attribute to a combination of youthful exuberance and poor communication skills.

"Yes!" I shouted. Then I climbed into the driver's seat, shut the door, and sped away. And I do mean "sped." I hit the gas, waved goodbye out the window, and disappeared from sight. I drove down the street for maybe a half mile before turning around and speeding back in the other direction, toward the Blitzes' house. I roared past them as they stood at the end of the driveway, waving frantically and shouting. I did not know what they were saying and did not really care. There were other cars in the neighborhood, and I realized they were all going much slower than me. The speed limit was twenty miles per hour in the neighborhood, and I must have been going close to fifty. I drove past the house for a block or two, then doubled back again, this time very slowly. I pulled up to the curb, stopped the engine, and got out.

"I'm a good driver," I declared proudly.

Before I could say anything else, Laurie was in my face. She was so mad.

"Blondy!" she shouted. "Are you crazy?"

"I don't think so."

"You don't have a license to drive a car," she said. "You don't have insurance. If you had gotten in an accident and hurt someone, you'd be history. The government could send you back to the Congo, or put you in prison."

I felt terrible. I had never seen Laurie so angry.

"What were you thinking?" she added.

"But Jared said 'park.' So that's where I went."

Laurie looked perplexed. "What?"

"The park," I explained. "Where I play basketball."

Terry and Jared started to laugh. Laurie remained angry for a few more seconds, but finally she smiled and shook her head.

"Okay, Blondy. Just don't ever do that again."

★

TIME MOVED QUICKLY IN the spring of my senior year. I passed my driver's test on the first try, and before I knew it, graduation day had arrived. It was a typically perfect Arizona day, the sun splashing across the Mesa High School football field as we marched into the stadium in our purple gowns. I thought about everything that had happened to me since I had arrived in America. It had been less than two years, but it felt like so much longer. There had been so many hardships and disappointments, but so much to cherish, as well. Think about it: two years earlier I was still in the Congo, dreaming of a life in America. I spoke not a word of English, and knew not a soul beyond my country. And now? Here I was, about to graduate from high school with my friends and classmates. Right on time!

I thought about my family back in the Congo and the sacrifices they had made for me—how hard it must have been for my mother to let me go. I thought about how lucky I was to have found a new family in Arizona, people who opened their hearts to me and took me into their lives and their home. I looked around the stadium, at my classmates and teachers, at the smiling faces in the crowd, so many proud and happy families.

I was one of them.

I belonged.

Throughout the ceremony I had trouble sitting still. I kept looking up into the crowd, waving to my American family: Terry and Laurie, and their sons, Brandon, Jared, and Travis. Laurie's mom, my American grandmother, even flew in from New Mexico. Finally, after speeches had been delivered and awards presented, it was time to hand out diplomas. I had trouble controlling myself during this portion of the ceremony. I kept yelling and jumping up and down and clapping my hands whenever the principal announced the name of one of my friends. And since I was friendly with just about everyone in the school, it happened quite a lot. I didn't mean to be inconsiderate; I was just so excited and grateful. Fortunately, everyone seemed to understand. They knew what I had been through, and what a long and remarkable journey it was that brought me from the Congo to this stage.

When my name was called, a roar went out from the crowd, just like at a basketball game. Only better. I walked to the center of the stage, shook hands with the principal and accepted my diploma. Rather than walk right back to my seat, I scanned the audience for Terry and Laurie. Then I held my diploma high above my head and shouted at the top of my lungs:

"Yes! Mom and Dad—we did it!"

CHAPTER 19

Most of my teammates on the University of Tulsa basketball team arrived on campus early in the summer, as is customary for Division I athletes. The summer serves as a boot camp of sorts, with incoming freshmen taking classes and training hard in the gym to prepare for both the academic and athletic rigors of college life. It gives everyone an opportunity to bond while accepting the realization that in the classroom and on the basketball court, college will be much more demanding than high school. It is, in short, an integral part of the indoctrination process.

And I missed it.

In order to qualify as an NCAA Division I student athlete, I had to make up some classes during the summer after my senior year. This was not exactly a surprise—I knew that by insisting upon trying to graduate with my classmates at Mesa, I would have to carry a heavy load and perhaps attend summer school. So that's what I did. Given what I had already been through on my journey to becoming a high school graduate, it was more of an annoyance than a burden; I wanted to be at Tulsa with my teammates. I wanted to make new friends and reunite with one of my best friends, Donte Medder. I wanted to prepare for basketball season by getting in the weight room and adding muscle and strength to my still slender frame. I wanted to get ahead in the classroom, like everyone else. Instead, I toiled away at Mesa High.

I left Arizona late in the summer, with Laurie as my traveling companion. I know that Terry wanted to make the trip, as well, but airfare was expensive and Laurie was more than capable of handling the move on her own. More than that, really. She was my American mom, and everyone knows that mothers are better suited to last-minute shopping and setting up dorm rooms. On the night before I left, however, Terry invited me to sit at the dining room table for another one of those important discussions I had come to know so well. This time there was nothing specific on the agenda. As my American dad, Terry merely wanted to make sure that I was okay before leaving the house. He wanted to talk about life and love; about respect and responsibility.

"Always remember where you come from," he began, and I noticed right away that his voice was softer than usual, his tone more measured. "Remember your family in the Congo, and everything you went through together. Remember that you have a family here, too. We know what you've accomplished, how you found a way to transform all the pain of your childhood into joy. You did it by having a great attitude, and by working hard. So keep doing that. Never quit, never give up."

"I won't," I interrupted. "I am not a quitter."

Terry smiled. "I know that, Blondy. But the thing is, Tulsa is going to be different. Everyone will be bigger, stronger, and faster than the players you saw in high school. Some of them have been there for a few years. They will test you. They will talk trash and they will knock you down. Don't say anything. Just get up off the floor and keep playing hard. Show them you are different from them. Show them you can't be intimidated. You have seen things and experienced things they can't imagine. Use that as a source of strength."

I nodded. "I will, Terry. Thank you."

There was a long pause as he lowered his head. When he looked up at me, I could see that his eyes were wet.

"I will always be here for you," he said. "I am so proud of you. I love you, son."

I reached across the table and put my arms around Terry. "I love you, too, Daddy."

★

ON THE DAY THAT I arrived at the University of Tulsa, I felt like I had made the best possible choice to begin the next chapter of my journey. I had visited during my senior year—even spent a night with Donte in the dorms—so I knew what to expect. But the campus seemed even prettier now, and everyone was so friendly and warm.

After we moved into my dorm, Laurie and I went straight to the athletic offices to meet with Coach Wojcik. Athletes often tell horror stories about coaches who have split personalities—sweet and sensitive during the recruiting process, and then angry and abusive once you begin playing for them. I still did not know Coach Wojcik well enough to have an opinion on this subject, but the man who greeted us that day seemed no different from the one who had offered me a scholarship.

"Tell Terry not to worry," he said to Laurie. "I'm going to be Blondy's dad for the next four years; we'll take good care of him."

My roommate was a 6-foot-5 freshman guard named Jordan Clarkson. He was smart and funny, and he was easy to talk to, so I liked him right away. We became close friends from day one. That first night in the dorm we stayed up for hours, just lying in our beds, in the dark, talking about school and basketball and life. Obviously, we had grown up under very different circumstances—Jordan was from San Antonio, while I was from the Congo—but still we connected like brothers.

The next day, during my first basketball workout at Tulsa, I felt slow and weak and out of shape compared to everyone else; it was instantly apparent that missing the summer session had put me at a deficit; I would have to work twice as hard as my teammates to show that I fit in. I didn't mind; hard work did not scare me in the least. But Jordan? Oh, my! He looked like a superstar from the moment he laced up his sneakers.

The interesting thing about Jordan was that he was so quiet and unassuming on the court. He led by example, not by words. The coaching staff would sometimes push Jordan to be more vocal, but it simply wasn't his style. He was the hardest-working player I had ever been around, and everyone on the team respected him and admired him. As players, we understood what Jordan brought to the game; we didn't care if he ever said a word. Coach Wojcik wanted him to be loud and demonstrative, to get in our faces and push us to be better, but it simply wasn't in Jordan's nature to behave that way.

I was the more animated half of our duo; unfortunately, I wasn't nearly the player that Jordan was, in part due to natural ability and in part because I hadn't played enough basketball yet, nor received the type of coaching afforded the best high school players in America. I had a steeper learning curve than my teammates, and having missed summer training it made the climb even harder.

But there was no shortage of teammates who set a good example, and whose work ethic made it clear that college basketball would be much more demanding than high school basketball. People like Jordan Clarkson and my good friend Donte Medder. Donte had torn his ACL, his anterior cruciate ligament, as a freshman, and was now working hard to get healthy and back into the lineup. I looked at Donte, whom I had always admired, and I realized: there are no guarantees.

I worked hard every day in practice; I worked hard in the classroom. Despite the fact that I still had some language issues, I became a strong student. Progress was slower on the basketball court. Although I was as athletic as anyone on the team, my game was less refined. And I was so skinny! Every night I would go to the dining hall and eat until I could barely move; still, I could not gain any muscle. I spent hours in the weight room, working with our strength and conditioning coaches, but gains were slow to come.

"Keep up the good work," Coach Wojcik told me a few weeks before the season started. "You're doing great. Just be patient."

I wasn't so sure.

In late October, as basketball season drew near, I decided to redshirt. In the world of Division I sports, redshirting means that a player will not be eligible for competition, but will continue to train with his teammates and take a full load of courses. This practice, common in college athletics, allows the student athlete to physically mature and remain in good academic standing, while preserving a year of eligibility. In most cases, it is the coaching staff that determines whether an athlete should redshirt. Sometimes, however, it is the player who makes the decision. Most athletes do not choose to redshirt because they view it as a setback of some sort—a determination that the player is not prepared for the challenges of college athletics. I did not view it this way. I looked at a redshirt year as a great opportunity to get bigger, stronger, and better, and to get ahead in the classroom. At the end of my freshman year I would have fifteen credits under my belt, I'd be a better basketball player from having worked with my teammates and coaches, and I'd still have four years of eligibility.

It all made perfect sense.

There was just one problem: the coaches weren't convinced that I should redshirt, as I was playing well in practices. Coach Wojcik even called my parents and told them how well I was doing. I knew that I was unlikely to get much playing time, so I remained committed to the idea of redshirting. Coach Wojcik eventually agreed, told me to keep working hard, and predicted that by the following year I would be a valuable and productive member of the team. Not that I wasn't a part of the team while redshirting; in fact, even though I played on the scout team during practices (the scout team mimics the plays and style of an upcoming opponent so the starters can adequately prepare), I was having a lot of fun. Being part of the scout team is an important, if somewhat thankless, role, but I embraced it fully, as I loved helping my teammates and knew that someday I would get my chance.

I treated every practice as though it was a game. I held nothing back, not even when playing against my best friends, like Jordan or Donte. If either of them drove into the lane, I would do my best to make sure they regretted it. I became known for my rebounding and shot-blocking prowess, just as I had been in the Congo and at Mesa High. Every day, I was among the most exuberant players in the gym—cheering on my teammates, talking a little good-natured trash, trying to win every sprint at the end of practice. Even if I wasn't suiting up on game nights, I was still a part of the team, and I wanted everyone to know it.

In fact, I was playing so well that the coaching staff started talking about pulling my redshirt and declaring me eligible for the remainder of the season. I protested and Coach Wojcik backed off, but only temporarily. When a couple of players got injured, and we started losing some games, Coach Wojcik had second thoughts. He called Terry and Laurie again (Coach Wojcik was always very good about maintaining communication with my parents, just as he promised) and explained that the team could no longer afford the luxury of having me redshirt.

"Blondy is playing so well in practice," he explained. "We need him on the floor."

I had already missed part of the season and was therefore reluctant to give up my redshirt, but I understood Coach Wojcik's position. And, of course, I wanted to play. If the team needed me, and the coaches thought I was ready to contribute, then I had no business withholding my services. That would have been selfish and weak.

"Okay, Coach," I said. "I am ready."

I made my collegiate debut on December 8, 2010, against a strong Oklahoma State team. Midway through the second half, as we fell more than twenty points behind, Coach Wojcik called my name.

"Let's go, Blondy."

I jumped from the bench and peeled off my warmups so quickly that I almost tripped and fell. Even though we were getting killed, Coach Wojcik smiled.

"Give us some energy out there," he said.

I nodded and walked toward the scorer's table; I was nervous and excited. As I entered the game I thought about what Terry had said to me before I left.

Always remember where you come from.

It was oddly comforting, the notion that nothing compared to the challenges of my past; this was just a basketball game. It was not a matter of life and death. It was supposed to be fun.

Less than a minute after I entered the game I scored my first basket—on a thunderous dunk, no less! It had no bearing on the outcome of the game, but it felt tremendous nonetheless. I played seven minutes in that game, scored three points, and had one blocked shot and one rebound. Not a bad debut for someone who was supposed to redshirt. But any happiness I might have felt was tempered by the fact that we were badly beaten, and destroyed entirely by the sight of my good friend Donte going down with another knee injury just a couple minutes after I entered the game.

This was a crushing thing to see, and it happened just a few feet away from me. I had thought often about how much fun it would be to play basketball with Donte again, for the first time since we were high school teammates. Like me, this was his first appearance of the season in a Tulsa basketball game. When he grabbed his knee and fell to the floor, I could not believe my eyes. Sometimes you can tell right away when an injury is serious; this was one of those times. Donte was in an extraordinary amount of pain; he also seemed keenly aware of exactly what had happened, as he pounded the floor and cried, "No, no, no!"

Within a day or two the diagnosis was confirmed: Donte had re-injured his reconstructed ACL. There would be more surgery, more rehabilitation, and many more missed games. I felt terrible for him; he had been through so much already, and he had fought so hard to overcome such a devastating injury. It seemed terribly unfair that he should have to go through it all over again. But I urged him to be strong, and I tried to be supportive, just as he had done for me when I first arrived at Mesa.

"You will be back," I said. "Have faith."

★

THE REST OF MY freshman season was a roller coaster. Some games I would play quite a bit; sometimes I would not play at all, or only play a couple of minutes. This type of scenario is among the most challenging for any athlete: there is insecurity in the unknown. If you are the last player on the bench, and you know there is no chance of getting into the game, you accept it and adapt. You might not like it, but you learn to live with it. Similarly, if you are a starter or one of the top reserves, you know that you will play a significant portion of the game, and this allows you to perform with a degree of comfort and confidence. But if you have no idea how much you are going to play—or if indeed you will play at all— every game is filled with tension and anxiety.

What if I make a mistake? What if I turn the ball over or take a bad shot? Will he pull me out of the game?

The truth is, uncertainty is a part of the athletic experience. Division I basketball is a business; careers are made and broken based on the performance of teenagers. It is a challenge, to be sure, and every player must learn to adapt to the whims of a coach who hears the wolf at his door on a nightly basis. If you find yourself sitting when you think you should be playing, you cannot take it personally. You just have to work harder and maintain a positive attitude. I will acknowledge that in the latter regard, I stumbled a bit as my playing time fluctuated. I became frustrated and angry with the coaching staff because I felt that I should have redshirted if I wasn't going to get a lot of playing time. But there are no guarantees for anyone; our roster had been depleted by injuries and the coaches needed me in uniform. Beyond that, there were no promises; nor should there have been. I had to earn every minute. From both an emotional and physical standpoint, it was endlessly challenging.

It was also a valuable experience in terms of understanding that life is a never-ending struggle—a series of tests and obstacles that must be met and overcome. The moment you start taking things for granted is the moment you get knocked off your feet.

In mid-January, we played at Arizona State University, a game scheduled by Coach Wojcik as a homecoming for Donte and me. Arizona State is located in Tempe, which is only about ten miles from Mesa, so my whole family and many of my high school friends came to the game. Donte sat on the bench in street clothes, which was incredibly hard for him, while I got a chance to show off for my buddies back home. Unfortunately, it was one of the worst games I played all year. Coach Wojcik put me in relatively early, and I responded with a tepid defensive performance. I don't know whether I was nervous or disoriented; regardless, I got dunked on twice in the first minute after I entered the game. Shortly thereafter, I was pulled from the lineup and took a seat at the end of the bench, where I remained most of the night. We lost the game and I played poorly, which was disappointing, but at least I got to see my friends and family.

My freshman season was a valuable learning experience, one that forced me to gain both emotional and physical strength as I learned to juggle the demands of school and sports, while trying to maintain a positive outlook during a season that was often frustrating. I played in thirteen games and averaged less than seven minutes per game. It's hard to show what you can do in such a small window of time, but I did my best. The coaching staff told me after the season that I had exceeded their expectations and they had big plans for me the next year. I was excited and eager to validate their confidence.

CHAPTER **20**

What is a happy ending? Is it the expected completion of a journey, exactly as it has been mapped out? Or is it something else entirely? I do not have the answer for this, but I do know that life is full of surprises, and that one must never accept defeat.

I arrived at the University of Tulsa in the fall of 2010 filled with hope and ambition. I dared to dream about a career in professional basketball. So what happened? I discovered that despite my physical talents, I was quite a raw basketball player and had a great deal of catching up to do if I was going to be an effective college athlete. But I wasn't discouraged. Instead, I vowed to work hard in the off-season and do better the next year. Unfortunately, there was no "next year."

Just three days after the season ended I walked into the gym to play some pickup ball. A lot of guys take time off after the season to give themselves a chance to recuperate, both mentally and physically. This is understandable—the season is long and hard, and by March you are sore and exhausted; you need a break.

But I didn't want to take any time off. I wanted to use every possible moment to get ready for the next season. So I went to the weight room the day after the season ended; I ran sprints on my own. I worked on my conditioning and my shooting form. And on the third day I jumped into a pickup game with players of disparate size and skill.

Some of them were my teammates, but some were just regular students looking for a good run. You might think that it would be hard to get excited about playing pickup ball in an empty gym, with no clock or scoreboard or referees, after you've spent the entire winter playing in front of thousands of screaming fans.

But you would be wrong.

If you truly love the game of basketball (as I do), then it really doesn't matter when or where you play. Sure, there is something special about playing in front of a packed house, but most of us first learn the game in solitude, just shooting and dribbling in the quiet of an empty court. It was that way for me, dating back to my introduction to basketball, when I was a little kid shooting around at Foyer Social, aching for a chance to get into a game. I embraced any opportunity to play, to compete, and to improve. So, as I peeled off my shirt that day for a simple game of full-court five-on-five, my heart beat a little faster. There were no coaches or spectators, but I was pumped about playing!

About five minutes into the game I took a pass from a teammate and made a sharp move to the basket, beating my defender by a step. Without hesitation I rose to the hoop and threw down a two-fisted dunk. It felt great—so smooth and powerful. But as I descended, I could sense something beneath me, a presence moving suddenly into my landing space. I tried to adjust at the last second, but it was too late. My right foot came down on top of a defender's foot. My ankle rolled sharply to the outside, sending a wave of intense pain through my body.

This is the unpredictability and randomness of life: never before had I suffered any sort of serious athletic injury. For goodness' sake—I had grown up playing in sandals or even bare feet! I survived a year and a half in the jungle without being injured. But there I was, rolling around on the gym floor, clutching my broken ankle, writhing in pain and cursing at the top of my lungs.

"FUCK! NO! NO! NO!"

All because I had inadvertently stepped on another player's foot while coming down after a dunk in a pickup game. It was the most common of basketball injuries . . . and among the most potentially devastating.

Even with surgery that summer and the insertion of a variety of hardware designed to strengthen my ankle, the injury never healed properly. For months, I endured rehabilitation and therapy, but by the time the next season began I was out of shape and, once again, woefully far behind my teammates. So, I took a redshirt year, which allowed me to continue rehab while enrolled in classes (so that I wouldn't fall behind academically), but without exhausting a year of athletic eligibility. In the end, it did not matter.

There is a difference between being merely "healthy" and being fit enough to play basketball at the highest level of intercollegiate competition. Pain was a constant partner as I tried to return to the program, and it dramatically impeded my progress.

By the end of the 2011–12 season, I began to have serious doubts about whether I would ever again play at Tulsa. This was mainly but not exclusively because of my physical issues. We had a mediocre season, with a 17–14 overall record and a 10–6 record in Conference USA. Had Coach Wojcik been in the first or second year of his contract, this might have been deemed an acceptable part of the rebuilding process. But he was in his seventh year and we were expected to challenge for the conference title and make the NCAA tournament. Neither of those things happened, and shortly after the season ended, following a four-overtime loss to Marshall in the quarterfinals of the conference tournament, Coach Wojcik was fired. He left the school with a career record of 140–92, which is quite respectable. In fact, Doug Wojcik remains the school's leader in career victories. This just further illustrates how competitive and cutthroat a business Division I college basketball can be. You can win more than 60 percent of your games—more than any other coach in the program's history—and still lose your job.

I knew the reality of the situation and wasn't shocked to hear of Coach Wojcik's dismissal. But I did find it disappointing. Despite my frustration over playing time as a freshman, and my injury as a sophomore, I liked Coach Wojcik and thought he would give me a fair shot if I could recover. He had been honest and thoughtful with me from the first time we met, and I appreciated the way he kept in touch with my parents through good times and bad. I was sad to see him go, and of course apprehensive about what his departure might mean for my career.

There was a lot of anxiety surrounding the basketball program at this time. Donte Medder had quit the team after just six games, unhappy with his lack of playing time following recovery from the second ACL tear. I thought Donte behaved rashly, and I told him as much when he announced that he was leaving school and transferring to another program.

"You are making a mistake," I said. "Give it time."

But Donte was impatient and frustrated, and by Christmas of that season he was gone. I had lost not only a teammate, but one of my best friends. Donte wound up at Cal State San Bernardino, where he eventually ruptured his ACL a third time, which not only ended his career, but also led to him withdrawing from school. He never did complete his degree.

Donte wasn't the only friend I lost that year. Jordan Clarkson, my roommate and the team's leading scorer, decided to transfer to the University of Missouri after Coach Wojcik's firing. With so many people leaving (we also lost three seniors to graduation, and another starter, Eric McClellan, transferred to Vanderbilt), I couldn't help but wonder whether I belonged at Tulsa. There was so much uncertainty surrounding the program.

The hiring of Danny Manning to replace Coach Wojcik less than a month after the season ended got my attention. Manning was the all-time leading scorer at the University of Kansas, and the No. 1 pick in the 1988 NBA Draft. To say the least, he had pedigree. And patience. After a long playing career, he had joined the basketball staff at his alma mater in 2003, and had spent eight years learning the job—first as team manager and director of student-athlete development, and then as an assistant coach. Now, finally, he was ready to become a head coach.

While Coach Manning had never run a program before, it was impossible not to be impressed by his résumé. And after meeting him for the first time, I couldn't help but like him, as well; he was personable and friendly. Still, he hadn't recruited me, worked with me, or even seen me play one second of basketball. He wasn't *my* coach, and I think a lot of the guys on the team felt that way. This is a pretty common response to the upheaval that comes with a change in coaching staff. Rather than making this decision in a vacuum, I called Terry and Laurie and told them I was feeling discouraged about everything that was happening at Tulsa—my injury, so many friends leaving, Coach Wojcik getting fired—and that I was thinking about transferring. They did not pressure me, but they did help me consider more clearly the benefits of staying: I was nearly halfway to a degree at Tulsa. I was comfortable. True, basketball had been a disappointment, but there was no guarantee that I would get more playing time elsewhere, especially considering my uncertain physical condition. My parents encouraged me to see the big picture, to remember why I was in college in the first place. It was fine to have a dream of playing in the NBA, but the important thing was to get a degree. Maybe everything would turn out well at Tulsa. Maybe Danny Manning would be a tremendous coach who saw value in my skill set. Maybe, with a few more months of therapy and treatment, my ankle would finally heal.

Maybe.

I decided to stay. To become part of the solution, rather than part of the problem.

Unfortunately, my ankle did not cooperate. Throughout the spring I experienced periods where I felt a return to full health was possible.

Then there would be a setback of some sort—a workout followed by swelling and pain and three or four days in which I could barely walk. Sometimes I would have to use crutches. And it wasn't like I twisted the ankle or took a bad step. I'd be playing and feeling okay, and then I'd wake up in the middle of the night with my ankle on fire. It was baffling and immensely frustrating.

There were more appointments with doctors and surgeons, more X-rays and MRIs. None of the scans offered conclusive evidence, and certainly no answers. Over the summer, our team made a trip to Canada for a series of exhibition games. I hardly played at all, and when I did play, I was ineffective, hobbled by a lack of fitness and persistent pain in the ankle. It was a vicious cycle: the ankle felt better only when I rested, and yet the constant rest resulted in diminished conditioning. Simply put, I was out of shape, at least by the standards of Division I basketball.

After that trip, I met with the doctor who had performed the surgery on my ankle. He was not encouraging.

"It's been more than a year since the surgery," he said. "You should be better by now. If you're still having this much pain, then it's possible you're not going to have a full recovery."

I suggested another operation, but the doctor was reluctant. The ligaments had been badly stretched and weakened.

"At this point, I wouldn't recommend surgery," he said.

"What would you recommend?"

He paused and glanced at the floor.

"I would recommend that you consider not playing competitive basketball anymore. You're risking long-term damage."

These words should not have come as a shock—after all, I had been sidelined for nearly eighteen months—but for some reason they took my breath away. I had assumed that eventually I would be healthy, that my body, which had withstood so much discomfort and abuse over the years, would win this battle as well. The evidence strongly indicated otherwise, and to hear such a grim prognosis from the man who knew my injury best was sobering, to say the least.

"But . . ." I began, and yet the words would not come out. My chest began to hurt.

I thought about how hard I had worked to get to this point—the beating I took back home at Foyer Social and on my club team, Molokai; the endless miles I had walked to get to basketball practices in which I nearly fainted in the 110-degree heat. How could it end like this? I had barely even played college basketball—and now my dream of playing in the NBA was over? Just like that? It felt like a cruel joke.

"No, no, no," I cried. "I'm going to recover and get back out there. I have a goal that I have to reach, and nothing will stop me!"

"I'm sorry, Blondy," the doctor said, shaking his head pitiably. "I wish I had better news, but I honestly think it's time for you to move on."

★

SHORTLY AFTER THE FALL semester began, I met with Coach Manning. He seemed legitimately sensitive to my plight, perhaps because he knew what it was like to experience a devastating injury. Coach Manning was one of the greatest college players of his generation. He led Kansas to a national title in 1988 and received both the Naismith and Wooden Awards as the the national player of the year. But he ruptured his ACL as a rookie with the Los Angeles Clippers, and while he spent many years playing in the NBA, injuries prevented him from ever achieving the kind of success most people had predicted. Like me, he spent a lot of time in doctors' offices and training rooms, struggling to recapture the strength and fitness that had been robbed from him. Along the way he learned that the end of a playing career did not signify the end of life; it simply meant that it was time to chart a new course. In Manning's case, that course was coaching. I had no backup plan. I was going to be a professional basketball player, either in the NBA or overseas. Of that I was one hundred percent certain.

"I know this is hard," Coach Manning said. "And I don't mean to pressure you. I'm just trying to get an idea of how you feel, and what you're thinking."

"I don't know what to do, Coach. I've tried everything. My ankle just isn't getting better, and the doctors say it's not going to get better."

Coach Manning nodded. He had already consulted with the medical and training staff.

"There is no shame in any of this," he said. "It can happen to anyone. And even if you can't play, that doesn't mean you can't still be a part of the program."

Coach Manning offered me two options: first, the opportunity to be a manager, which might sound demeaning, but is actually a fairly common training ground for aspiring coaches; second, I could take a medical retirement, which would relieve me of all basketball responsibilities, but I would get to keep my scholarship.

"Can I have a few days to think about it?" I asked.

Coach Manning smiled. "Sure, Blondy. Take your time."

Both of these scenarios were fair to me and beneficial to the team, as in either case I would continue to get a free education, and my scholarship would no longer count against the NCAA limit of thirteen scholarships per team. My spot would be taken by a healthy body. If I stayed on the team, in a state of perpetual recovery, then my scholarship would remain on the books and my presence would be a liability. This was the reality of the situation.

Before making a decision, I turned again to Terry and Laurie, for I knew I could count on them to offer advice based on nothing more than love.

"What do you want to do?" Laurie asked.

"I want to play basketball, but if I can't play, then I don't think I can be around the program," I explained. "It's just too painful."

Terry and Laurie understood this completely, and so did Coach Manning. When I told him that I was going to take a medical retirement, he shook my hand and wished me well. There would be other opportunities, he said. Other ways to channel my energy.

The doctor's words too kept echoing in my head: *It's time for you to move on.*

But where to? And how would I get there?

CHAPTER 21

The answer came through prayer.

For weeks after my medical retirement became official, I was despondent. I could not even walk past the gym without feeling as though I was going to break down in tears. I missed playing the sport I loved, the game that had sustained me for so many years and through so many hard times. But I did not regret the decision, for I knew with each stinging step that my body had nothing left to give. While I grieved for the loss of my basketball career, I knew I had made the right decision. I just needed another outlet for my creativity and passion.

"Please, God," I said each night. "Help me find the way."

And just like that, like a bolt out of the blue, it came to me.

Acting!

Before basketball, there had been soccer. Before soccer there had been theater. I had been involved in a very good program while in middle school, and I had shown promise as a young actor. And I had loved it. What if I were to rekindle that interest? What if I were to allow myself to be bitten by the acting bug all over again? It isn't so different from sports, after all. Athletes and actors are both performers, plying their trade in front of an audience. And both are part of a team, reliant not just on their own skill, but on the camaraderie and support of those who share the stage or court with them.

It seemed not just plausible, but logical.

I leaped immediately into the deep end of the pool, starting with a meeting with the director of the theater program at Tulsa. It is not unusual for college students to dabble in drama, taking either an elective class or even helping out backstage with a production. My plans were somewhat more . . . *ambitious.*

"I'd like to major in theater," I explained.

He looked at me like I was crazy.

"I thought you were a business major."

"Yes, that's right. I want a double major."

Practically speaking, this was almost impossible. I had just started my junior year and had not taken any theater courses. I would have to rework my schedule, and take extra classes in theater, while also maintaining a rigorous load of business courses. When I told my friends what I was doing, they could only laugh.

"Dude, you must be nuts," one of my former teammates said. "You're going to be even busier than when you were playing basketball."

Tulsa is a demanding school academically. Majoring in one discipline is hard enough, but adding a second major? To my teammates, this seemed crazy, but in my eyes it was simply another challenge, and one that was far from insurmountable. I figured if I could survive civil war and the hardship of the Congo, I could handle a heavy academic load. It also felt logical to me: a business degree was practical in the outside world; a theater degree was more about pursuing something I loved. With basketball gone, I needed something that provoked passion.

Sure, I'd be busy, but that was the point, wasn't it? To fill each day with work and fun and ambition, to strive for something glorious and seemingly unachievable. In the same way that playing professional basketball is out of reach for all but the fortunate few, so, too, is the world of professional acting. That was my goal, you see—not merely getting a degree in theater, and learning the craft of acting, but using that degree as a calling card.

While once I dreamed of being in the NBA, now I dreamed of being a movie star, and I was determined to do everything possible to make that dream come true. It was a massive commitment, but one that helped ease the pain of losing basketball. While there were times I missed playing, and I certainly envied my teammates on game nights (sometimes I attended as a spectator), most of the time I was too busy and tired and immersed in the fantastic world of drama to give it much thought. Overnight, it seemed, my life had been transformed.

There were many wonderful teachers in the Theater Department at Tulsa, in particular Professor Steven Marzolf, who was himself an experienced stage and film actor. In both the classroom and onstage, Professor Marzolf pushed me and challenged me; like any great mentor, he gave generously of himself but also held me to a high standard.

"You can make a living at this, Blondy," he told me. "But you have to work harder."

Professor Marzolf had performed with the prestigious Steppenwolf Theatre in Chicago; he had appeared in a couple of movies. He was at once practical and ambitious. Like any great teacher (or coach), he constantly raised the bar of expectations, imploring his students to never settle for mediocrity. He told me that I had talent and charisma; he also told me that if I didn't reduce my accent, the challenge of finding roles in Hollywood might be insurmountable. This was a harsh reality of the business, and there was no point in pretending otherwise.

Like anyone else in the Tulsa Theatre Department, I had to pay my dues before earning a role in a legitimate production. In fact, it wasn't until June of 2013, shortly after the end of my junior year, that I made my debut, in an ambitious production of Shakespeare's *Much Ado About Nothing*. Part of Tulsa Shakespeare in the Park, the free production ran for more than a week and drew big crowds every night. Updated to the 1940s and set in Tulsa, our version of *Much Ado About Nothing* retained the play's trademark humor and language, but updated for a modern and local audience. I had a modest but not insignificant part as a guard, and each night when I first appeared onstage, the crowd would gasp and applaud; I guess I did not look like the typical Shakespearean actor! I had quite a few scenes and lines, and felt I performed well. My castmates said so, anyway. A few people told me afterward that they were surprised by my performance. Performing Shakespeare is almost like performing in a different language; since English was already my third language, I guess you could say Shakespeare was my fourth. In a strange way, maybe that made things easier.

Regardless, on closing night, as we all stood together onstage and took our final bows, I felt both sadness and excitement. I did not want the magic to end; indeed, I would have happily performed *Much Ado About Nothing* every night for the rest of the year. It was an odd feeling, knowing that for many of my castmates, this was not only the end of their college theater careers, but the end of college, as well. I was fortunate. I had another year of school, and yet already I felt no ambivalence or confusion about the future. I knew exactly where I was going and what I wanted to do.

★

MY SENIOR YEAR WAS exhausting and rewarding and filled with more work and fun than I ever could have imagined. I took public speaking classes, spent endless hours in the library, and continued to work on the craft of acting. I also worked on a draft of my autobiography that eventually stretched out to more than three hundred pages (forming the backbone of the story you are reading now). I wrote out of a sense of obligation, not just for a creative outlet. You see, I felt like I had a story worth telling; a story that might one day inspire others, especially young kids living in poverty or trying to survive in a war-torn country. *There is hope*, I wanted to say.

I spent a lot of time in my car as well. Sometimes I would drive six hours in the snow to Missouri to watch my friend Jordan Clarkson play basketball; then we would hang out afterward and talk about our plans. Jordan still hoped to play in the NBA; I was going to be an actor. We believed in each other and supported each other.

Dream big, my brother.

But the person with whom I was closest at this time was Serge Ibaka. After playing for two years in Spain in the European professional leagues, he had been drafted by the Seattle SuperSonics. We had kept in touch throughout my time in America, and when the SuperSonics relocated to Oklahoma City in 2010, the same year that I enrolled at the University of Tulsa, it was a wonderful and unexpected twist of fate. Here we were, old basketball buddies from the Congo, now both living in Oklahoma, and separated by only a hundred miles of interstate.

We spent a lot of time together, especially once I got my first car, a beat-up Suzuki unfit for someone my size, but surprisingly resilient given its age and odometer reading. Serge was a warm and generous man; his door was always open to friends and family, the ranks of which seemed to swell with each passing year in Oklahoma City. Serge liked having me around, and I will admit to enjoying the perks that came with being a good friend of an NBA star. I could get passes to any Oklahoma City Thunder game, with great seats and VIP access. I hung out with Serge and his teammates after games, went out to some of the best clubs in town, and ate at the finest restaurants. Beautiful women would routinely find their way to our table, and always Serge would introduce me in this way:

"I'd like you to meet Blondy. He is my brother."

This was not meant to deceive. It was simply the way we felt about each other. And before long I came to be known around town as Serge's brother. It was a fun and intoxicating lifestyle.

For a while.

As Serge's posse expanded, I began to feel uneasy about my place in this universe. At one point, I couldn't even keep track of the number of people who seemed to rely on him for financial support. There were aunts and uncles, brothers and sisters, friends I did not even recognize, all living in his sprawling home, or in nearby homes or apartments. There was pressure from his management team to cut expenses, to stop the never-ending flow of cash. I was not part of this circle, for I was still a college student on scholarship, living in a different city. Serge certainly did nothing to make me feel unwelcome. We were friends . . . *brothers.* I was, however, wary of falling into the trap of exploitation and laziness. I would look around at all the people who depended on Serge, some of whom appeared to be taking advantage of his generosity, and I would think to myself, *I do not want to be like that. I want to be independent and find my own way in the world.*

Midway through my senior year I told Serge of my plans.

"Bro, after I graduate, I am going to L.A."

He smiled quizzically. "L.A.? What's in L.A.?"

"I'm going to be an actor," I said. Serge knew of my love for theater, and I had told him of my plans to pursue a career in the film industry. But I don't think he believed me or took me seriously.

Serge shook his head. Then he threw an arm around my shoulder.

"Look, Blondy. Everyone in L.A. is an actor. You know that, right?"

I shrugged, smiled. "Yeah, but most people aren't very good at it."

Serge laughed. "I don't know, my brother. You're going to have a college degree, you're a smart guy. Why do you want to be an actor?"

"Because I love it. I want to entertain people. It's like when I was playing basketball. When I'm up there on the stage—I'm alive!"

Serge nodded sympathetically. "Okay, I get it. But why not take your time? Stay here with me in Oklahoma for a while. I'll help you find a job, make some money. Do that for a year or two and then go to L.A. Be smart about it."

I understood what Serge was doing; he had my best interests at heart. To him (and to many other people who knew me), packing up and moving to Hollywood, without a job or connections, seemed like the craziest thing in the world. His advice was sound. I would have a business degree as well as a degree in theater. I had friends in both Tulsa and Oklahoma City who could help me get started on a potentially lucrative career in finance. But the very thought of that life made me queasy.

"That's just not me," I told Serge. "I can't get up every morning, put on a suit and tie, and sit behind a desk all day. I would be so depressed."

"A lot of people would be grateful for that life," Serge pointed out. Again, I could not argue with him. With all that I had been through, prudence and security should have been appealing. But it wasn't. "I know it sounds crazy, bro," I said. "But this is what I was meant to do."

CHAPTER 22

I moved to Los Angeles just a few days after graduating from the University of Tulsa in May of 2014. A friend from Oklahoma City agreed to make the drive with me, just to help the time pass. By now I had upgraded to a 2007 Cadillac CTS. A big, gas-guzzling boat of a car, with some heavy mileage on the engine, but sturdy and reliable enough to make the trip from Oklahoma to Los Angeles, and to provide transportation for months to come. But even the Caddy couldn't run on empty, and somehow during the marathon drive, while singing African songs with the windows down, I had neglected to keep a careful eye on the gas gauge. I was at the wheel and my buddy Devon was asleep when the car began to sputter. Next thing you know, there we were, pushing a 3,500-pound car down the highway, me on the driver's side, holding the steering wheel, my buddy Devon on the passenger side.

"How far to the gas station?" Devon asked roughly twenty minutes into the ordeal.

"No idea," I said. "It can't be that far."

It turned out to be approximately three miles from breakdown to refill, which really isn't all that far—unless you're pushing a Cadillac the whole way. It took us almost two hours, by the end of which we were both exhausted. It wasn't until we began filling up the tank that we realized we had chosen the most ridiculous solution to our problem.

"Why didn't you just walk here and get some gas, then walk back and fill up the car?" the station attendant asked. "Would have been a lot easier."

I looked at Devon. We both sighed.

Soon enough we were in Los Angeles. I had saved roughly a few thousand dollars (and by "a few" I mean less than five) from my scholarship money, and originally thought this would sustain me long enough to get established in L.A. Obviously my budgeting skills were in dire need of refinement. Again, however, I was fortunate to have love and support. I did not ask the Blitzes for assistance. They had done too much for me already. As it turned out, though, another family stepped in to help.

A couple of years earlier, you see, I had a met a woman named Marissa Brownlee, whose close friend dated Serge Ibaka. We hung out a few times, just as friends, and when Serge broke up with Marissa's friend, we lost touch. Midway through my senior year at Tulsa, I got a text from Marissa. She had recently married and just wanted to catch up, to see how I was doing.

"You should come over for dinner," Marissa said. "I'll introduce you to my husband, Kyle. You guys would get along great."

One dinner became a friendship that deepened over the next few months. Marissa's husband worked in finance. They had a comfortable life rooted in faith and family, and they wanted to share some of their good fortune.

"We prayed about you," Marissa said one night after dinner. "And we want to help you with your dream of becoming an actor. We feel like God would want us to do that."

To my astonishment, they offered to set up a bank account from which I could draw living expenses while I looked for work both within and outside the industry. That they were willing to offer anything was a surprise; the amount—$3,000 per month, for the next six months—was breathtaking.

"I don't know what to say."

Marissa smiled. "You don't have to say anything. Just work hard and follow your dream."

So it was that I arrived in Los Angeles on May 16, 2014, armed with a confidence born of love and support, and a completely unexpected financial safety net. At the same time, I must admit that I was completely and utterly clueless.

The first mistake was moving into an apartment in Hollywood—specifically, near the intersection of Sunset and Vine. An iconic location, to be sure, and convenient if you work in the business or merely want to soak up the intoxicating Hollywood atmosphere. But also completely stupid when you have a limited budget and zero connections. The one-bedroom apartment rented for $2,100; and I spent most of my savings to buy a bed and other furniture. When I think of this now, I feel shame and embarrassment. What I should have done was find a cheaper place to live, along with a roommate to split expenses. But I figured $2,100 was a reasonable price for Hollywood. That would leave me $900 to buy food and gas; soon enough, I'd have a job anyway. Isn't that what everyone did when they came to Hollywood? Go to auditions during the day and wait on tables during the evening. I could do that. How hard could it be?

Like I said—clueless. Utterly clueless.

I had learned how to budget my time and work hard in college, but this was different. Living on your own, as an adult, requires another skill set, and I had not developed those skills. Moreover, I had never held a job. I was always too busy playing basketball and taking a full load of courses and working in theater productions to hold a part-time job. As a result, I made some rather egregious and humiliating mistakes. For example, I applied for a job at a hotel. Nothing special, just working the front desk. In filling out the application form, I came to a question about "salary requirements." I thought for a moment, and then pulled a number out of thin air.

"Thirty-five dollars per hour."

Yes, that seemed like reasonable compensation—for the manager of the hotel, perhaps. I did not realize that this was a minimum wage position, which at the time was nine dollars per hour (although I was unaware of that threshold, as well). I did not get the job or any other job. Repeatedly I would fill out applications with salary requirements that must have appeared to employers as some sort of joke or exercise in ridiculous grandiosity.

For the longest time, I couldn't even get an interview. Eventually I got a call from AFLAC, the insurance company. At first it sounded like a good job, with the potential to earn several thousand dollars per month. There was just one catch: income was derived entirely from commission sales. I took the job anyway. They gave me a packet of information, a short training session, and then sent me on my way to find new clients. I made a couple of cold calls, went to one meeting, and quickly realized I wasn't cut out for this line of work.

After two or three months, I figured out that my salary demands were out of touch with reality, so I stopped including that information on job applications. It didn't matter. No one would hire me. I would get up in the morning, put on a suit, and walk to Target . . . or Walmart . . . or Best Buy . . . or Bed Bath & Beyond. You name the big box retail outlet, I probably applied there. Never got a callback from any of them. My appearance probably didn't help. Too tall, too dark, too heavy an accent. And completely inexperienced. I applied for jobs as a busboy and waiter. Again, with no success whatsoever.

I wasn't even looking for acting jobs. I didn't have an agent or a manager or any friends in the business who could give me a boost. I had presumed that I would be able to get a part-time job quickly to pay the bills. I convinced myself that no one would hire me as an actor unless I could demonstrate stability in other aspects of my life—by getting a job, for example. When that didn't happen, I became depressed and unfocused and things began to spiral out of control. I wasn't eating much or going to the gym. I began to lose weight. I had trouble sleeping. I could feel anxiety and panic creeping around the edges of my life.

Near the end of Month Three, bad turned to worse, in the form of a phone call from my friend Marissa. Her family had experienced a financial challenge and they would have to abort their plans to provide me with assistance.

"How soon?" I asked.

"One more month."

What could I say? They had already extended to me kindness and generosity well beyond anything I expected or deserved. I thanked them for their help and said that I would be fine. *Plenty of leads on jobs, acting gigs around the corner. No need to worry about Blondy.* I was trying to convince them as much as myself.

Even though I had less than $500 left in my bank account, I decided to use almost $300 to buy a plane ticket to attend draft day with Jordan Clarkson in his hometown of San Antonio. Jordan was like family to me, and this was one of the biggest days of his life; I couldn't miss it for anything. Jordan and his family and I all celebrated together when he was drafted by the Washington Wizards midway through the second round. The Wizards, in turn, quickly sold his rights to the Los Angeles Lakers.

When we were freshman roommates, we talked all the time about playing in the NBA. I was considered a stronger prospect than Jordan coming out of high school, simply because I was so big, and so raw and inexperienced—there was the assumption that I would improve greatly in college. That, of course, did not happen. My career ended before it had barely begun; but my friend was in the league, which was the next best thing. And best of all, he would be coming to L.A. Finally, I would have a friend in town!

Jordan moved out west in July, and the Lakers put him up in a hotel. Many second-round draft picks do not even make an NBA roster, but the Lakers were confident that Jordan had been underestimated. Once he began summer workouts with the team, their confidence only grew.

Still, Jordan wasn't happy living in a hotel, so I invited him to stay at my place.

"I'm only going to be here another month or so," I told him. "I'm running out of money. But you can stay here as long as I have the place. Then once you get your own apartment, maybe I can crash for a couple months while I look for a job."

Jordan said no problem. We were like brothers, and brothers take care of each other. Before long he had moved into my apartment. I gave him the bedroom while I slept on the couch because I figured he needed the rest more than I did; after all, he was the professional athlete. Pretty soon I was out looking at houses with Jordan and his mom, since I was at least somewhat familiar with the area. They ended up renting a nice but not extravagant three-bedroom place in Lawndale, about fifteen minutes from the Lakers' practice facility. I was happy for Jordan and relieved that I would have a place to stay for a little while.

Or so I thought.

The strangest thing happened after Jordan moved out of my apartment and into his place. He became a ghost. He ignored my texts and did not return my calls. By this point I had already informed the leasing office in my apartment building that I would be moving out. I began to panic. I thought perhaps Jordan was merely busy and hadn't seen my messages; eventually he'd get back to me. But as the weeks went by, it became apparent that something was wrong. I couldn't imagine what I had done to offend him. We were such close friends, with so much shared history. I had let him crash at my place, and he had promised to reciprocate. I had made it quite clear that this would be only a temporary arrangement; just as I did not want to ride Serge Ibaka's coattails in Oklahoma, I had no desire to exploit my friendship with Jordan in Los Angeles. I knew that if he made it in the league (and I was confident that he would), the hangers-on would come out of the woodwork. I was not going to be part of that group. I simply wanted a place to stay for a month or two while I tried to line up a job.

"Jordan, please tell me what's up," I texted him. "I'm going to be homeless. Can I at least crash in your garage for a little while? Please . . ."

There was no response.

In desperation, I reached out to a former high school classmate named Connor who was now living in L.A.

I explained my situation to Connor, told him that I needed a place to stay for a while and to store my stuff.

"Come on over," Connor said.

In the next few days I moved into the apartment with Connor and his three roommates. I brought a bed, sofa, and TV, but they made room for all of it. The only catch was that Connor said he expected me to stay for six months, since they were going to get rid of some of their furniture to make room for mine. I agreed because I had no choice. I needed a place to stay.

A few weeks later I began getting interviews for some jobs, including one as a retail clerk at a Louis Vuitton store. I thought I was going to get the job, and told Connor I might be moving out, and that I'd have to take my stuff with me. It never occurred to me that my leaving might upset Connor; in fact, I thought it would make him happy, as the apartment was crowded and I was a nonpaying tenant. So his response caught me completely off guard.

"Who do you think you are?" Connor shouted. "You told me you would be here for six months, and now you're leaving? Fuck you!"

I was speechless. I had never seen this side of Connor before. He had always been so laid-back and friendly. But since moving in, I also had discovered that Connor smoked a lot of weed, and maybe this wreaked havoc with his emotions. For whatever reason, he flipped out on me.

"You ain't shit, Blondy. Why don't you go back to Oklahoma? No, why don't you go back to Africa?"

I couldn't believe what I was seeing or hearing. Connor's girlfriend was there at the time, and she did her best to get him to calm down, but he was completely out of control.

"Bro, why are you talking to me like this?" I asked. "We're friends."

"Fuck you! Get out of my house, you stupid . . ."

That's when he dropped the N-word.

Now, I am not a fighter. I mean, I am a fighter; I am a survivor. But I am not one to throw down at the slightest provocation, or even at a severe provocation. I believe in love and peace and brotherhood. I believe that good triumphs over evil, and that anger and hostility accomplish nothing. Still, as I stood there in front of Connor—my friend!—I could feel my blood beginning to boil. That word is so ugly, so repulsive, so filled with contempt and hatred.

I looked down at Connor. He was much smaller than me; he did not provoke fear. I felt my hands curling into fists, and the adrenaline coursing through my veins. This happened to me sometimes like with Patrick and my coach at Golding. Confronted by aggression, I would be transported back to my childhood, and the helplessness I felt. I had learned over the years how to swallow the fear, to beat back the obvious symptoms of post-traumatic stress disorder. I learned how to walk away from confrontations whenever walking away was an option.

And yet, there I was, ready to launch.

One punch and he's out cold, and this whole thing is over. And he deserves it.

I took a few deep breaths. Connor's girlfriend implored me to leave, before I did something stupid. I thought about what might happen, how the temporary satisfaction of hitting him would quickly be replaced by regret—not just regret over hurting my friend, but over consequences sure to follow. It was not my apartment, after all. I was a black man in-volved in an altercation with a white man, in the white man's apartment. And I was 6 feet, 8 inches tall. I wasn't even a citizen, for goodness' sake. I tried to imagine the police showing up, and how I would be treated. I would be viewed as the instigator, the troublemaker. I might lose my visa. One punch and I'd be arrested and deported.

Slowly, carefully, I let my hands drop and unclenched my fists. Then I began to cry.

"Okay . . . okay," I said, my voice barely above a whisper. "I am leaving."

As I turned to walk out, Connor went into one of the bedrooms, grabbed my clothes, and threw everything outside.

I was beaten. There is no other way to put it. With tears running down my face, I went into my bedroom and picked up my laptop computer. Then I went outside, scooped up my clothes and put them in my car. Everything else—my bed, couch, and television—I left behind.

I had less than $50 in my bank account, so it wasn't like I could go find a hotel room. Instead, I drove to a McDonald's in a commercial area not far from Jordan Clarkson's house. I hung out in the parking lot for a couple hours, crying and feeling sorry for myself. Eventually I went inside, ordered a chicken sandwich and a cup of water, and sat down at a table. I stayed there for quite some time, nibbling on my sandwich and using the free Wi-Fi to scour the Internet for jobs. When darkness fell, as people were beginning to wonder whether I'd ever leave, I went out to my car. I cradled my phone in my hand for several minutes before opening my list of contacts. I scrolled down to Jordan's name and began writing a message.

> Brother, I am homeless. I have no place to go. I am sleeping
> in my car tonight outside a McDonald's. It would be nice if
> you could remember where we came from, and what we went
> through together. I just need a roof over my head for a little
> while. I promise it won't be long. Please . . .

I took a deep breath and hit "send." Instantly, the word "delivered" appeared below the message. Not long afterward, so did the word "read." But there was no response. Not that night. Not the next day. Nor the day after that.

For the next two weeks, I slept in my car at night, moving from parking lot to parking lot around L.A., and killed time during the day by hanging out at fast food restaurants. I would order a chicken sandwich and fries, and make it last all afternoon, and sometimes into the evening. I was always hungry, always scared and depressed. I managed to land a job as a delivery person for a restaurant, but the job paid only a small salary.

"You'll do well with tips," the owner explained. "Just smile a lot. That's how you make the real money."

He was wrong. There was no real money. Most people either didn't tip at all, or such a meager amount that it seemed like a joke. Drivers were expected to pay for their own gas as well, which is why most of them owned compact cars or hybrids. Great gas mileage, more money in the pocket. I must have been the only delivery man in L.A. driving a Cadillac. After expenses, I hardly made anything at all.

Sometimes I would tap away on my laptop, working on the screenplay of my life story, but the very act of putting it in words just made me sad. I couldn't envision a happy ending.

Around this time I got a call from Laurie Blitz. She and Terry had been checking in on me periodically, but I did not want to burden them with my problems. They had done enough for me, so I kept telling them everything was fine. I was going out on auditions, working a part-time job. All good.

"Do you need any money?" Laurie asked.

I swallowed hard. I could feel the tears coming again.

"Maybe a little," I said. "It's very expensive out here."

"Are you okay, Blondy?"

"Yes, Mom. I will be all right."

They wired me $300, which helped enormously for a couple more weeks. Then another friend from Oklahoma helped arrange for a place where I could stay for a few days. Her sister was married to a Los Angeles plastic surgeon, and she had told me before I left Oklahoma to look them up if I ever got in trouble. Well, much as I hated to admit it, I was in trouble. I needed help and reached out to them, and they offered to put me up for a while, which was a godsend. But it's strange how the worst things can arise from even the most considerate of deeds.

One night as I was leaving their place for the last time, I stopped to get gas at a Chevron station near the UCLA campus. As I stood by the car, wearing a hoodie, I noticed a police cruiser parked across the street, not more than fifty feet away. Behind the wheel, staring at me, was a white officer for the campus police department. I tried to ignore him and go about my business, but something about the way he was looking at me felt wrong. I finished pumping the gas, got back in my car, and pulled slowly out onto the street. As soon I pulled away, the police cruiser pulled out behind me. I drove very slowly and cautiously, no more than fifteen to twenty miles an hour. The officer shadowed me for maybe half a mile before hitting his lights. Suddenly, my heart began pounding.

Oh, this is not good. Why is he pulling me over?

I pulled slowly to the edge of the street and put the car in park. I had seen enough of the racial unrest in America, and was familiar enough with the escalating tensions between black Americans and white police officers to know that I was in a potentially life-threatening situation. I kept my hands on the steering wheel and my eyes facing straight ahead. I did not want to do anything that would give the officer the mistaken impression that I was some sort of threat. But as I looked in the rearview mirror, I could see him approaching from behind. His gun was already drawn.

"Out of the car!" the officer shouted.

Frozen with fear, I did not move a muscle. I envisioned the officer's reaction as a 6-foot-8 black man emerged from a Cadillac in the dark of night. *Was it even safe to get to get out of the car?*

"I said get out of the car! Now!"

Still, I did not move, did not say a word. As the officer kept his distance, another police cruiser arrived on the scene, lights flashing. And then a third. Suddenly the entire block was afire with strobelike red and white lights. Predictably, the spectacle attracted attention, and pretty soon a crowd of onlookers had gathered at the scene. The presence of so many potential witnesses gave me a small sense of security. I slowly opened the door and got out of the car. As I stood to full height, I could see the officers stiffen with apprehension. With guns drawn, they remained several feet away. I noticed that the crowd was comprised mostly of young people, probably UCLA students since we were basically on the campus. Many of them had taken out their cell phones and were now recording the incident. I wanted to believe that this was an insurance policy, but I also knew that more than one black person had been killed by police officers in the preceding months, and each time the incident had been captured on video by onlookers. There were no guarantees.

"Officer, may I ask what I did wrong?" I said through a voice rattling with fear.

The first officer stepped forward. "Shut the fuck up and get on your knees!"

"Why?" I began. "What did I do?"

"On the ground!" the officer shouted. "Right now!"

I fell to my knees, with my hands above my head. Instantly the officer was on me, driving my face into the asphalt. I felt a foot pressing against my back as they handcuffed me and told me to keep my mouth shut. Out of the corner of my eye, I could see the barrel of a gun just a few inches away. I began to pray.

"Please God . . . forgive all my sins . . ."

As this was happening, I could hear some of the students yelling.

"Leave him alone!"

"He didn't do anything!"

I worried that the crowd was adding fuel to the fire. The situation was unstable enough without the officers worrying about a riot.

"I need your license," one of the officers finally said.

I told him it was in my wallet, in my back pocket, and that I could not retrieve it while handcuffed. He removed it, took out the license, and walked back to his car while another officer helped me sit up on the curb. I was scared and shaken.

After a few minutes, the officer returned.

"Sir, did you know you're driving with a suspended license?"

"What? No, sir. I mean . . . why?"

"You have an outstanding violation."

And then it hit me. When I had first moved to L.A., I had gotten a ticket for running a red light near the intersection of Hollywood and Vine. The officer had told me that I was to appear in court at a particular time, and that I would have to pay a rather steep fine. I did not appear in court. I did not pay the fine because I did not have much money and I did not understand the seriousness of the infraction. I realize this was a rather huge and inexcusable mistake on my part, and I have no way to rationalize it except to say that I was scared and lacked financial resources. And once the date passed, and I heard nothing, I simply put it out of my mind.

Now, months later, the penalty was much greater. The police had no reason to pull me over, aside from the fact that I was a physically imposing black male wearing a hooded sweatshirt while driving in an affluent, mostly white community. That they lacked probable cause was irrelevant now. I was, in fact, driving with a suspended license, and nothing else mattered.

As the officer removed my handcuffs, I felt a sense of relief. At least I wasn't getting arrested. Then he asked me a question.

"Do you have someone to drive your car for you?"

"No, sir. It's just me. I am alone."

The officer shrugged. "Well, then, we're going to have the car impounded."

I was shocked. I was so ignorant of American laws that I did not realize the cascading series of events that would arise from my failure to pay a traffic ticket. By not appearing in court and paying a fine, I had lost my license. And since my license was suspended, I could not legally drive a car. As a result, I was about to lose my car. As the reality of the situation sank in, I began pleading with the officer.

"Sir, you don't understand," I said, trying to stifle my sobs. "That car is my home. I live in that car."

The officer seemed unmoved, so I pressed on.

"Look inside," I pleaded. "My whole life is in that car. All my clothes, my computer. Everything."

The officer walked to the car, peered inside, and then looked at me.

"Do you have anyone to drive the car or not?"

"No, officer," I repeated. "I am alone."

The officer opened the door and began tossing my belongings out into the street.

"Sir," I pleaded. "Please don't do that."

He told me to shut up and continued to clear out the vehicle. Eventually, everything I owned was on the ground. A few minutes later a tow truck arrived and my car was hauled away.

Desperate, I called a friend of mine named Damien White. Damien and I had met when I first moved to L.A.; he had installed cable service in my apartment. It was a huge imposition for me to ask him for help, but he was generous to offer me a ride and a place to crash. I stayed with Damien for a few days, but I realized pretty quickly that couch surfing was no way to live, especially when I had no car, no job, and no plan for a better future. I decided to reach out to the Blitzes and tell them the truth. It was time to admit defeat.

"I'm sorry," I said. "I haven't been honest with you."

I proceeded to tell Terry all about my Hollywood adventure, and just how horribly wrong everything had gone, almost from the moment I arrived. I told him I had been unable to find a job, that I was completely broke, and that I had been living in my car for the better part of a month, until my car was towed. And I told him that I now needed money to get my car back. Terry listened patiently and quietly, just as he always did when I came to him for help. When he finally spoke, it was mostly to express sadness and concern.

"I just wish you had told us sooner," he said.

"I know. I let you down."

"No, you didn't," he said. "You gave it your best shot, and we're proud of you." There was a long pause. "Blondy, sometimes in life you have to take one step backward before you can take two steps forward."

"What do you mean?"

"I mean, maybe L.A. isn't the best place for you right now. You're welcome to come home. You know that. There's no shame in it. We're always here for you."

CHAPTER **23**

As usual, Terry was right. It was impractical for me to continue
living in L.A., one of the most expensive cities in the world,
when I had no income and no prospects for furthering my acting career. While the dream was not completely out of reach, I realized I had
to pursue it in a different way.

I appreciated the Blitzes' generosity, but I simply couldn't imagine
moving back into my old bedroom in Mesa. Terry and Laurie understood this so they did not pressure me to return to Arizona. Rather,
they paid to get my car out of impoundment (I left it with a friend in
LA; the tickets would take some time to clear up), and offered to pay
my airfare to Oklahoma City, which had come to feel like home, and
where I still had quite a few friends. So in mid-December, I returned
to Oklahoma—just seven months after I left for my big Hollywood adventure. It would not be inaccurate to say that I came home with my tail
between my legs. After all, I had told everyone about my plans to make
it as an actor in Hollywood. Now I was home, penniless and jobless.

And quite embarrassed.

The Egan family, whom I had gotten to know before leaving, welcomed me home with open arms and even offered me space in a spare
bedroom, which I gratefully accepted. I spent my days working on my

résumé and looking for work, while also continuing to write my life story. At night, I prayed.

"Please, God, help me find a way back to Los Angeles. I do not want to be a failure. Tell me what do, and I will do it."

If this sounds like a self-serving attitude toward prayer, well, it wasn't; it was merely a cry of desperation. Even though I had many friends in Oklahoma City, I rarely left the house. It would have been easy to call Serge and tell him I was back in town and immediately become part of his posse. But I did not want to do that, for I knew that the comfort and security it provided would have sucked the ambition from my heart. I had to find my own place in the world.

Eventually, Marissa Brownlee and her husband found me a job working the front desk at a hotel in Oklahoma City. I wanted to learn how to do the job well, so that when I moved back to L.A., I would have some practical work experience and the potential to earn a living while looking for acting jobs. I spent roughly a month on the job before a strange turn of events prompted my departure.

Marissa and Kyle played no small role in all of this. It was through them that I had been introduced to a woman named Becky Switzer, who was the wife of Barry Switzer, the legendary former football coach at the University of Oklahoma. Becky ran a small talent agency out of Oklahoma. Becky and I met before my first trip to L.A., and she put me in touch with a man named Erik Logan, who worked for Oprah Winfrey's production company. Becky felt that if Erik could hear my story, he might be interested in making a movie about my life. We did in fact meet, but nothing came of it. Such is Hollywood.

As my life began to unravel in California, I neglected to reach out to Becky, which was probably a mistake in judgment caused primarily by shame. But I was not thinking clearly. Becky, as it turned out, was even more deeply connected than I had realized.

Roughly a month after I returned to Oklahoma, I got a text from her.

"Are you still in Los Angeles . . . or back in Oklahoma?"

I said that I was in Oklahoma, and I apologized for being so quiet.

"No problem. I think I might have something that would interest you. Let's talk."

As I dialed Becky's number, my heart began to race. I did not want to get my hopes up. I also fretted that I had made a mistake by leaving California. Although I was a novice, I knew something about the employment process in Hollywood. It isn't unusual to get a call about an audition with almost no time to prepare. This is why aspiring actors live as close to Hollywood as possible—so that they are free to interview or audition for a job on short notice. At that very moment, I was in Oklahoma City, more than a thousand miles away from the center of the entertainment universe. I might as well have been on another planet.

"I hope you aren't too busy," Becky said by way of introduction.

I laughed. "No, I have plenty of time. What's going on?"

"There's an audition for a lead role in a pilot for ABC. They've been trying to cast a specific part, and they can't find anybody. They went to South Africa. They went to Kenya. They went to China."

Becky had certainly piqued my interest. I mean, really, she had me at "ABC," but the notion that there seemed to be an international component to the role was even more intriguing.

"What are they looking for?" I asked. "Who is the character?"

There was a long pause.

"Well . . . he's a basketball player. And he's from another country."

Oh, my goodness.

"He's supposed to be very tall and have an accent, too. Can you handle that?"

I laughed. "Yes, I think so."

"Good," she said. "I'll send you the sides and you can look them over. Then we can talk again. We're going to have to move fast. The audition will be in a few days."

That night I looked over the material that Becky sent over from ABC. "Sides" usually refers to actual pages from a script or screenplay, but in this case the sides were accompanied by an overview of the show. As I read it, I couldn't believe my eyes. It was like I was reading my own life story!

Although it did not yet have an official title (this is not unusual for a pilot; our show was known simply as "Untitled NBA Project"), the arc of the series had been clearly drawn, and what I saw of the pilot was not only well written and funny, but so close to my own life that I felt as if I'd barely be acting. As originally written, the lead character was from Botswana. He was very tall, with seemingly limitless, if unrefined, talent for the sport of basketball. Based on potential and athletic ability, he is drafted by the Golden State Warriors (who were, at this time, just on the cusp of becoming the NBA's best and most popular team).

The character, whose name is Mo Gosego, speaks virtually no English. So not only does he have no understanding of American culture and tradition, but the team has no way to communicate with him. This is problematic in ways large and small. Simply negotiating a typical day is challenging for Mo; but even more challenging to his employer is Mo's apparent indifference to his job. He does not work as hard as some of his teammates, and he allows opponents to push him around on the floor. The Warriors' coaching staff and management can't figure out how to motivate Mo, nor can they adequately communicate their expectations. To remedy the situation, they hire a translator—a young man named Jason who has just returned from Africa after serving a stint in the Peace Corps. Jason speaks Lingala, which presumably will allow him to act as an efficient intermediary between Mo and his American teammates and coaches. But of course, things are much more complicated than that, as Jason's unfamiliarity with basketball is nearly as big an obstacle as Mo's unfamiliarity with English. Their working relationship becomes a deepening friendship, one that is complicated, funny, and human. What I saw of the pilot and the overview was funny and smart; I wanted so badly to be a part of it.

And not just because Mo seemed to have been written with me in mind. I knew in my heart that this was an A-list project. Most of the cast, after all, had already been assembled: Skylar Astin (one of the stars of the hit film *Pitch Perfect*); Jami Gertz, whose career included starring roles in the films *Sixteen Candles* and *Twister*, along with recurring roles in the series *ER, Ally McBeal*, and *Entourage*, among others; and Golden Globe winner Ving Rhames. The executive producers were a group of industry heavyweights: Dan Fogelman, who had written the screenplays for *Crazy, Stupid, Love* and the Pixar animated hit *Cars*; Mandalay Sports Media's Peter Guber and Mike Tollin; and Aaron Kaplan of Kapital Entertainment. The series was being produced in cooperation with both the NBA and the Golden State Warriors, which would allow for mutually beneficial cross-promotional and licensing opportunities.

It was, in every way imaginable, a big-time project.

As soon as I finished reading the pages, I called Becky.

"Okay, I'm in. When do I have to be there?"

"Two days," she said. There was a pause. "And Blondy?"

"Yes?"

"It's an audition. They won't pay your expenses."

I swallowed hard. "That's okay. No problem."

Actually, it was quite a large problem. I had a couple hundred dollars to my name, money that the Blitzes had sent me to get home and to rebuild my life in Oklahoma. This was less than half of what I needed to fly to Los Angeles; and I'd need a cheap hotel room, as well. Eventually I told Becky of my fiancial concerns. She offered a possible solution: instead of auditioning in person, we could just shoot some video and upload it on a laptop.

"No," I said. "I want them to meet me, and to see who I am."

I knew there was only one way to get the job: to sit in a room with the producers and read from a script and explain to them that there was no one else for this role; that indeed I was born to play the part.

If you've spent much time traveling, you know that buying a plane ticket on short notice can be a brutally expensive proposition, and so it was in my case. As soon as I got off the phone with Becky I went online and began hitting all the airline websites, as well as the wholesale sites like Kayak,

Travelocity, and Priceline, searching for a bargain. Alas, there was none to be found. The cheapest flight, on less than forty-eight hours' notice, was roughly $700. Which was several hundred dollars more than I had. I did not want to impose upon my parents again, so instead I reached out to a friend named Drew Faulkner and his wife, Brittany, whose family worked in the oil industry. I hated doing this again—it seemed like I always had my hand out, asking for help—but these were desperate times and they called for desperate measures. I called Drew and explained the situation. I hid nothing, including the possibility that I would not be able to repay him.

"It's just an audition," I said. "There is no guarantee that I will get the job. But if I don't go to the audition, there is no chance at all. If I get the part, I promise I will pay you back—with interest."

Drew just laughed.

"Don't worry about it. I would be honored to help you. How much do you need?"

"Well, I have about three hundred and the ticket is seven hundred, so I need four hundred."

There was a pause on the other end of the line. Drew wanted to know where I would be staying, and how I would pay for it. I said something about crashing on a friend's couch.

"Look, I'll get your ticket, okay?" he finally said. "You keep your money. Get a hotel room. You need to do this right."

"Drew," I said. "I can't thank you enough."

★

TWO DAYS LATER I walked into the Disney offices in Burbank for the most important meeting of my professional life. I signed in at the office of Susan Vash, a casting director, and took a seat in the waiting room, along with a half dozen very tall young men who looked like basketball players, all holding sheets of paper in their hands, and mumbling lines to themselves.

This was my competition. Interestingly, two of the candidates were white, a result of the producers leaving open the possibility of changing the lead character's background from African to Eastern European. The most important thing was finding the right actor, someone with a unique combination of stage presence and athletic ability. Once they found that person, they would shape the story accordingly. But I knew they preferred someone of African descent, which gave me a measure of confidence. Honestly? I figured the two white guys were long shots.

The more formidable presence was offered by Ger Duany, a Sudanese actor who had a significant role in *The Good Lie*, a 2014 film starring Reese Witherspoon about a group of African refugees and their struggle to adapt to their new life in the American Midwest. This was a serious and well-received film, and Duany was a talented actor who, like me, had also played college basketball and survived a tumultuous childhood in Africa (in his case, Sudan). His bio also included roles in *I Heart Huckabees* and *The Fighter*, so it would be an understatement to say that his résumé was deeper than mine. After all, I had no résumé.

We briefly made eye contact, but said nothing. This was my first audition, but already I got the sense that they are intensely weird and competitive. Everyone in the room is fighting for the same job. There is nothing collegial about it. I kept my head down and focused on my lines. I tried not to think about the fact that I was the least experienced actor in the room.

One by one we were summoned from the waiting room. I was one of the last, which was unnerving. Some of the candidates ahead of me were in the room for only a few minutes, while others were inside for considerably longer. The shorter the audition, I noticed, the more despondent the actor appeared when he emerged. This also was unnerving, for I knew that when my time came, the relative success or failure of my audition could be clearly measured by its duration. If they showed me the door quickly, I was done. If they permitted me to stay and chat for a while, I had a chance. To improve the odds, I presented the most upbeat and affable version of myself that I could possibly muster. I did not want them to know that I was terrified and broke and fighting the urge to flee. I wanted them to think that I was confident and friendly and eager to be part of their team.

I wanted them to believe that indeed I was Mo Gosego.

As I had so many times in my life, when faced with a challenge, I reflected on my experience in the Congo. I will admit that upon first seeing Ger Duany in the waiting room, my reaction was one of despair.

Oh, shit. He's a real actor. He will probably get the job.

But then I realized, what was the worst that could happen? I would survive this experience. Win or lose, I would learn from it. I would grow and become a better person.

"Blondy?"

Finally, it was my turn. I stood to greet the woman who was standing in the doorway, smiling broadly, hand extended.

"Pleased to meet you," she said. "I'm Susan."

I nodded. "Blondy Baruti. I am the kid from Africa."

She laughed. "Yes, I know. Come in, we'll get started in a moment."

There was only one other person in the room: Susan's assistant, Melissa, who was recording the audition on a video camera. I literally jogged into the room, bouncing on the balls of my feet, shaking my arms out like a boxer getting ready to fight. But smiling . . . always smiling.

"Tell us a little bit about yourself," Susan said.

"I'm Blondy Baruti, I'm from the Congo, I played college basketball, I'm still learning the language here in America, and I feel like this story is mine. This is my life!"

Melissa peered out from behind the camera, smiling. She and Susan looked at each other and laughed.

"Okay, well . . . that's great," Susan said. "Show us what you've got."

I had been given one scene to prepare, an emotional interaction between player and translator. In the scene, Mo, having drawn the ire of everyone in the Warriors' organization for his passive approach to the game of basketball, finally breaks down and explains to Jason why he seems to lack fire. Susan read the part of Jason; before we started, she asked if I need the pages, since I was empty-handed.

"No, thank you. I have it memorized."

Susan smiled. "All right, then. Whenever you're ready."

We ran through the scene together; Susan was a total pro. And near the end, I went for broke, throwing every ounce of energy into an emotional payoff.

"I know you're from the Congo and this is hard to understand, but in America, when you play basketball, you have to fight for every rebound and every loose ball," Susan (as Jason) read. "Nothing is easy. You have to work and fight every minute."

I looked off into the distance, and then into Susan's eyes. In that moment—in that little room with just the three of us—she became my translator.

"Why is everyone here always telling me to fight?" I cried. "I have been fighting all my life in Africa. I am tired of fighting. This is just a game!"

Afterward, they congratulated me on doing a good job and thanked me for my time. I could not tell how long I had been in the room. Just as I was getting ready to leave, Susan stopped me.

"Blondy, can you wait outside for a little while?"

"Yes, of course."

"Thanks, we're going to finish up with the others, and then we'd like you to do another scene."

Oh, my goodness.

I was no expert, but I figured this had to be a good thing. There was just one problem: I hadn't rehearsed or memorized any other scenes. This was the only one I had been given. Susan handed me several pages.

"Pick a scene," she said. "Don't worry about memorizing. We'll just read it."

I went back outside and waited for the last two candidates to finish their auditions. They were in and out quickly, and soon enough I was back in the room, stumbling through a scene that had neither context nor meaning. All the confidence I had brought to the first scene had evaporated as I stuttered and stammered. Susan, meanwhile, patiently delivered her lines as professionally as she had the first time around. Soon enough, the scene was over. I rolled up the pages and tried not to cry. My shirt was soaked with sweat.

"I'm sorry," I said, certain that I had played my way out of the starting lineup (to borrow a basketball metaphor).

"That's okay," Susan said, waving a hand dismissively. Then she talked with her assistant for a moment before turning to face me once again.

"When are you going back to Oklahoma?" she asked.

"Tomorrow," I said.

She seemed disappointed. "Is there any chance you can stay a little longer?"

I was confused. I had just botched the second audition, and she wanted me to stay in town?

"How long?" I asked.

She shrugged, then smiled reassuringly. "A few days. Maybe a week. We'd like to set up another meeting, so we can introduce you to the producers and the writing staff."

For an instant, I felt the urge to leap forward and wrap Susan in a hug. But I managed to squelch that urge and respond in a more professional manner.

"Sure, I can stay as long as you'd like," I said, trying to sound casual. "No problem at all."

Inside, however, my stomach did a tap dance, veering from unbridled joy one moment to utter panic the next, as I tried to figure out how I was going to finance another week in Los Angeles. I had only been there one day, and already I was broke. But I was not broken, and that was all that mattered.

CHAPTER 24

With a week to kill in L.A., I decided to take care of some unfinished business and repair my friendship with Jordan Clarkson. I still had not spoken with him since the day we looked at houses together many months earlier. He was doing well with the Lakers and I was happy for his success, but there was a hole in my heart at having lost one of my best friends for reasons I could not fathom.

When Jordan again did not respond to my texts or phone calls—"Hey, brother, I'm in town again and wanted to get together; miss you"—the situation seemed hopeless. I called my parents several times that week to give them updates, and during one of the calls they told me that they had heard from Jordan's family. Jordan, apparently, had told his parents that I was trying to reach him, and they all were concerned that I was looking for a place to stay. Now, finally, came the explanation for Jordan's disappearance. His parents had felt that as a rookie in the NBA, with serious professional and financial obligations, Jordan had to focus entirely on his career and his job. They were worried that I was unemployed and in need of help, and they felt this was too great a burden for Jordan to take on under the circumstances.

"Jordan is very young and he is going to have enough trouble taking care of himself," they explained to the Blitzes. "He can't take care of someone else."

Now it all made sense: the disappearing act, the lack of communication, the coldness of it all. Jordan did what his family told him to do, and no doubt felt bad about it, so bad that he couldn't even tell me to my face. That was unfortunate, because I would have understood. I mean, it was messed up and wrong, in my opinion, and did not take into consideration the depth of our friendship and what we had been through together. Part of this, naturally, is cultural. I had grown up in a world that was at once cruel and communal. Family and friends in Africa are raised under a guiding principle of generosity. This is not true of everyone, of course—in times of great strife, people can and do behave selfishly—but I saw many times over the goodness inherent in my fellow man. I believed then and I believe now that there are few things stronger than the bond of friendship. If you are my friend, you are like family. And if you are family, what is mine is also yours. If we are both hungry, and all I have left is one tiny piece of bread, and you have nothing? Then I will give you half of my bread. There is no question about that. It is a simple moral obligation.

Still, I understand that we all come from different places. I do not fault Jordan's family for worrying about him and making recommendations based on what they felt was in his best interest. I do wish my friend had taken the time to be honest with me, rather than withdraw suddenly and completely from my life, at a time when I really needed his help.

But I didn't want to stay with Jordan now, and I sure wasn't trying to interfere with his life in any way; I just wanted to get together for a cup of coffee and tell him how much I loved him, and that he would always be my brother. I wanted to share the news of my audition. I wanted to tell him: life is good, my friend. And soon we will be reunited here in this magnificent city.

In order to get this message across, I first had to get clearance from Jordan's parents, so that they would know that I had no intention of squatting in their son's home or otherwise interfering with his progress. The next day, Jordan and I did meet, and after a few awkward moments, everything was fine.

"This thing happened to us," I said. "But now it's over. I just want you to know that you are still my brother, and nothing will ever change that. I love you."

"I love you, too," Jordan said.

★

A FEW DAYS LATER I returned to Susan Vash's office. Oddly enough, though the stakes were even higher, I felt strangely calm as I walked into the building. Three of us had returned for a second audition (although not Ger Duany, which surprised me a bit), but this time I made eye contact with the others, even smiled and said hello. It's hard to explain, but already I felt as though I had accomplished more than I ever imagined, and I realized suddenly that it was important to get that point across to the people who were waiting in the office.

When it was my turn to audition, I walked in wearing a broad smile and with my hand extended.

"Hello, I am Blondy Baruti," I said to each person. It was a much busier room than it had been one week earlier. In addition to Susan and her assistant, the group also included writers Casey Johnson and David Windsor and producer Aaron Kaplan. They were all about to settle into their chairs when I asked them for a favor.

"Before we start the audition, I'd like to tell you my story," I said. This, I was later informed, is not typically a part of the audition process. Producers and writers and casting directors are busy people; protocol dictates that an actor stay on task: read your lines, say thank you, and get out of the room. But that seemed insufficient under the circumstances. As Susan smiled at me—she wanted enthusiasm, and I was going to give it to them—I began to talk.

"I don't know if I will get this job or not," I said. "But I want you all to know that I am thankful for the callback. Looking back on my life, it seems hard to believe I am even here—standing in front of a group of writers and producers from Hollywood, auditioning for a role in an ABC pilot. This is a dream to me. I grew up very poor in the Congo. I escaped the violence of my home by running away with my mother and sister, for days and nights and weeks and months on end. Somehow, I survived. I moved to the western part of the Congo and started playing basketball, even though people told me I wasn't good enough. I came to America, to this great country, and I went to college. I've had to go through a lot of struggle, but I am still here. And for me to be able to audition in front of you guys . . . it means everything to me. Whether I get the job or not, I feel like I have done something with my life, and I'm grateful to you for giving me the chance."

There was even more to the monologue than this; it went on for three to four minutes and included a bit more detail about my time in the Congo and the loss of my basketball career. But you get the point. I hoped that they would, as well. I did not want to waste their time; I just wanted to let them know who I was and how much this meant to me. When I finished, the room fell quiet. Finally, Aaron broke the ice.

"Okay, I guess we're done here. Congratulations, Blondy, you've got the job."

Again, there was a moment of silence, before laughter filled the room. He was kidding, of course. I might have had the appropriate real-life background for the character of Mo Gosego, but I still had to prove I was capable of getting the job done. In short, I had to prove that I could act. Again.

Susan and I did the same scene we had read a week earlier, and again it went very well. They asked me to make some adjustments, to do it with more feeling, or more "action." The audition went on this way for at least twenty minutes, with subtle changes and shading—I got the sense that they were not only testing my range, but my ability to take direction under pressure. This would help them know whether I was a professional actor, or an amateur with an interesting story.

When the audition ended, there was little fanfare. Everyone was polite, but noncommittal.

"Thank you for your time, Blondy," Susan said. "We'll be in touch."

I walked out not knowing whether I would ever see any of them again, or if indeed my career was over before it had even begun. Frankly, it didn't matter. Just to have made it this far was an accomplishment beyond anything I imagined.

And yet . . .

Oh, how I wanted the role!

★

THAT AFTERNOON I GOT a call from Becky Switzer.

"They loved you," she said.

"Great! What's next?"

"They want you to come back for one more audition. Can you stay three more days? Dan Fogelman is going to be in town, and he will be there, as well."

I did not hesitate to answer. "Of course, I can stay. Thank you, Becky!"

"You're welcome. Good luck, Blondy."

I called my friend Damien and asked if I could stay with him for a few more days. He cheerfully said no problem. He also said he'd give me a ride. I was grateful for the help—until his car got a flat tire on the 405 on the way to the audition, several miles from the ABC offices in Burbank. At first, we tried to change the tire ourselves, but with seven lanes of traffic in each direction, it was much too dangerous. Damien decided to call Triple A, but as we stood by the car on the side of the road, with traffic backing up the way it often does in L.A., I felt a surge of anxiety.

"I'm going to be late, bro. I'm going to be late. This is so bad."

Damien put an arm around my shoulder, tried to calm me down.

"It'll be okay. Relax. The truck will be here in no time and we'll be back on the road."

"No, no, no. You don't understand. I can't be even one minute late for this meeting. Not one minute or I will be screwed. You can't be late for an audition."

"We won't be late. I promise."

I admired Damien's optimism in the face of such a catastrophe, but he was wrong; there was no chance that we would get there on time. Gripped by panic, I reached out to Becky for help. Why? Because that's what actors do when they're in trouble: they call their agent! Instead of calling, though, I texted her a photo of our car on the side of the road, with a blown tire leaning up against the vehicle.

"I'm going to be late," I texted. "What should I do?"

Her response was almost instantaneous: "Call Uber and get there as quickly as possible. I'll let them know what's going on."

I felt bad about leaving Damien, but he understood, said he would be fine, and wished me good luck. My Uber ride arrived quickly, and we got to Disney only a few minutes late for the audition. I must have looked a mess, but everyone was gracious and understanding (Becky had forwarded the photo of our three-wheeled car).

This time there were only two of us left to audition. I went second, which was good, since it gave me time to stop sweating and gather my composure. Susan once again led the audition. As she guided me into the room, I was immediately struck by the size of both the venue and the audience. It was a huge conference room, and this time there were more than a dozen people in attendance: Susan and her assistant; Dan Fogelman; executives from ABC and Disney; the director, John Fortenberry; the writers, Casey Johnson and David Windsor; and the star of the series, Skylar Astin, who gave me a rather long and perplexed look. You see, when I had entered the building, I saw Skylar walking ahead of me. I had been alerted to the fact that he would be part of the audition, and I had read quite a bit about him online as part of my preparation. When I saw him outside, I had tried to get his attention.

"Hey, Skylar! Skylar Astin!"

He had turned briefly, then continued walking.

"Skylar!" I shouted again. "It is me—Blondy Baruti!"

There wasn't a hint of recognition. I'm not sure Skylar even heard me, or if he simply thought I was a *Pitch Perfect* fanboy who wanted an autograph. Regardless, he did not respond. Instead, he disappeared into the building. By the time I reached the lobby, he was already gone. But now, here we were again, face-to-face in a Disney conference room, getting ready to share a scene together. As I shook Skylar's hand and introduced myself, he smiled shyly. I could tell he was embarrassed.

"Wait . . . did I just see you outside in the parking lot? Yelling my name?"

I nodded. "Yes, sir."

"I'm sorry, Blondy. I didn't know who you were."

I told him it was fine, no harm done. Sometimes I get carried away with excitement.

We did exactly the scene I had performed in each of the two previous auditions, so I felt like knew the dialogue verbatim, and had a pretty good understanding of the emotion and character development it was meant to convey. But the real test was not to see whether I could act, but what sort of chemistry there was between Skylar and me. The success or failure of the pilot—and indeed the entire series—rested largely on the interaction between our characters. It was an improbable friendship between two young men from vastly different worlds, and if the audience did not invest itself in this relationship, then the story would crumble. I liked Skylar right away, and I think he liked me. Rather than feeling intimidated by his experience and résumé, I took comfort in it. Despite the obvious pressure of being a finalist for a role that would have a profound impact on my life, I felt oddly at peace. This was partly due to the fact that I had studied hard and knew my lines so well, and felt like I understood the process. But it was also because of Skylar, and the feeling of brotherhood he projected. I had been acting only a few years, and only in live theater, but I knew what it was like to work with performers who were selfish and insecure, and I knew what it was like to work with performers who were confident and generous.

Skylar, I could tell, fell into the latter category. He gave me lots of support and encouragement throughout the audition. By the end, I felt completely comfortable working with him. If there was one concern that everyone seemed to have about our working relationship, and how it translated to the screen, it was physical and not artistic. You see, interestingly enough, they were worried that there wasn't enough of a height discrepancy between the two of us. As written, Mo Gosego was well over seven feet tall, while Jason, the translator, was supposed to be somewhat shorter than average height. In reality, Skylar was a solid 5-foot-10, and I was 6-foot-8. Never before in my life had someone told me that I wasn't tall enough, but that was the impression I got on this day. We ran through our lines once; then, before filming the scene for studio executives, Susan rigged a makeshift platform for me to stand on, effectively adding three or four inches to my height. The idea was to present the appearance of Mo absolutely towering over his American counterpart.

We went through the scene a few times, modifying it according to the director's suggestions. By the end I felt comfortable and confident. Afterward, we all stood around for a few minutes and chatted informally—some of them had questions about not only my life in the Congo, but my theater background, as well. And then I was on my way, with no more assurance or resolution than there had been after the first two auditions. Just a pleasant but perfunctory "Thank you for coming, Blondy. We'll be in touch." This time, though, I tried not to read too much into it. This was the way things worked in Hollywood. All communication was done through representatives—agents and managers—so I did not expect anyone to tell me I had or had not earned the job. That information would come soon enough.

★

THE NEXT DAY I flew back to Oklahoma. Shortly after I arrived, I got a call from Becky, who proceeded to give me a crash course in Hollywood protocol. Susan had called Becky to suggest that I meet with a woman named Adena Chawke, a manager at Greenlight Management and Production in Beverly Hills. Here's the thing about the entertainment business that many people do not realize (certainly I was unaware). Most actors employ not just an agent, but a personal manager, as well. There is considerable overlap between the two roles, and together they help an artist form the strongest possible team when trying to build a career. Since my agent was based in Oklahoma, it made sense for me to connect with a Hollywood manager. Susan and some of the others involved in our pilot were familiar with Adena's work, so they recommended her to Becky.

Within two days, Adena was in Oklahoma City, sitting across a table from me, explaining the particulars of a management contract, and what she would do to earn her 10 percent commission. I was also paying Becky 10 percent, which meant I was giving up 20 percent of my income, which might sound like a lot, until you consider that my income at that point was . . . well . . . zero. If having an agent and a manger meant I'd be more likely to secure work, then I was on board. Once Adena and I came to an agreement, she shifted the conversation to another topic.

"ABC is going to offer you the role," Adena said. She said this matter-of-factly, as if it were not one of the most amazing things I had heard in my entire life. Which obviously it was.

"That's fantastic!" I yelped. "When do I start?"

Adena held up a hand. "Slow down. It's not that simple. We have to settle on a contract first, and frankly I'm not happy with the offer."

"What is it?" I asked.

"They want to pay you ten thousand dollars per episode—"

I know there were words that came after this, because I could see

Adena's mouth moving. But something happened that prevented me from hearing exactly what she said. The shock of those words—*ten thousand dollars . . . per episode!*—had apparently cut off the flow of oxygen to my brain. I was about to pass out.

"I'm sorry, Adena . . . did you say ten thousand dollars?" This was more money than I had earned in my entire life.

She nodded. "Yes. I know that sounds like a lot, but trust me, it's not. It's very low for a starring role in a network sitcom. I'm going to push for more based on your value to the project. Whether you have experience or not is irrelevant. They want you for this role and they know you're the best person to play the part. It took them forever to find the right person, and now they've found him. You should be paid accordingly."

"What does that mean?"

Adena smiled. "I'm going to ask for forty thousand."

I nearly fell out of my chair. "Forty thousand! A week?"

"Well, per episode, yes. It's not every week, but still . . ."

Yes . . . still.

"So, what next?" I asked.

"You let me handle everything," Adena replied. "If anyone from Disney or ABC calls you, just refer them to me. I'm your manager now, and I will negotiate on your behalf. I know you are the first choice, so have faith. And try to be patient."

I was not patient. In fact, I could not have been more impatient. Every day I woke and checked my email and text messages, praying for some news on the pilot—confirmation that I had gotten the job and that a fee had been settled. And each day there was no news, so I'd wait a few hours and then call both Becky and Adena, just to see if they had an update, which of course they did not.

"Sorry to bother you," I'd say.

"No trouble at all, Blondy. Just relax. It's going to work out."

Three weeks passed and I was out having dinner with my friend Drew—I'd been staying with his family while in Oklahoma City. We were at a nice restaurant with the entire family: Drew and his wife, their kids, and his wife's parents. It was a pleasant and fun evening. For a change, I wasn't obsessing about work and acting. I was just trying to have a good time.

Until my phone lit up. It was Adena. Before I even answered, I held up the phone for everyone to see.

This is it!

I stood up from the table and began pacing around the restaurant, trying to find a quiet space.

"What's up, Adena?"

"I just wanted to say congratulations," she said. "ABC has agreed to thirty thousand dollars per episode."

I was speechless.

"Blondy? Did you hear me?"

"Ummmm . . . yes. This means they want me?"

I could hear her laughing. "Yes, Blondy, it means they want you. And it means you are going to be a star."

I held the phone above my head and turned to Drew and the rest of the table. By this point I was halfway across the room.

"Drew!" I shouted. "I got it! "I got the part!"

As Drew came running toward me and everyone in the restaurant stared in disbelief at the sight of a 6-foot-8 black man screaming at the top of his lungs, I fell to my knees. As tears filled my eyes, I looked up at the ceiling.

"Finally," I said. "Thank you, God."

lmost overnight, it seemed, my life was transformed. My name and my photo appeared in the trades—*Hollywood Reporter* and *Variety*—and on Internet sites devoted to following every tidbit of gossip or legitimate business that comes out of the entertainment industry. There were enticing feature stories in which the parallel lives of performer and character were highlighted. It was an intoxicating time, to be sure. I was going to be a Hollywood star, making more money in a single week than I had seen in my entire life.

Of course, this was dependent on the pilot getting picked up by ABC and finding a place on the network schedule, but wasn't that almost preordained? I mean, everything had happened so quickly and smoothly, in almost fatalistic fashion. My very first audition had led to an offer to star in a network sitcom. Looking at Mo Gosego was like looking into a mirror. The cast was stellar, the writing both heartfelt and humorous. Additionally, we had on our side that elusive thing known as synergy— thanks to the recent rise in popularity of the Golden State Warriors and their best player, Steph Curry. Our show was an ABC property, and ABC/Disney was a broadcast partner of the NBA.

When the stars are so properly aligned, how can anything possibly go wrong? Production began with a "table read" at ABC studios in Burbank. A table read is exactly what it sounds like: a group of actors sitting at a large table, reading a script, while the director, writers, and producers look on, occasionally making suggestions or otherwise offering notes. The table read is a warm and pleasant experience—a way for the cast and crew to familiarize themselves with the material, while also getting to know their coworkers in a casual setting. There are no costumes or sets for the table read. There isn't even much acting. Just a lot of reading and laughing, and an enormous amount of coffee.

Since now I was under contract, ABC arranged to put me up in a Sheraton not far from the studio. Meals and transportation were covered, as well. I felt blessed to have no financial stress—a rare circumstance for me! At least in the short term, all I had to do was concentrate on my work. Memorize my lines, get into character, and become familiar with the rest of the cast. This I did before even arriving. I spent endless hours on Google and IMDb, committing to memory the film and television credits of of Skylar Astin, Jami Gertz, and Ving Rhames, along with a dozen other actors playing supporting roles. I streamed video of their work, which made me feel both honored to part of this cast, but also a little intimidated. Still, excitement was the predominant emotion.

When I walked into the room for the table read, Jami was the first person I saw. She was every bit as beautiful as she appeared on the screen, and even warmer and friendlier than I had imagined.

"Jami Gertz!" I yelled from several feet away. She saw me, smiled, walked over, and gave me a big hug.

"Nice to meet you, Blondy."

"Nice to meet you, too," I said. "I am a big fan."

"Really?"

"Yes, I loved your movie, *A Better Life*."

Jami seemed genuinely surprised by this. Most people know her as a performer in mainstream movies or television shows, but in my research I had discovered that Jami's production company was responsible for one of my favorite movies of the last few years. *A Better Life* tells the story of a Mexican laborer struggling to raise his son as a single parent in Los

Angeles, while worrying about the possibility of deportation and the influence of gang violence on his impressionable teenage boy. It is a strong and emotional film that struck a chord with me for obvious reasons, and I loved it before I even realized that Jami's company had produced it. So, I wanted to let her know what it meant to me.

"That's very nice of you, Blondy. Thank you. You've really done your homework."

The table read was fun, but uneventful. I was eager to get to the actual production, but that would be a week or more down the road. A few days later, bored from spending too much time in my hotel room and eager to bond with my castmates before we began shooting, I sent an email to Jami, asking if she might want to get together for coffee or dinner.

"Sounds great," she wrote back. "How about dinner first, and then we can go to a Lakers game? I have seats."

We met at a restaurant near the Staples Center and spent nearly two hours talking about work and family and personal history. Jami, I learned, was not just a successful actor and producer, but the mother of three boys, two of whom were out on their own; the third was a junior in high school. She talked and acted like a Supermom—with tons of energy and insight. She was one half of a seriously accomplished marital partnership: her husband, Tony Ressler, was a businessman whose many eclectic interests included an ownership stake in the Atlanta Hawks. This might partially explain Jami's interest in the *Untitled NBA Project* for ABC. She was a huge basketball fan and her husband, as an NBA owner, was basically part of the Disney/ABC empire.

The conversation was comfortable; Jami wanted to hear all about my life. She is a good listener, and also asks great questions. She wanted to know all about my plans for trying to build a future in the entertainment industry. My answers were enthusiastic, but somewhat vague, as you might expect, for I really had no clue. My hope was that our pilot would lead to a series, which would then lead to several years of consistent and lucrative work, followed by movies and more series. You know—the career arc of a superstar. I'm sure it sounded both innocent and arrogant, but in reality, I was just eager to show what I could do. Jami, playing the role of both mom and Hollywood veteran, gave me some gentle advice and encouragement. I was struck mainly by what an incredibly nice person she was.

The game was great, and it was fun to be at Staples Center, even though the Lakers weren't exactly tearing up the league in those days. Jami is a knowledgeable basketball fan, and she got a kick out of the fact that Jordan Clarkson had been one of my best friends in college. When the game ended, we walked out, still talking about hoops and Hollywood. Once we got to the parking lot, Jami asked me if I had any plans.

"Just going back to the hotel," I said.

She smiled. "I don't think so. Why don't you follow me back to my house. You don't have to stay in a hotel."

The offer took me completely by surprise. Despite being familiar with the enormous generosity of many Americans (the Blitzes, for example), I had seen nothing that led me to believe such behavior was common in the entertainment world. Jami and I hardly knew each other. We were merely coworkers thrown together by circumstance; despite our shared involvement in this project, we were from different worlds. And it wasn't like I was out in the street, as I had been on previous sojourns to Los Angeles. I had a comfortable bed in a perfectly nice hotel room. I had an expense account! Jami's offer was so kind, and so unnecessary, that I found myself tongue-tied.

"Huh?" I said. "What do you mean?"

Jami laughed. "Get in your car and follow me."

I shrugged. "Okay."

I knew only that Jami lived somewhere in Beverly Hills, so I tucked in behind her big Mercedes sedan and followed her closely as we began winding through the hills, climbing past ever more opulent and glorious neighborhoods, with spectacular views of the lights of L.A. Eventually we came to a neighborhood known as Beverly Park, a gated community where the homes all have the size and muscle of a shopping mall (although most are much more attractive). I would later find out that Jami's neighbors included Eddie Murphy, Sylvester Stallone, and Mark Wahlberg. When I got out of the car and looked around, I could barely speak, so impressive was the home and the landscaping, and the view to the city below.

"Oh, my gosh," I said. "This is so beautiful."

Jami said thanks and invited me into the house, where I was introduced to her youngest son, Theo. Jami had assured me that Theo knew all about me, as she had told him some of my life story after we met at the table read. Although just sixteen years old, Theo was poised and confident and charming. Sometimes I wondered if all American teenagers are this way, but of course they are not. It is a matter of luck and genetics and fine parenting. I liked Theo right away. There was just one problem: I could not pronounce his name properly. For some reason, whenever I tried to say "Theo," the "Th" became "Ph," resulting in something that sounded like "Phil."

The most amazing thing about that night was the fact that Jami did not even tell her husband that she was bringing home a guest; and not merely a guest for dinner, but one who might be staying for a while. She simply made a decision that came from her heart, knowing that her equally generous husband would support the invitation. At first, I did not know what to make of this, and I worried that Tony might be offended. Once I got to know him, that assumption was almost embarrassingly inaccurate. And once I got to spend time with both Jami and Tony, and as I watched them together, they struck me as the best kind of couple. Partners in the truest sense of the word, they had been married for more than twenty-five years. They had raised three sons together and built successful careers. Owners of professional sports franchises have the reputation for having massive egos and a tendency to want to control everything, as they often do in their other business interests. I don't know what Tony is like in a boardroom, but I do know that around the house in Beverly Hills, he is an extremely interesting and laid-back guy.

I also have come to know Tony and Jami as a couple who are devoted to the concept of philanthropy, on both a global level, and in their personal lives. With the 2014 initial public offering of his company, Ares Management, Tony had been transformed from a wealthy man into a billionaire. He continued to work in the wealth management field, while also exercising his passion for sports and philanthropy. The Ressler/Gertz Foundation addresses many of the issues that are of personal interest to Jami and Tony, most notably education, with a particular focus on the Los Angeles area. Tony was a founding board member and cochair of the Alliance for College-Ready Public Schools, a group of L.A. charter schools. The foundation also has supported Homeboy Industries, which provides education, employment training, and other programming for former gang-involved and incarcerated men and women—something I did not know when I first saw Jami's film, *A Better Life*, but that makes perfect sense in retrospect. The foundation also supports the arts and various youth sports activities.

But Jami and Tony are not just quiet and distant philanthropists, far removed from the beneficiaries of their largesse. Some people don't like to get their hands dirty with this sort of work. Jami and Tony did not fall into that category. At the same time, it's worth noting that Jami later made it clear to me that she was not in the habit of bringing home strays to the family mansion in Beverly Hills. When we went out for dinner that night, and to the Lakers game, she had no intention of inviting me into their family.

It just sort of happened.

But once Jami makes up her mind to do something, she is not easily dissuaded. When she finally called her husband later that night, after I had already accepted the invitation, and said, in effect, "Hey, just so you know, we have a new kid in the house," it was no surprise that Tony responded with little more than a shrug.

"Okay, looking forward to meeting him."

Needless to say, there was plenty of room in the house—even a 6-foot-8 basketball player from the Congo would barely be noticeable.

Jami gave me two options: I could stay in the bedroom formerly occu-pied by her oldest son, Oliver, who had since relocated to New York City. It was a huge, sprawling room, bigger than the house in which I had grown up, and I would have been perfectly comfortable there. Even more appealing, though, was the second option, presented as we walked outside and toured the grounds. A short distance away, tucked into the backyard and near the pool, was a guest cottage.

"You can stay here if you'd be more comfortable," Jami said. "But I want you to know that you're welcome to stay in the house, as well. Whatever you'd like."

I didn't quite know how to respond. I did not want to be rude in the face of such a grand display of hospitality, and I was concerned that by declining an invitation to stay in the main house, I would risk offending Jami. But I had to be honest. We barely knew each other and I did not want to impose or do anything that might put a strain on either our working relationship or our new friendship. Sometimes, I had learned, a little space is necessary for a healthy living arrangement.

"I understand, and I can't thank you enough for your kindness," I said. "If it's okay with you, I will stay in the guesthouse."

Jami smiled. "Of course."

The next day I retrieved my belongings from the Sheraton and be-came a temporary resident of Beverly Hills. With a separate kitchen and bathroom suite, and a family whose kindness seemed to rival that of the Blitzes just a short walk away, the guesthouse felt like a gift from heaven.

And it was just one of many that I received from Jami and her family.

When Jami found out about my still-outstanding traffic tickets not long after I moved into the guesthouse, she was at first aghast that I'd been foolish enough to drive around the busiest freeways in America with a sus-pended license. But then she went into mother mode by hiring an attorney who was able to help me clean up the whole mess. I'm sure it cost a lot of money—more money than I could imagine. I knew only that I was over-whelmed by her generosity, and so grateful to have stumbled into her life.

CHAPTER 26

H ollywood tends to be fueled by momentum. When there is significant buzz surrounding a project, it quickly gains speed and support. Similarly, a young and inexperienced performer can become a hot
commodity based on little more than physical appearance or potential.
To some extent, both of these scenarios applied to me when we began
filming the pilot for our series. There was a lot of talk around town
regarding the series, and how it seemed destined to not only make it on
the ABC prime-time schedule, but to become a hit. Yes, it was basically
a fish-out-of-water story (not a unique concept), but there were so many
things that it made it interesting and unusual, not least of which was the
casting of a complete novice in a costarring role. My backstory became
the engine of publicity for the series, which was at once flattering and
disorienting. While I was not lacking in confidence, I understood the
reality of the situation: I had been given the opportunity of a lifetime.
Most people don't realize that for every pilot that gets the green light
and is developed into a series, there are dozens that fail miserably. Many
pilots are never viewed beyond the privacy of an executive suite. That is
simply the truth of the matter: the odds against getting picked up are
long, and the obstacles plentiful. Most actors who appear in a pilot know
better than to get their hopes up. They keep their options open and continue to audition for other parts.

Not me. I was one hundred percent invested in the pilot. It was my big break, and I knew it. With such a great cast and writers, and the obviously enthusiastic backing of the network and the NBA, we were poised for success in a way that evades all but the most fortunate of newly hatched series. This fact was not lost on those of us who were involved, both in front of the camera and behind it. We all knew we were in an unusual position, no one more so than me. Throughout the process I kept hearing about how lucky I was to be part of such a great project, and I did not dispute this observation. Rather, I held it close to my heart and used it as a daily reminder of where I had been, and how beautiful the future appeared to be.

"We are a lock to get picked up," they would say. "And you are going to be a star." I would smile and nod, and think to myself, "If God is willing."

Although development took several months—casting, writing, acquiring licensing agreements—the actual shooting of the pilot required only a few weeks of work. While movies are usually developed and shot at a glacial pace, scripted television series are often produced with great speed and efficiency. This is not surprising, I suppose. After all, a movie is a single, self-contained story, perhaps two hours long, while a television series might stretch out over ten or twenty episodes in a single season. There is no room for dawdling or self-indulgence.

The approach is intensely professional and workmanlike. This is not to say that a series lacks artistic integrity. But it is true that everything is ruled by the clock and the calendar. We were shooting a pilot; if the pilot was picked up, we would immediately begin production on a full season. Every week would bring a new script, a new show, a new challenge. If making a movie is like running a marathon, then making a television series is like running a series of sprints, one right after the other, with very little rest in between. It is both exhausting and exciting. I wanted that challenge in the worst way.

On the first day of shooting at the studio in Burbank, I was so pumped up that I was worried I might forget my lines. But I wasn't scared. Quite the contrary. I couldn't wait to get started. It was similar to the way I used to feel in the locker room before a big basketball game, when the adrenaline was pumping furiously through my body. You need that adrenaline to prepare for an intense and challenging situation, but too much of it can ruin a performance—on the basketball court or in front of a camera.

To be honest, I think other people were more nervous than I was about how I would handle the pressure. Until the first day of shooting, I did not realize what a busy and crowded place a television set could be. There must have been fifty or sixty people hanging around—cast, crew, technicians, studio executives—all of them watching the production. I had acted onstage in front of more than a thousand people, but this was different. This was not an audience in the traditional sense of the word. Some of these people were my coworkers; some were my employers. All of them were deeply invested in the proceedings, and more than a little curious about the unknown actor from the Congo.

"How are you feeling, Blondy?" the director, John Fortenberry, said to me, just moments after I arrived. "Are you okay?"

A legitimately nice and thoughtful man, as well as a talented director, he probably (and not unreasonably) presumed that I would be nervous on the first day of shooting and wanted to help ease any anxiety by letting me know that we were all in this together.

"Don't be shy," he urged. "If you have any questions, just come to me and ask. You're going to do a great job."

"Thank you," I said, but I couldn't help wondering which of us he was trying to convince. There was a lot of money riding on this pilot. I had done well in the audition, but this was different. This was the real thing. What if I screwed up? What if it turned out that I wasn't ready to star in a network sitcom? That would be a problem not just for me, but for everyone on the set.

An image crossed my brain—that of a freakishly tall former basketball player standing in front of a camera (several cameras, actually), his face blank, eyes wide, the victim of a sudden and crippling case of stage fright.

"Line, please," I imagined myself asking in a desperate plea for help.

And I could see everyone shaking their heads in disappointment; or, worse, pity.

No, I would not let that happen. A new image came to mind—that of a ten-year-old boy walking barefoot through the jungles of the Congo, picking at festering insect bites and holding his nose to avoid the ever-present stench of death. What here could possibly compare to that horror? This was not a punishment; this was a gift, a chance to do something I loved. I had survived a genocidal massacre; I had survived being homeless.

This was a walk in the park.

"Do not worry," I said to John. "I am good."

I made some mistakes that day, but I did not embarrass myself. We worked for close to twelve hours, rehearsing and filming one scene after another. And so it went for the next several days. I found it to be utterly exhilarating. I was proud of the work I was doing, and everyone seemed to have a positive feeling. Not only was it funny and emotional, but we were developing a camaraderie that reflected the characters on screen.

The star of this fictional version of the Golden State Warriors was Derek Gates, a brilliant but aging superstar (think LeBron James or Kobe Bryant) played by LaMonica Garrett. LaMonica, who would go on to star in the hit drama *Designated Survivor*, was actually almost forty years old when we shot the pilot, but he is a beast of an athlete, as well as a terrific actor, so he was more than believable in the role. From the moment that Mo Gosego shows up in a Warriors uniform, Derek Gates is frustrated and angry. Gates wants to win a title before he retires, and he wonders why the team has used the No. 2 overall pick in the NBA draft on an un-proven player. Mo's laid-back demeanor only makes matters worse.

"I'm getting old," Derek says to Mo. "I need your help. This team needs your help. You're a first-round draft pick, and you need to bring it every day. You need to work harder and you need to be tougher."

Derek's frustration, shared by coaches and management, leads the team to hire a translator, in the hope of getting their motivational message across more clearly. Enter Skylar Astin's character, Jason, the translator who knows nothing about basketball. He is also reeling after being dumped by his girlfriend while they were working together for the Peace Corps in the Congo. The job of translator pays six figures and is a big break for Jason, who wants to prove to his parents—especially his father—that he is capable of doing something worthwhile with his life. But as Mo stubbornly refuses to embrace a stronger work ethic, and to "fight" the way his teammates and coaches want him to fight, Jason begins to lose faith in both himself and his client.

At one point the two men get into a heated disagreement, as Jason grows weary of Mo's apparent complacency, and Mo grows weary of being nagged and cajoled. Part of this scene involves the exchange that was so crucial to my audition—with Mo crying and expressing confusion and sadness over everyone's disappointment with his attitude: "Why do they want me to fight? I am tired of fighting. I had to fight for my life in the Congo." But it also features a heartfelt plea from Jason, who makes it clear to Mo that their lives are intertwined. If Mo does not become a fighter, and subsequently a better basketball player, then he will quickly find himself out of the NBA. If that happens, then Jason will lose his job, as well.

"You're getting paid millions," Jason says. "You have to show them you are worth it. You have to work harder. If you get cut, you won't have a job, and you will have to go back to Africa. I will get cut, too. And I'll have to move back in with my parents."

As a result of the argument, Mo and Jason are drawn closer and being to develop not just a working partnership, but a legitimate friendship. This sets the stage for one of the funniest and most emotional scenes in the pilot, which we filmed during halftime of an actual Golden State Warriors game, against the Phoenix Suns, in front of a packed house at Oracle Arena. The pressure in this scenario was daunting. While the NBA gave the series its stamp of approval, and the Warriors let us use their logo and uniforms, they were not about to let us interfere with the rhythm of an actual game. We had perhaps ten minutes in which to film this pivotal scene. If we didn't get it right, the director could not just yell "Cut!" and ask us to do it again while the Warriors and Suns hung out in the locker room waiting for us to finish. We'd have to come back on a different night and start all over again.

We all knew our lines and our jobs. The delicate choreography of acting within the framework of a basketball game had been carefully laid out. As written, the scene involves the revealing of a pivotal piece of information: the fact that Derek Gates had gotten into an argument with Jason earlier in the day, resulting in the NBA All-Star using duct tape to pin Jason to a basketball backboard. Jason reveals this information to Mo during the game, which so provokes Mo's anger that for the first time since joining the Warriors, he plays with great passion. He becomes, for the first time, a true fighter.

There is just one problem: the person with whom he chooses to fight is his own teammate, Derek Gates.

"He is my friend!" Mo says to Derek, as the two are running down the court. "And I am from the Congo. And in the Congo, we take care of our friends!"

With that, Mo throws a punch at Derek. The two begin to wrestle as teammates and officials rush in to break it up. The NBA obviously frowns on fighting and typically imposes huge fines on players who engage in such behavior. But it rarely, if ever, happens among teammates, which is what made the scene so funny. I'm sure it was all a bit bewildering to the twenty thousand spectators at Oracle Arena. An announcement was made, informing the crowd that we were filming a pilot for ABC, and asking for both the cooperation and enthusiastic involvement of everyone in attendance. In other words, they were supposed to act like normal fans. To that end, nothing was divulged about the nature of the scene. When I began trading punches with LaMonica Garrett, there was an audible gasp in the arena.

Wait . . . what's going on? Why is he fighting with his teammate?

It was perfect! The crowd's shock was exactly what the scene required, and LaMonica and I perfectly executed both the verbal exchange and the physical confrontation, the upshot of which was a winking admonishment from team management. You see, while it wouldn't be appropriate for a coach, or a general manager, or an owner to tolerate such an egregious display, in this case there was tacit approval. For the first time, Mo Gosego had demonstrated a fighting spirit. Regardless of the circumstances, this was cause for celebration.

For the cast and crew, there was reason to celebrate, as well. The scene at Oracle Arena was the last we filmed for the pilot. It was a bit of a strange sensation, saying goodbye, for no one expected the hiatus to last very long. At the end of a play or movie, everyone exchanges gifts and vows to keep in touch. It is a bittersweet feeling—a mix of melancholy and joy that comes with completing a long journey. This was different; we all felt that the journey had barely begun. We would go our separate ways and reunite in a couple of months, after ABC had picked up the pilot and ordered a dozen or more new episodes.

After we left Oakland, Jami invited me to join her family on a short trip to Aspen, Colorado, where she and Tony had a vacation home. I had never skied, but accepted the invitation anyway. It was a great trip to one of the most beautiful places I had ever seen. In all ways, I felt truly blessed.

★

FOR THE NEXT MONTH, we played the waiting game, while network executives went through the annual ritual of putting together their fall schedules. On each network, the lineup would include a handful of new shows whose pilots had tested well and that for one reason or another appeared to be worthy of a deeper investment. Based on everything I had heard, we would be one of the lucky few. Some of the people around me took a more cautious approach. Jami, for example, had been in the business a long time. She had experienced her share of triumphs and disappointments, and knew all too well the gambler's axiom (which applies to Hollywood, as well)—that there is no such thing as a sure thing. But even she was confident.

I filled most of my days with physical activity: coaching youth basketball or training like crazy in the gym. When I first was offered the role of Mo Gosego, I weighed 185 pounds. The producers immediately assigned me a trainer and a new diet, designed to add at least thirty pounds of muscle to my angular frame. I had made progress, but there was still plenty of work to be done. I didn't mind. Whatever they wanted me to do—take acting lessons, lift weights, improve my accent, consume more than five thousand calories a day—I was willing and eager to do it.

One evening in early May—on the day that the networks were going to announce the names of pilots that had survived the selection process—I was sitting with Jami, waiting to hear our fate. I couldn't stop checking my phone or looking online.

"Relax," Jami kept saying. "It will be okay."

I couldn't relax. I was too nervous. Finally, an email appeared in my inbox. Immediately I recognized the sender's address; it was from one of the producers of our pilot. I hesitated for a moment. Was this good news or bad news? If it were good news, wouldn't he call? Actually, wouldn't he call even if it were bad news? What would he possibly share in an email? With my finger twitching in anticipation, I opened the message. As I started to read, the words blended together. A few jumped out at me at once, like a collage:

Sorry . . . network . . . pass . . . pilot.

The note was brief and to the point, which somehow crashed through the fog enveloping my brain. Holding my laptop, with the screen propped open, I stood up. Jami could tell by the look on my face that something was wrong.

"What is it, Blondy?"

I handed her the laptop.

"We're not getting picked up."

Jami's eyes widened. "What! How? That's not possible."

"I guess it is. Read the message."

Jami stared at the screen for a moment, until her eyes started to well with tears.

"I'm so sorry, Blondy," she said. "I feel terrible for you."

This was a significant disappointment for Jami, as well, but it was typical of her to be more concerned with how the news might affect someone else. I was almost too numb to cry at that moment, for I could not believe what was happening. The pilot was so strong, and everyone was so confident. I was not foolish enough to begin writing checks I could not cash, but I was certain that this time my luck had changed.

And now it was all gone? Just like that? Instead of being the star of a network sitcom, I was, well . . . nobody.

The realization hit me hard. I felt exactly the way I had felt when my eligibility was stripped away in high school. Or when I fractured my ankle in college. But this was even worse. It is one thing to be tested by God; it is quite another to be teased and taunted. And that is the way I felt. Suddenly the emotion began pouring out of me. I cried so hard that I could barely breathe—great, heaving sobs, with tears rolling down my cheeks.

"Why?" I muttered. "Why, Jami?"

"Hang on a second," Jami said, wiping away her own tears and reaching for her cell phone. As she walked out of the room, I could hear her talking to Tony, who was in his car.

A little while later, Tony arrived home from work. Tony is a compassionate man, but less emotional than me, which was a good thing at that moment. I needed a sturdy shoulder to lean on, and he was there for me.

"Blondy, I know this is really disappointing," Tony said, his voice calm and reassuring. "I know what's going through your head. But I want to you to look around right now. Look where you are. Look at what you have. You have a lot of people who care about you. You have us, and we're not going anywhere." There was a pause. "Do you understand what I'm saying."

"Yes . . ."

"Good. This is not the end of anything, Blondy. Don't give up."

CHAPTER 27

For the better part of two weeks, I barely came out of my room. I would sleep late, and the moment my eyes opened to greet a new day, I was engulfed by sadness. I would stare at the ceiling for hours, thinking about what might have been—what *should* have been!—fantasizing about the life I was going to lead. I would have my own home, perhaps a mansion with room for all my relatives—African and American. There would be cars and money; there would be security, something I had never really known.

Sometimes I'd log on to my computer and peruse the myriad websites devoted to the television industry. I'd shake my head in frustration and jealousy at the descriptions of shows that had secured a place on the fall schedule. This was an exercise in self-flagellation—at once pointless and painful. It accomplished precisely nothing. Hollywood is a maddening town, and its chief export—entertainment—is an almost indecipherable commodity. I was hardly the first person to have his dreams crushed after they were seemingly within reach, and I wouldn't be the last.

But what to do now?

As I had so many times in the past, I turned to God for help. He had been there for me in the jungle; he had been there for me when I needed help getting out of the Congo and going to America; he had been there for me when I was on the verge of being deported; he had been there for me when I suffered a career-ending injury in college; and he had been there for me when I was living in my car in Los Angeles. Each time I was at an impasse, and in desperation had sought help from God. And each time he had taken me by the hand and guided me out of the darkness. I wondered sometimes if I had exhausted my quota of divine intervention, but I prayed nonetheless.

"What now, Father? What do I do?"

Finally, the answer came to me one morning:

"Stop feeling sorry for yourself. Get your butt out of bed. And get back to work."

That morning I went to the gym and pushed myself so hard that I nearly passed out. It felt great to sweat out all the anger and frustration, and to do something productive. I made a vow to myself to stay in shape, because, let's face it, when you are a 6-foot-8 African man, and a former Division I athlete, you are primarily going to be considered for roles that have a highly physical component. This is another way of saying that I do not look like a typical Hollywood leading man—in either drama or comedy. I had to play to my strengths, and my greatest strength was also my biggest weakness: I looked different. But I couldn't change that. All I could do was be the best possible version of myself.

There was no shortage of people eager to offer condolences and support in those days—friends and family members, business associates, all of whom expressed some mix of shock, sadness, and anger over the network's decision to pass on our pilot. For a while I was obsessed with getting more information—a specific reason for our failure. Were the characters not believable? Was the writing not as sharp as it seemed? Was it me? Was it simply too much of a gamble to put a complete unknown at the center of a network sitcom?

No answers were forthcoming. At one point, I heard that a particular executive, who was a native of Great Britain, could not get his head around the idea of a show set in the world of American professional basketball. European soccer, perhaps, but not basketball. This was merely innuendo, but it seemed as reasonable as any other rationale. Eventually I stopped seeking answers, for it was no more productive, and perhaps just as painful, as banging my head against a wall.

Complicating matters further was the fact that ours was an unusually proprietary project. It's fairly common for a pilot to be written, produced, and shopped to multiple networks. If one passes, there is always another potential suitor down the block. Alas, this was not the case with *Untitled NBA Project*, as the name so clearly indicates. From the moment of conception, we were an ABC/Disney project, with the full cooperation and support of the NBA. What we were going to do now that ABC had passed? Take the pilot to CBS or NBC? Or Fox? Solicit interest from a network that does not have broadcast rights to NBA games?

Unfortunately, there were no other options. The moment ABC decided to pass, our project ceased to exist.

But that did not mean I had to disappear, as well. The truth was, I had gotten the break of a lifetime on my very first audition. As Jami said to me, "A lot of actors work their entire careers and never get a chance to star in a network series. You almost made it on your first try." This was Jami's way of saying that I should be both grateful and realistic. As usual, she was right. I've never known anyone who is as good as Jami at being both mother and mentor. She was capable of hugging me one moment, and giving me a good kick in the behind a few minutes later. She and Tony raised their family in a world of privilege and luxury. But you would never know it by meeting their children. They are humble and hardworking. As long as I was part of their extended family, I was held to the same standard, and for that I am forever appreciative.

I even became close with Jami's father, Walter Gertz. Jami's family called him "Zayda," which means grandfather, but I preferred to call him "Big Z," because he was a little bit overweight. I love Big Z. He would introduce me by saying, "This is my grandchild," and people would look at me quizzically, as if thinking, *How can a tall black man be related to a white Jewish person?* We all thought it was funny.

Still, it is an indisputable fact that relationships rule the business world, and this is as true in Hollywood as it is in any other industry. ABC's decision to pass on our pilot was not universally applauded, and one of the people who expressed dismay was Disney CEO Bob Iger, one of the most powerful men in the entertainment business. Mr. Iger's son, Max, happened to be a close friend of Theo Ressler. (The world is sometimes a very small place indeed.)

A few weeks after the pilot was spiked, Theo and Max were texting. According to Max, Mr. Iger was surprised and saddened to hear of what happened, since he had been a fan of the project. He was not about to ride in like a white knight and rescue the pilot; it would have been inappropriate to usurp the creative control of those beneath him. But he did have some thoughts on the matter, according to Max.

"My dad wants to meet Blondy," Max said. "You should come over to the house."

"What do you say?" Theo said, showing me the text.

I smiled. "Let's go!"

And just like that, I found myself at the Brentwood home of Bob Iger. This, again, was a completely surreal moment for me. Less than a year earlier I had been sleeping in my car; I couldn't get a job as a retail clerk, let alone as a professional actor. I was homeless and penniless. And now, here I was, having dinner with one of the smartest and most influential men in all of Hollywood. A person who, like Tony and Jami, believed wholeheartedly in the power of philanthropy—both large and small.

It was a brief and casual meeting, more of an introduction than anything else. But I have come to understand the importance of such meetings, and of making the most of every opportunity. Mr. Iger had seen the pilot and thought it had great potential. Sometimes though, he said, things just don't work out. He urged me to keep working hard and to maintain a positive attitude.

"I'm going to keep an eye on you, Blondy."

"Thank you, sir."

A week later I got a call from my manager, Adena. ABC wanted to sign me to an exclusive talent holding deal. This meant I could only work for ABC, but it also meant the network was serious about making a creative and financial investment in my career. It was, at the time, a much needed show of support. Was it a coincidence that the offer came shortly after I visited Bob Iger? Of course not. This is a universal truth: who you know sometimes means more than what you know. ABC would not have offered this deal if it did not think I had potential, but sometimes a little prodding from above helps the process along.

The truth is, we are all part of a larger community. The more you give, the more you get back. I truly believe that. I was blessed to have a family in the Congo, another family in Arizona, and a third family in Beverly Hills. I called Terry and Laurie regularly to give them updates about my Hollywood adventure, and while they were disappointed to hear of the pilot's demise, they were relieved to know that I still had a place to live and a growing network of support within the industry.

A few weeks later, Jami initiated a conversation about my future.

"I want you to know that you are welcome to stay here as long you'd like," she said. "You're part of our family now."

"Thank you, Jami."

"But I've raised three boys and I know sometimes you need space. Tony and I have talked, and we have a proposition."

"Okay." I wasn't sure where this was going.

"We think you have the talent to become a successful actor, and we want to support you in that endeavor. And we don't want you to have to worry about how you will pay your bills while you're trying to find work."

What came next was truly incredible. Jami and Tony offered to set me up in an apartment in Koreatown, with the rent prepaid for three full years. They would also pay for a car and health insurance, and give me a monthly stipend so that I could buy groceries and gas and other assorted necessities. In other words, they would pay for my life so that I could concentrate fully on trying to make it as an actor.

"Jami, I don't know what to say."

She smiled. "You don't have to say anything. But it's not free, Blondy. What we expect in return is that you will work your butt off. Show us what you can do. Make something happen with your life. No excuses."

"No excuses," I parroted back. Then I gave Jami a hug and thanked her again. I no longer felt sorry for myself; in fact, I was rather embarrassed for having ever indulged in such behavior. How many struggling young actors in Hollywood would have wanted to trade places with me at that moment? I knew what it was like to be alone in this town. I knew what it was like to have no friends, no contacts, no home, and no food.

I knew what it was like to have no hope.

But now?

Anything was possible.

CHAPTER 28

My job was to find a job, and I embraced it with all the energy and enthusiasm I could muster. For a young actor on the hunt for work, one of the biggest challenges is creating a productive rhythm to your life. The temptation is great to let inertia win the day: sleep in, take meetings over lunch, do some surfing, hit the clubs at night. Work when there is work, and spend a lot of time playing. I tried hard not to fall into this trap. I wanted to make Jami and Tony proud; I wanted them to think they had made a wise investment. So I filled my days with acting classes and auditions and meetings; I coached youth basketball and took a very intense class designed to reduce my accent. *Untitled NBA Project* notwithstanding, writers in Hollywood are not sitting around and dreaming up parts for unusually tall African actors with thick, almost unintelligible accents. I had to make myself more marketable.

It's fascinating the way things work. I had no experience whatsoever, and a résumé that was virtually blank when I earned the lead role in an ABC pilot. Now that I had that rather impressive line on my résumé, along with some hard-earned insight into the casting end of the business, I couldn't get a job. There were nibbles, to be sure. I went out on auditions and did my best. Sometimes I would get a callback; sometimes not. But there were no offers. I could usually tell when I arrived at the studio whether I had a chance. If the other actors were all white and under six feet tall, I knew I was a long shot. Often, I could tell simply by reading a synopsis if I was a legitimate candidate. I was not blind to my own weaknesses, or to the peculiarities of my physical appearance and voice. Sometimes, if I was completely honest with myself, I knew within the first page of dialogue that I was inappropriate for the role. Nevertheless, I accepted every opportunity to audition.

After a while I came to realize that this was the new normal. As with just about every other aspiring young actor in Hollywood, rejection became a staple of my diet. And I learned to swallow it without complaint. Each unsuccessful audition—to say nothing of roles for which I was not even considered—took me further from the rarefied atmosphere I had come close to occupying. After a while I began to wonder, Was I really a good actor? Or had I merely been lucky? The stars had aligned so perfectly with the pilot. I mean, how often does an actor stumble across a part that seems to not merely have been written with him in mind, but is almost like a reflection of his own life.

Perhaps it was fate, or a fluke, and it would never happen again. But then I reminded myself that I had earned the role through a series of auditions. If I could convince the creators of an A-list project such as that, then surely there were other roles for which I would be a reasonable fit. It was a matter of perseverance.

At the same time, it never hurts to have a friend in high places, someone who can open doors with a single phone call. Once the door opens, you have to walk into the room and act like you belong there, but I have learned the first step is much harder than the second.

In October of 2015 I received an email from Bob Iger.

"How are things going?" he asked.

I responded honestly. Email, like texting, often has the unfortunate effect of putting a particular emotional spin on something that might not be accurate, so I merely stated the facts.

"I'm working hard, going on auditions. So far I have not been able to get a job."

Bob's response was short and succinct, but it nearly made me fall off my chair.

"You're going to be getting a call from someone at Marvel."

Marvel?

As in Marvel Studios, the film company responsible for many of the biggest blockbusters of the last decade? Marvel? One of the most lucrative brands in the entertainment industry? Home to Spider-Man, Iron Man, the Incredible Hulk, the Avengers, and so many others?

Yes, that Marvel.

And then I remembered: Marvel was also a subsidiary of the Walt Disney Company.

"Hang in there," Bob wrote.

A couple days later I got a phone call from the office of Kevin Feige, the president of Marvel Studios. The call came from his assistant. There was a role available in one of the upcoming Marvel movies, a sequel to the wildly successful *Guardians of the Galaxy*.

"We think it might be right for you," she said. "Would you be interested in coming in to read?"

Was it this easy? Is this the way world worked? The CEO of Disney calls the head of Marvel Studios, and just like that I get an invitation to read for a part in a multimillion-dollar movie? I could barely spit out my answer.

"Yes, I would like very much to come in and read. Thank you."

It all happened so quickly. The next thing I knew, I was in the office of Sarah Finn, one of the top casting directors in Hollywood. I had been told absolutely nothing in advance beyond the fact that I would be reading for a role in the second film in the *Guardians of the Galaxy* franchise (the movie did not even have a title yet; or if it did, I wasn't told). I did not know the name of the character or his importance to the movie. I knew nothing about the story or who else would be appearing in the movie (although I presumed that Chris Pratt, the star of the first film, would be returning). Marvel productions tend to be shrouded in secrecy, and this one was no different. Marvel fans are both zealous and resourceful. Any leaked information can be quickly disseminated through social media and spun in ways the studio might not find desirable. Every aspect of a Marvel production, therefore, is withheld from all but a small circle of studio executives and creative personnel. It's not unusual for the actors themselves to know almost nothing until the production begins. And even then, they are often provided only information that is pertinent to their own characters.

This was much different from my experience auditioning for the ABC project. To help with preparation, I had been given a series overview and a character synopsis, along with a full scene to rehearse. I went into that audition feeling like I knew my character intimately. I *was* Mo Gosego. But when I walked into Sarah Finn's office, I had no idea what to expect. It was like walking into a college exam without having studied. You know you aren't going to get a good grade; you just hope that you can somehow manage to avoid failing and embarrassing yourself.

I cannot honestly say that I left Sarah's office that day feeling strong or confident. This wasn't really even an audition; it felt more like an interview, and while I got the impression that they liked me, I had no idea whether I was a serious candidate for the job. I still didn't even understand the job. A broad range of possibilities existed, everything from *You're the only person we are considering for this role . . .* to *. . . We're bringing you in as a favor to Bob Iger, but you have no shot.*

Then came the waiting game. It's never a good idea to sit around waiting for the phone to ring, so I jumped right back into the routine of classes, teaching basketball, working out, and trying to line up more auditions. Finally, about two weeks after I read for the role, I got a phone call from my manager, Adena.

"Marvel just called. The part is yours."

For a moment, I did not say anything. I simply held the phone to my ear and stared out the window of my apartment. And then I began screaming.

"YES! YES! YES! I am going to be in a Marvel movie!"

I was so loud that I must have frightened the neighbors. But I could not help myself. There was so much pent-up energy flowing through my body looking for an exit. I found myself dancing around the apartment, singing out loud. I could not get over the idea that I was going to be in a Marvel movie. Whether the role was large or small, whether I would play a villain or a hero, I did not know. And I did not care.

When I got off the phone with Adena, I waited approximately two seconds before sharing the wondrous news with friends and family. The first person I called was Jami. Without her I would not have been in this apartment. Without her I would not have met Bob Iger. Without her, I would not have gotten this job. As I waited for her to answer the phone, I was struck once again by the wonderful unpredictability of life, and the blessings that come to us in ways large and small, and the importance of finding people you love and trust.

"Jami, guess what?" I blurted out as soon as she picked up. "I am going to be in a Marvel movie—*Guardians of the Galaxy*! Can you believe it?"

There was silence for a moment, and then the sound of Jami crying softly.

"Blondy, I'm so happy for you," she said. "You deserve this."

★

ON MY FIRST DAY in Atlanta for principal production on *Guardians of the Galaxy Vol. 2*, in March of 2016, I woke to the sound of an alarm clock bleating across the blackness of a hotel room. I opened one eye and looked at the numbers. It was 2 a.m. The world is eerily quiet at that hour, as even the biggest of cities slows its breath while resting up to greet another day. Most people hate getting up early, especially so early that when you peel back the drapes in your hotel room it still looks and feels like the middle of the night. Not me. I had barely slept at all the night before—or for most of the previous week. Not because of anxiety—although I'll admit to a small amount of nervousness—but simply because I could not wait for the day to begin.

On that first day, and for most of the next two months, while I was on location, I felt no sluggishness. It was almost as though I didn't need to sleep. I jumped out of bed, put on some lively African music, and began dancing around the room, singing out loud. I'm sure this did not make me the most popular resident on my floor of the hotel, but I simply could not contain myself. In less than an hour, a car would arrive to take me to the movie set. That alone was enough to blow my mind. Never mind that I still had not seen a script and knew almost nothing about the story of *Guardians of the Galaxy Vol. 2*, or my role in it. I was a performer in what was sure to be one of the biggest movies of the year.

What more could I ask?

I discovered almost immediately that the process of making movies, particularly special-effects-laden blockbusters, is an extremely slow and tedious affair that bears almost no resemblance to shooting a network sitcom. Every day for me (and for many others in the film) began with several hours in the makeup chair. It took roughly three hours each morning to transform me into the character of Huhtar, an alien who is part of the villainous Ravagers. I knew almost nothing of the *Guardians of the Galaxy* universe when we started filming, and only marginally more by the end. Even as filming commenced, I was privy only to that which I needed to know for the scenes in which I was included.

And that was perfectly fine. It was better to aim small, and to concentrate on my little corner of the film, rather than get caught up in the sheer massiveness of the production. I came away from the whole experience with an immense amount of respect for the director, James Gunn, whose job was so vast and demanding that I couldn't imagine how he ever got a moment's rest. In a television sitcom, you can shoot an entire episode in a single day; in a movie like *Guardians of the Galaxy*, you might exhaust weeks shooting a single scene. And when it was done, James and his team of special effects wizards and tech masterminds would apply all manner of digital tweaks and enhancements. Like so many current Hollywood blockbusters, *Guardians of the Galaxy Vol. 2* was a movie created both on the soundstage and in darkened rooms filled with computers and other technological gadgetry.

My training came on the stage, which is about as literal an experience as an actor can have. Even my brief foray into television was decidedly low-tech and human. To suddenly be thrown into a situation where I was covered in makeup and instructed to deliver lines or complete a physical task while standing in front of a blank green screen, which would later be replaced by digital images, was quite an eye-opening experience. In some ways, especially in the beginning, it did not feel like acting, but I soon realized that this type of performing is almost more demanding, for it requires an extraordinary amount of discipline and imagination.

Despite my comparative inexperience, and despite all the pressure he must have faced, and the large number of stars and studio executives with whom he interacted on a daily basis, James Gunn treated me with respect and endless patience.

"If you have any issues, or any questions, don't be shy about speaking up," he said. "We're all on the same team here."

In the end, though, it was incumbent upon me to put forth the best possible performance under the circumstances. If I needed help understanding a particular plot point, or a technological element, the crew was more than happy to oblige. But the actual performance—the *acting*—was on me. I had to bring it every day, regardless of how large or small my role might have been.

The fear of embarrassment or failure can be a powerful motivator, and I used it to my advantage. For a while I was somewhat starstruck not only by the scope of the production, but by the presence of so many famous actors—from veterans like Kurt Russell and Sylvester Stallone, to younger stars like Chris Pratt and Zoe Saldana. They were all extremely nice and friendly; they were also intensely professional when it came to their work. I was not about to be revealed as the amateur in the crowd. Pages were usually distributed a day in advance, and I made sure that I showed up each morning thoroughly prepared. I would study my lines or choreography well into the night, and again while sitting in the makeup chair. By the time the cameras were rolling, I had memorized every second of my scene, including every line, whether spoken by me or someone else.

Movie acting, especially when special effects are involved, can seem like silly, almost childish work. But it is work nonetheless, and it takes significant preparation and focus to do it well. When you put $200 million into a movie, as was the case with *Guardians of the Galaxy Vol. 2*, the stakes are high indeed. And everyone knows it. For me, there was the added pressure of knowing that my presence in the film, while not necessarily unwarranted, was certainly facilitated by a phone call from Bob Iger. I suppose it's possible I was not the only person in the cast or crew who got his job based on a recommendation from a Disney executive, but it sure felt that way. As a result, I left nothing to chance. I might not have been the best actor in the cast, and I certainly wasn't the most experienced or best-known; but no one was better prepared for his job. I couldn't control much, but I could make sure that no one outworked me or had a better attitude. If motivation was ever a problem—which it wasn't—all I had to do was imagine someone calling Bob Iger and saying, "Why did you recommend this guy?" I felt like I had to prove that I was worthy of the job, not just for myself, but for Bob; I didn't want to let him down.

Huhtar, I was told, would be in several scenes throughout the movie, though it was difficult at times to get a feel for the overarching story and my place in it. But it felt like I had a fairly substantial role, albeit one that was mostly physical in nature. A lot of running and jumping and fighting, including a showdown near the end of the film involving the Ravagers and the Guardians. This was my death scene (actually, it was the death scene for all of the Ravagers), and while it wasn't exactly an emotional showcase, I did my best with the exit.

On my last day, I made a point of personally saying goodbye to as many people as possible. A movie set is a remarkable machine, dependent on the contributions of countless professionals of wildly disparate talents. Everyone plays a vital role. Some are just more visible than others. I sought out James Gunn before leaving. He thanked me for my time and effort and gave my work a solid review. Maybe he was just being nice, but it felt genuine.

"Thank you, James," I said while shaking his hand. "Don't forget about me."

"Don't worry. I won't."

EPILOGUE

More than a year passed before the release of *Guardians of the Galaxy Vol. 2*. In the meantime, I continued to take classes and work on my accent and maintain my Huhtar-like physique with long sessions in the gym. You never know when a call will come, so you must be ready on a moment's notice.

I filmed another pilot for ABC—a reality show based upon a popular Swedish television program called *Six Degrees (of Separation)*. I was one of two hosts (the other was Erik Anders Lang) who would travel the world in an attempt to bring together people who have some sort of connection that they might not even realize. In the pilot, we began by introducing a woman in a small town in Nepal. Our goal was to connect this woman and her life to that of a Hollywood celebrity—Rob Lowe, in this case—in six steps or less. I won't tell you exactly how we did it, but we were successful, and we had a lot of fun along the way.

Still, every project is a dream, every pilot a long shot. That much I had already learned. Although ABC was happy with the pilot and it tested well, we still had not found a home for the series by the time *Guardians of the Galaxy Vol. 2* was released on May 5, 2017.

Nevertheless, what a night that was. I attended the premiere with Joe Fria, one of my fellow Ravagers, and an actor with a long list of credits. After the pageantry of the red-carpet entrance (which seemed to go on forever), the entire cast was seated together in the beautiful and sprawling Dolby Theatre. There were more than three thousand people in attendance, and every one of them seemed to be intimately familiar with the Marvel universe in general and *Guardians of the Galaxy* in particular. They cheered wildly each time a favorite character appeared on-screen for the first time. They laughed and applauded in all the right places.

What many people do not realize is that a premiere represents a great unveiling, not just to the general moviegoing public, but to the performers as well. There are a handful of stars who get to see an early screening, but most actors do not see their work until the premiere. Until that moment, they don't know what the movie will look like, or even how large or small their role will be. They do not know how much of their work will appear on-screen, or how much has been left on the floor of the editing suite. I approached this experience, therefore, with both enthusiasm and trepidation. It was impossible not to get caught up in the glamour and excitement of the evening; and yet, as the lights went down and the screen lit up, I could feel my heart beating faster. And as the movie rolled on, for ten, twenty, forty minutes, I began to worry.

What if I didn't make the cut?

Stranger things had happened. Every actor in Hollywood has felt the sting of the editor's knife. It's inevitable. A director typically shoots hundreds of hours of film, then pares it down to roughly two hours for theatrical release. What you see on the screen is a distillation of months of work: a puzzle assembled using only the best pieces in the box; everything else is jettisoned.

Maybe Huhtar was a casualty of this process.

Maybe my performance was deemed lacking.

Maybe . . .

Suddenly, roughly an hour into the movie, there I was, larger than life, walking across the screen, unrecognizable in Huhtar makeup, with thickly padded cheeks and brow, and a silver skullcap, grunting ominously. The character seemed big, strong, menacing, exactly as he was meant to look. Reflexively, I sat up straight in my seat and smiled. For the briefest of moments, I had to stifle the urge to cry out triumphantly.

"That is me—Blondy Baruti! I made the cut!"

Instead, I took a deep breath and sat quietly as the scene unfolded. For the final hour, I was more relaxed. Huhtar wound up with roughly five lines of dialogue and perhaps ten minutes of mostly silent but action-packed screen time. He did not stand out; neither was he invisible. He was simply part of the team.

But what a team it was!

As the final credits rolled and the audience cheered and applauded, I remained in my seat, reflecting on the strangeness of it all. I thought about what Jami had said to me after I got the part:

"You deserve this."

I do not know if that is true. Who is to say what we deserve or do not deserve? The randomness and unpredictability of life is so often bewildering. Who knows what is determined by fate or luck or karma or hard work? Did I deserve to be ripped from my home in the Congo and nearly die in the jungle? Did I deserve to be given the opportunity of a new life in America when so many of my friends were far less fortunate? Did I deserve to be homeless in L.A.? Or to be rescued by Jami and Tony, just as I had been rescued by Terry and Laurie Blitz?

I think about those things even now, when I drive through certain parts of the city, and see the blank faces of shattered men and women living on the streets, carrying signs, pleading for help. I think about it when I read accounts of the ongoing atrocities in the Congo, or when I speak to my family back home, which I do on a weekly basis. I tell them how much I love them and miss them. I send money to my mother each month to help support her and my nieces and nephews, since they do not have much in the way of material possessions, nor a father in their lives. I think of them sometimes and my heart aches.

Why is that not me? Why have I been so blessed?

I have no answers, of course. But I will forever try to prove myself worthy of the grace of God, and the kindness extended to me by strangers. I will continue on the never-ending journey, with wonder and appreciation for each and every step.

ACKNOWLEDGMENTS

There are so many people I would like to recognize for helping me along my journey.

First, my family in Africa: To my grandmother: when I was hungry, she cooked for me and told me everything will be all right. To my uncle, Joseph, for giving me a sense of direction and a father figure while I was growing up in the Congo. He was there to guide me and lift my spirits up when I was down. And to my father, who wasn't there for me while I was growing up, but who gave me life; for that I will always be grateful.

To all my friends back home in the Congo. They supported me and pushed me very hard, mentally and physically, which made me a better basketball player down the road. I thank you all.

Thank you to the Blitz family, who took a chance on an unknown kid from overseas and loved me unconditionally as their own son. Terry Blitz is the father I never had. Thank you, Terry, for loving me and being there for me no matter what the situation was. When I was down, you led me along the right path; when I needed a shoulder to lean on, you were always there for me; when I was afraid, you told me everything would be okay. I love you and Laurie, and the entire Blitz family.

Thank you, also, for the love and support of the Brownlee, Faulkner, Egan, and Moncho families. I'm proud to call you guys family and nothing will ever change that.

To all my friends in Arizona, especially Mesa High School; Mississippi; Oklahoma; and Los Angeles—your love means the world to me.

Thanks to the Iger family for the love and support you have demonstrated since I first met you guys. To the Ressler family—thank you for accepting me into your home and making me part of your family.

A big and special thanks to Jami Gertz for opening your home to someone you had just met behind the scenes of a TV show. The care and guidance you provided helped me become the man I am today. I thank you and your family from the bottom of my heart.

To my manager, Adena Chawke, the best any actor could ask for. Thank you for believing in me. You have always been there for me, throughout the roller coaster of ups and downs.

Thank you to everyone who helped make this book a reality: my coauthor Joe Layden, and our literary agents, David Doerrer and Frank Weimann; my editor, Christine Pride (and everyone at Simon & Schuster). Thank you all for your patience and for believing in me and in my story.

Lastly, and most importantly, I would like to express unending thanks to my Lord and Savior, the King of Kings, Jesus Christ. If not for him, I would not be here today. He loves me and protected me throughout my life. And he never left my side.

Glory to God forever.